REVOLUTIONARY DEMOCRACY

Vol. XXII, No. 2   April 2017

Contents

**Views expressed in signed articles are those of authors and not
necessarily of the Editorial Board.**

Published Half-Yearly for *Revolutionary Democracy* by Vijay Singh from K-67, FF, Jangpura Extension, New Delhi-110014, and printed by him at Progressive Printers, A-21, Jhilmil Industrial Area, G.T. Road, Delhi-95. Editor: Vijay Singh.

RELEASE ALL MARUTI-SUZUKI WORKERS NOW!

New Trade Union Initiative

13 Maruti-Suzuki Workers Sentenced to Life Imprisonment for Forming a Trade Union

The Conviction

The Gurgaon District and Sessions Court handed down sentences of life imprisonment to 13 Maruti-Suzuki workers on 18 March 2017 convicting them on charges of criminal conspiracy, murder and destruction of evidence for the 18 July 2012 incident at the company's Manesar plant in which a manager lost his life. The court also served commuted prison sentences of five years each to 4 workers and of three years to 14 workers variously convicted for trespass, unlawful assembly, mischief and rioting and possession of deadly weapons.117 workers who were kept under arrest for at least 31 months and more have been acquitted of all charges.

Of the 13 convicted of murder, 12 – Ram Meher, Sarabjeet Singh, Sarvjit Dhillon, Ram Vilas, Pawan Kumar, SohanLal, Ajmer Singh, Sukh Kumar, Amarjeet, Yogesh, Pradeep Gujjar and Dhanraj Bambi – were the office bearers of the Maruti Suzuki Workers' Union, who were in place on the day of the incident. The thirteenth, Jiya Lal, was the worker who was the subject of the disciplinary action on the day of the incident, when he protested against casteist abuse by a supervisor against him for being a dalit.

The Incident

The Maruti-Suzuki Manesar plant workers – both permanent and contract – had sought to form a union of their choice in 2011. The Maruti-Suzuki management with active support of the Government of Haryana first denied them union registration. Following months of sustained militant struggle, frequently put down by the police acting admittedly at Maruti-Suzuki management's behest, government finally acceded to union registration in early 2012 but, the Maruti-Suzuki management refused to recognise the union and negotiate with them in good faith. The escalation of the incidents on 18 July 2012 was employed by Maruti-Suzuki management to rid themselves of the union, its leadership and 2,300+ workers who were summarily dismissed.

The Case

The criminal conspiracy apparently occurred despite the fact that the judgment acknowledges that the investigation was weak insofar as: there was a change of the assault weapons (from lathis and rods to car parts) in the course of the investigation, lack of forensic examination of the assault weapons, failure to hold an identification parade of the accused and false medico-legal reports and delays in recording witness statements. The charge of criminal conspiracy including of murder and destruction of evidence is based entirely on the testimony of prosecution witnesses, entirely negating the testimony of the defence witnesses, including references to the sustained attack by the Maruti-Suzuki management on the workers' right to freedom of association and collective bargaining. By negating the testimony of all defence witnesses the court also completely denied the presence of external bouncers, who brought in the lathis and rods that caused the violence. The prosecution witnesses, apart from two policemen and one labour department officer, are all managers or labour contractors of the company. It is noteworthy that the prosecution could not find a single worker as witness from a workforce of 2,700+.

There was a common charge against all 148 workers who were arrested in July 2012. By a slight of hand, the judgment acquitted 85 of the accused on grounds of the poor investigation; another 22 were acquitted as they could not be identified by prosecution witnesses. In fact the same court had denied the acquitted bail.

This also brings to the fore an important condition of contract labour wherein labour contractors cannot identify their own 'employees' making it abundantly clear that they are 'sham and bogus' labour arrangers that give companies the avenue to violate labour laws.

In a macabre turn of events on 17 March 2017, the prosecution counsel called upon the court to award a death sentence to the 13 convicted of murder. The prosecution claimed the Punjab and Chandigarh High Court order of 22 May 2013 while denying bail formed the basis for the death penalty. The judgement says: 'The incident is most unfortunate occurrence which has lowered the reputation of India in the estimation of the world. Foreign investors are not likely to invest the money in India out of fear of labour unrest' as grounds for the death penalty. The public prosecutor was not just transgressing the very clear law on death sentences laid out by the Supreme Court, but also laying out the agenda of a blood thirsty government signaling to employers that it is willing to send workers to their death if they defy their employers and in particular foreign capital.

The principal basis of the conviction of murder is based on the alleged presence of 13 workers in a particular room of the factory. This amounts to handing out collective punishment in the absence of material evidence. The judgment blindly or without application of mind acknowledges the Maruti-Suzuki management position of the violence caused by workers without even as much as recognizing the events of the day which were part of the persistent attack of the Maruti-Suzuki management on the workers right to form a union of their own choice and its refusal to negotiate with the union, over fair and just, workers' demands.

This judgment has arrived at its conclusion by association and not by evidence severely compromising the independence of the judiciary. This judgment is a fundamental attack on workers right to freedom of association. It also confirms that the judiciary is entirely conjoined with both employers and government in pushing the working class towards criminalisation for even their just and fair demands that are protected by the constitution.

As, the NTUI stands in solidarity with entire membership of the Maruti Suzuki Workers' Union and especially the comrades convicted of murder and their families for their extraordinary sacrifice and forbearance in this struggle. We also salute the determination of the upwards of 100,000 workers within the Gurgaon-Manesar industrial belt who have boycotted their factory canteens on successive days in a show of solidarity in advance of the judgement and almost immediate tool down, after the judgement, by all 25,000 workers at all plants of Maruti-Suzuki.

This is not just the struggle of Maruti-Suzuki workers. This is not just the struggle of workers of Manesar-Gurgaon industrial belt. This is our struggle too. This is the struggle of the entire working class. This is a struggle we must win.

As we go forward from here we call upon:

Maruti-Suzuki India Limited to immediately reinstate the 117 acquitted workers with Back Wages with effect from 18 July 2012.

The Government of Haryana to

1. Compensate the 117 acquitted workers for their unfair and illegal incarceration,

2. Withdraw the case of the prosecution in the Appeal court

3. Appoint a judicial enquiry, headed by a retired judge of the Supreme Court, into the police investigation of the dispute and the conduct of the public prosecutor and that such enquiry should be completed within 60 days.

RELEASE ALL MARUTI-SUZUKI WORKERS NOW!

DEMONETISATION IN THE LARGEST DEMOCRACY

A case study of complete cooperation despite terrific sufferings

Dr. N. Bhattacharyya

Bharatiya Janata Party and some regional parties formed the National Democratic Alliance 2 (NDA2) and are ruling at the centre since 2014. The National Democratic Alliance 1 (NDA1) ruled at the Centre during 1997-2003. Governments both in the states and at the centre have to protect interest of every Indian both resident and nonresident irrespective of caste, creed, religion, culture, language etc. The Supreme Court and Election Commission recently ordered all political parties not to use 'religion' in any electoral issue! The British policy which was accepted by politicians of undivided India to divide India on a 'religion' basis in 1947 proved absolutely a stupid policy. The poor people of East Pakistan defeated Pakistan in the '1971 war of independence' and created Bangladesh only on the issue of language spoken by people of that country. However, even after 70 years of independence the constitutional provision of 'secularism in India' is still to be implemented wholeheartedly by all political parties. All of us know that such 'basic structure' can't be written off, but why are the political parties are not punished for ignoring it. The present Prime Minister of India as Chief Minister of a State failed to perform his Constitutional duty of 'Raj Dharma' as mentioned by Sri Atal Behari Vajpayee, Prime Minister of the NDAI Government, when people of one minority religious group was mercilessly butchered (Godhra- anti-Muslim pogrom, 2002).

Since the NDA 2 came to power at Centre after ten years in 2014, people around the country including some supporting parties were protesting against the 'intolerance' and 'harassment' by the activists of the party in power. Some eminent persons respected in the country for their independent constructive opinion were eliminated by anti social elements. Protests by people on any issue in a democratic country are declared antinational and condemned by police as act of 'sedition' in different states. Many intellectuals returned their decorations conferred by the State. University Professors and their PhD scholars are feeling insecure to speak the truth. India is rated as 'oppressive and unsecured' for the students in Higher Educational Institutions. JNU Student's Union was the target to teach students community in the country a lesson. JNU Student Union President, Sri Kanhaiya Kumar and other activists were sent to jail on charges of 'sedition' for some 'demonstration' in the campus. Learned lawyers in a capital's court mercilessly beaten him in the court complex. Recent happenings in JNU with members of faculty clearly establish beyond doubt that some unseen hands are officially engaged to destroy this particular University in north India. A University without a VC can run efficiently but without students and Professors what will happen to that institution. It is the responsibility of people of India to see to it that institutions of higher learning are not destroyed by vested interests. The suicide of Rohith Vemula a PhD student of Hyderabad Central University clearly showed a deep sense of hatred and humiliation towards 'dalit' students in Central Universities funded by taxpayer's money. After one year of his death Rohith's friends and family members were disallowed from expressing their grief and respect to departed hero of that University. One PhD student of JNU evaporated from its campus in 2016 and the Ministry of Home Affairs responsible to maintain law and order in Delhi is still clueless! The people of this vast country are suffering from deep sense of uncertainty and insecurity even in 2017.

II

On November 8, 2016 at 8 pm the Prime Minister of India suddenly (!) announced from Delhi the 'demonetisation' of Rs 500 and Rs 1000 currency notes. The vast majority of daily wage workers in north India's extreme winter cold were in bed after a day's hard labour. Waking up on 9th morning they found that world for them had completely changed. Many went to work to earn a daily wage, but gradually they found themselves on the streets as employers became 'cash less' and gradually many small traders, small and medium manufacturers and people working in various occupations of informal sector became unemployed due to the scarcity of working capital. In Delhi's Jumma Masjid area, rikshaws were parked but the scarcity of cash reduced the number of customers. Rickshaw pullers left for their villages. Millions of people of this vast country from Kanya Kumari to Kashmir, from Gujarat to Nagaland had no idea what to do with those old notes, they could not be used to purchase their day to day requirements. Those who had these 'big value notes' started waiting as beggars before banks and ATMs to get back their own money lying with banks in trust under RBI Act 1934. This is a new experience in India in 2016, around 70 years after independence.

The writer of this small story was 7 years old when the British Prime Minister in 1943 (in the middle of the 2nd world war) ordered to put all the foodgrains in warehouses to be used exclusively for the army. People were ordered to take rations from shops. Despite a bumper crop people used to wait in long queues before ration shops to take some rice even unfit for animal consumption. That was the inauguration in India of 'Queue' in 1943. 4 million people died in 1943 'Bengal Famine' and the British Prime Minister wrote: 'to teach a lesson to the country men of Mr. Subhas Chandra Bose'. In 1952 after first general election in independent India Mr. Rafi Ahmed Kidwai, Minister of Food and Agriculture allowed the selling of grains in the open market and Queues before ration shops started declining. Demonetisation 2016 revived that back breaking 'Queue' of the forties. Senior and super senior citizens in 2016 don't have the courage to go and stand in queues, even then there were people old and sick who tried to stand in queue and around 100 persons died in undergoing such cruel ventures! A bench is constituted in Supreme Court to examine the Constitution validity of 'Demonetisation'. Who will examine 'the torture and mental anxiety' that millions suffered quietly during those 50 and odd days and continuing till in mid January, 2017 it is yet to be normalized. Are not banks under legal obligation to compensate for such loss of life? Can any democratic Govt. without approval of Parliament undertake such 'actions' affecting life and livelihood of all people of this vast country? What Supreme Court says in England on role of Parliament on Brexit issue, though it was approved by 'referendum'? The word 'secrecy' in law is to be examined.

The publicity machine of the government claims that a section of black money holders happily converted their ill gotten wealth in gold ornaments at any price during the night of 8th November. A question was raised why did the government allow this to occur, after 12 at night. Why were the shops permitted to continue business till the early hours of 9th November, 2016 to carry on such illegal activities? Has any agency recorded these transactions and taken necessary actions as per law? It is also charged by the press that unemployed workers were deployed by people to stand in the queue for a price. From time to time press reported that XYZ officials of this or that Bank were detected for illegal activities involving new and old currency notes. Most amusing is the report the government showed that 'terrorists' killed in Kashmir during the demonetisation period was carrying new 'Rs 2000 notes' before it reached public for distribution! Both the print and visual media of the entire world were busy since 9th November, 2016 to show to the people around the world for 50 days that 'Indians are not trust worthy', they are punished for 'funding terrorism', 'accumulating black money' and 'circulating counterfeit notes' etc. At the same time Indians are grateful that a section of national and foreign media refused to buy such widely publicized defamatory charges against the citizens of this vast country. People rather criticized the politicians for such an unplanned adventure that caused immense hardship to the poor of this country! High value currency notes are no longer used in the 21st century and India reintroduced Rs 2000/- value of currency notes! However, in the Public Accounts Committee meeting held recently with the RBI Governor, an honourable member of the Rajya Sabha handed over new Rs 2000 notes (fake) to the RBI Governor! The government announced on 8th November that their 'operation demonetisation and remonetisation' will be over by end of December, 2016 but it failed on both the fronts.

Though the RBI and the Central Government is yet to accept the findings of the International Financial Press like Bloomberg that around 97/99 percent of the demonetised notes were returned by people by 30th December, 2016. According to reports there was hardly any so called 'black money' at least in form of cash (!). The people are angry and demanding from the government why they were compelled to undergo such inhuman humiliation and what is the compensation for such sufferings for all and sundry! People working in the unorganized sector never thought that from morning of 9th November they may face starvation as gradually their 'employment' evaporated into thin air and in next fifteen days they had to decide to stay in cities without any income or go back home where too they had to starve with members of their family. Recent reports by organisations like the Manufacturers Associations clearly brought out how production suffered from 9th November, 2016 for a cash crisis brought about by their own government. Loss of production created huge losses to mainly small scale and medium scale producers. Huge increase in demand for daily wage work under MGNREGS in November/ December 2016 over corresponding period last year clearly shows return of village labour due to chaos created by 'demonetisation' in the cities and semi urban centres.

In January 2017 cultivators were totally frustrated that winter fruits and vegetables including onion and potatos etc. had no demand due to shortage of cash and there were reports of a huge wastage of agricultural products throughout the country. The unorganized sector suffered tremendously and the government is behaving in the 21 century like that 'monkey' who advises people 'not to hear', 'not to see' and 'not to speak'. No one is uttering a single word to compensate for this well planned loss/ sufferings imposed on millions of poor workers and farmers. The move of demonetisation will be remembered for long time how poor and middle class in India suffered immensely for no fault of their own. No one is explaining how many new people have entered into already existing 'unemployment market' in India. Without making arrangement for the relief and rehabilitation of these unfortunate people and their family members how our policy makers can go to bed to sleep and rest?

III

Already the Banks in India are shattered by huge unrecovered loans called 'Non Performing Assets' (NPA). On June 2016 the total non Performing Assets was around Rs 4 lakh crores. Due to demonetisation large numbers of small and medium industries will fail to repay their loan to banks and that will increase the value of outstanding loans. On the other side the government has succumbed to the pressure to reduce interest rate on bank loan as banks are flooded with newly returned currency. Banks are in hurry to lend new loans and forget to collect old outstanding loans and interest thereon. So banks and their old debtors- friends are playing a beautiful game to cheat public institutions. This is called Indian capitalism in 2017. The big money bags never suffer! In demonetisation ordinary people have suffered the maximum loss both physically and economically.

School text books say the Reserve Bank of India (RBI) is responsible for 'Monetary policy' in India under the RBI Act of 1934. The Government decides the financial policy of India. Government appoints Governors to run RBI. In 2015 a new Committee on Monetary Policy was formed and till to-day people are kept in dark whether this monetary policy committee was taken into confidence or not. RBI Board Members knew in January 2016 that demonetisation will take place. Why proper arrangements were not planned to collect illegal tender of around Rs 15.44 lakh crores of high value notes and simultaneously distribute new notes through branches of banks and ATMs? The role played by RBI as a statutory autonomous monetary policy organization on 'Demonetisation—2016' has attracted criticism from all concerned citizens of the country. Various committees of Parliament are busy finding out the role of RBI on demonetisation and subsequent remonetisation. People, male and female, young and old are waiting to know how far 'demonetisation' was able to locate 'black money, terror funding and counterfeit currency rackets'. We have to answer to rest of the world how far we were successful to locate the criminals who are engaged in 'money laundering' in India. The BJP president's claim that the demonetisation issue was decided by NDA2 after the 2014 election victory and after all preparations it was implemented after 2 long years. So what we saw during last 70 days was the result of well planned foolproof preparations \ by the RBI and government! The RBI was asked its opinion on demonetisation on 7th November, 2016 to reply by the next day!

Zero balance *Jan Dhan* accounts were also opened throughout the country by the NDA 2 Govt. while this preparation for 'demonetisation' was going on since 2014. Many such accounts were without any balance till demonetisation was announced on 8th November, 2016. Govt. claims that some of these zero balance Accounts were used successfully to hide 'illegal income' or black money. Suspicion is natural that why such accounts were opened before 'demonetisation', it provided holders of black money to defeat the main purpose of 'demonetisation': small amount each in zero balance *Jan Dhan* acoount can hide huge black money. Why it was not thought of while opening *Jan Dhan* Accounts?

The government is trying to explain why remonetisation is lagging behind the scheduled last date of demonetisation. The RBI Governor informed the Parliamentary panel that the exact amount of currency returned was under calculation, but till middle of January, 2017 The government circulated only Rs 9.2 lakh cores worth of new notes or around 60 percent of demonetized notes. It is clearly evident that after declaring 86 percent of currency in circulation as 'illegal tender' on 8th of November, 2016, it was planned to remonetise only 60 percent of the value of currency withdrawn. Once RBI calculates the amount of money returned by people we shall be able to calculate the gap between currency collected and currency circulated. If only 60 percent of the demonetised currency was remonetised and that created a virtual social crisis for more than 60 long days, the authorities involved are accountable to people of this country.

IV

As part of 'Globalization', our government agreed with the World Bank and IMF to increase digital payment and to allow MNCs to increase their plastic card transactions in India. Indians particularly in rural India are under pressure by foreign agencies to increase the quantum of cashless transactions. The government of India implemented in 1991 the 'Globalisation' plan of World Bank and IMF. WTO was introduced in India in 1995 and opened all gates of import to India from developed world. Our export market and manufacturing industry suffered from acute competition from China and other developed countries. MNCs have successfully exploited huge market in India of 1300 million people and high profile advertisement that 'globalisation' will create huge job opportunities to millions of our unemployed youth remained a day dream! Yes, our youth are used as contractors' labour by e-commerce industry funded mainly by MNCs. Only information technology cannot solve this huge problem of unemployment in India. 'Cashless transactions' are increasing every day.

Plastic card traders like 'Visa', 'Master Card' etc. are trying to take advantage of 'demonetisation' and the government is helping them by delaying its programme of 'remonetisation'. Why there should be rationing on withdrawal from banks even after 15th of January, 2017, around 70 days have passed and the bona fide customers of banks are deprived of their right to withdraw their own hard earned money. International plastic money industry is thanking the present government for creating such huge opportunities to earn unscheduled income from this vast country.

The World Bank and IMF are there to look after the interest of only limited a number of developed countries and to pressurise the governments in the rest of the world to allow only the MNCs to operate at the cost of local initiative. It is their initiative to hand over the Indian market of the second largest populated country to 'digital payment' companies. Visa Card, Master Card many other payment systems are there for long time but they refused to accommodate the need of not so rich customers. Recently Govt. ordered petrol pumps to go for card payment business, petrol pump owners refused to accept cards because of the 'high transaction charges' of these card companies. The government of India appears committed to fulfill the demand of the World Bank and IMF. It wants a 'Cashless economy' in a country of 1300 million population where 70 percent of people still live in villages devoid of all modern infrastructure required for civilized living. Most of them are small and marginal farmers and landless labourers. They only know currency issued by RBI and some metal ornaments, may be needed in emergency. Hardly one-fifth of Indians are using the so called 'smart phone' and for card selling companies it is not an average Indian they are interested, rather they are searching only 'money bags' who are still not in their net. These Digital Payment companies want laws to compel these big fish only to carry on exclusively 'digital payments'. These MNCs are in India for a long time and charging huge charges from their customers. Is there any law to fix their various charges or they are allowed to trade as our private money lenders do? What is the interest rate they charge from defaulters? Is there any statutory authority to supervise the activities of these digital companies engaged in monitory services? Can the RBI ignore supervision of their transactions? Is there any one in the country to see that unorganised customers are not exploited by these MNCs in third world countries? Village moneylenders are criticized in India for extortion and the suicide deaths of their clients due to harassments. These Plastic card companies have to gain the confidence of people that they are not oppressive in their dealings with customers.

In the capitalist system of the 21st Century international trade is operated mainly through the **well planned geographical distribution of 'Tax Heavens'.** India and many emerging economies are officially treated as 'aid receiving countries' because without Foreign Direct Investments (FDI) the emerging countries will remain poor. History tells us these poor colonies in Asia, Africa and Latin America helped the economic growth of the now rich countries in Europe and America who pretend to help the emerging countries by trade and aid. Colonies of yesteryear are now bad words but what is the role of the MNCs and international trade agreements? Oil producing companies are all from developed countries and by reducing oil production recently are they helping poor countries or taking away what they gave them as FDI? 'Over and under invoicing' is treated as a modern scientific means to cheat countries where these corporations are registered. If fair calculation is done by some impartial international agency the result will show that what is written in textbooks is never practiced in real life. Rich countries never help by investing in poor countries, rather poor countries get poorer by the well planned exploitation of their natural resources and unorganised labour by these foreign corporate. Recent experience in India will be remembered for long time.

A particular foreign company did transaction in one of the Tax Heavens, earned Capital Gain and escaped capital gain tax as it was earned in one of the Tax Heavens. When the law was amended to give effect retrospectively eminent lawyers irrespective of political affiliation supported the foreign company, though such actions are criticised as 'antinational' publicly. Thus it is not very difficult to prove that though so much advertisement is made that rich countries are responsible for the development of poor countries through FDI transfer etc. but in real life poor countries are getting poorer and rich countries are accumulating more wealth. In December, 2016 the USA Federal Reserve increased the interest rate, immediately all investments of the world migrated to USA. Foreign investors in India withdrew Rs 66,507 crores in November and December, 2016 and Rs 5145 crores in January, 2017 or a total of Rs 71652 crores during the demonetisation period. (Indian Express 23.1.2017) This is their love for emerging countries. What role these tax heavens are performing in 21st Century? Poorer countries are cheated both ways: their export price is manipulated and they receive less foreign exchange as 'receiving countries' and even then so called rich countries are treated as 'donor' countries. However, it is yet to be agreed that without huge contribution from emerging economies so called 'rich countries' cannot maintain their 'richness'. The disturbing factors are many in the capitalist system; role of Tax Heavens and invoicing methodology have proved beyond doubt that it is not rich countries that help emerging countries but in reality it was working in reverse direction. What India lost during colonial rule for 200 years and helped the developed world of today it lost a larger and larger amount by allowing malpractices in invoicing mechanism and international trade through 'Tax Heavens'. This is explained in detail in a recent article: Aid in reverse: how poor countries develop rich countries | Jason Hickel *(https://www.theguardian.com › Business › Trade and development)*

V

Demonetisation has opened a Pandora's box. What was the compulsion to drag all the Indians throughout the country to line up before banks and ATMs? We have various organizations and judiciary to implement laws of the country. If it is proved that 86 percent currency as on 8th November which was demonetised and returned by the holders, then the government has to answer where black money in form of cash is? Wait for the result. The government has agreed there was no counterfeit currency received by banks. Already new notes are available which are counterfeit. So technology has to improve. Tax Heavens and their role is now going to stay, if the government of India feels they are functioning against the interest of the country, the necessary changes in our Tax laws are to be made to discourage transactions through tax heavens to stop loss of taxes. Demonetisation has taught a good lesson that average Indians are basically honest and peace loving citizen, they suffered without protesting. Unreasonable harassment in the hands of bureaucracy, they are still silent not that people are weak, but they are waiting for the expression of 'sorry' by the government for such inhuman torture of millions of people all these days. All political parties know that in a democracy citizens are masters and each and every citizen should be respected irrespective of age and gender. Accumulators of wealth through illegal means in India are known to bureaucrats. Many politicians in India are working as paid agents of some institutions and groups who are working against the interest ordinary people of this country.

VI

The discussion will remain incomplete if it is not mentioned here that during the demonetisation issue period one felt the absence of our 'trade unions' and the heroic role of the Trade Union Movement of the 60s and 70s. The repressive mechanism has totally destroyed the will power of workers to fight against oppression. Some efforts were made by employees and officers' association of RBI to question the 'deaf and dumb' behaviour of the RBI administration, but it was very mild. The rest of the Public Sector Bank Employees Unions remained silent while working from morning till late night all these days and ordinary citizen appreciated sincere and hard work done by them. People wanted more constructive suggestions from their organisations because they fought for the people on many occasions a long time ago. It is good that workers of Indian Banks have decided to go for one day strike on 7th. February, 2016. We desire Trade Union Movements in the country to be more active at this moment to retain whatever workers gained from their oppressive employers after long sacrifices all these years. We should see the clear writings on the wall.

25.01.17

TWO BUDGETS, DIFFERING CONTEXTS, BUT SINGLE THRUST FISCAL CONSOLIDATION AND REDUCTION IN SOCIAL DEVELOPMENT
PART I (BUDGET 2016-17)

K.B. Saxena

Budget exercise in India carries importance disproportionate to its contribution in economic governance of the country. Policy pronouncements relating to macro-economy which provide signals about the direction of the economy are far more important Budgets are indicative of only the priorities during the year. Budget provisions are, however, looked at eagerly by various interest groups to see how they would affect them during the financial year. The budget last year, became relatively more important due to slowing down of economy notwithstanding a reasonable GDP growth rate, and the crucial choices that have to be made to revive it. The factors contributing to the economic slowdown included, on the external side, falling oil prices, depressed demand across the world particularly from developed countries including China and dwindling exports, and, on the national side, manufacturing sector showing no signs of picking up (except in mining and electricity), lower growth rate of many industries compared to the preceding year, unutilized capacity in some industries such as steel and aluminum, slowing down of demand for industrial credit and little sign of enthusiasm in private sector to invest. This was further compounded by lack of growth in agriculture, consecutive drought for the preceding three years, persistent agrarian crisis with no respite in farmers' suicides, falling commodity prices, declining output of important crops and increasing cost of agricultural inputs. The combined effect of depression in industrial and agricultural growth resulted in absence of employment opportunities, low purchasing power of a large section of people and very weak domestic demand for goods and services. The situation demanded increased public spending in infrastructure and social sectors to boost rural economy and generate domestic demand. Government, however, responded to these challenges by choosing to pursue the path of fiscal consolidation initiated during the preceding year with the assurance of further reduction in fiscal deficit and reduced public spending with a view to placating international investors, rating agencies and international financial institutions and incentivizing foreign direct investment which is Government's main strategy to accelerate investment and generate jobs.

The reduction in fiscal deficit was pursued by slashing subsidies rather than by raising taxes. Thus, growth fundamentalism emerged as an overarching feature of the Budget.

But the budget also claimed to have made provision for boosting rural economy to generate domestic demand by increased public spending. The claim was supported by the increased outlay for agricultural sector and rural development and enhanced budgetary expenditure (in absolute numbers) of Rs. 1.93 lakh crore. This claim, however, does not stand the test of scrutiny. With regard to the enhanced expenditure, 2/3 of it is non-plan i.e., interest payment, pensions, defence etc. which does not have any developmental dimension. Only 1/3 of government expenditure is on the plan side which includes infrastructure and social sectors, with the former getting far more weightage than the latter. This again is projected as an aid to growth. Besides, in overall terms, the government expenditure as percentage of GDP (after accounting for inflation) fell from 13.2% (2015-16 RE) to 13.1% (2016-17 BE) (CBGA, 2016). The decline was more when compared to 2012-13 when it was (14.2%) and 2009-10 in which it was 15.9% of GDP. Its developmental dimension gets diluted as the expenditure profile in the Union Budget also showed a lower priority to social sector. This was achieved by two methods, direct and Indirect. The direct method was by failing to provide sufficient allocation for Social Sector. Though allocation for social sector in 2016-17 BE was higher at 3.15% of GDP compared to 3.05% in the preceding year, the actual spending to sustain this only at the RE stage as usually expenditure cuts were resorted to during the second half of the year, particularly as the expectations regarding the tax receipts failed to materialize. Besides, Social sector expenditure by virtually all States had been around 36% of the total state expenditure except, surprisingly, for Bihar and Jharkhand where it had been higher (CBGA, 2016). It was therefore, unlikely that States would be able to push this expenditure substantially. This level of spending in social sector was very low, given our dismal position in the HDI which is lower than some of our much smaller neighbors and lower than even the level promised to people (for education and health for example) during 2014 elections. This appeared to be by design rather than stemming from constraint of resources per se since the Government was unwilling to increase taxes to raise resources despite a very low Tax – GDP ratio in the country which in 2016-17 (BE) continued to be at 10.8%. and no growth over last year's level of tax revenue was anticipated or projected in the budget. The implication was that not only there was little scope for public expenditure being raised during the year but also that, if the estimated revenue generation did not materialize, the axe would fall on social sector expenditure as it had happened in the past.

Public expenditure in social sectors was also reduced through indirect method, i.e., transferring greater financial responsibility for social sector schemes to the States which was justified on account of increased devolution of resources to the States by the 14th Finance Commission. This was effected by 1) Central government shedding its responsibility of funding some schemes altogether leaving the States entirely to decide whether to continue with them and, if so, to fund them. These schemes were most likely to be discontinued due to paucity of resources with most of the States 2) schemes which were transferred to the States with reduced central share of 60% instead of existing 75% thereby increasing state share to 40% in place of existing 25% and accordingly reduced allocation in the Union Budget 2016-17 for them. The schemes so affected related to major social sectors – Education, such as ICDS, Sarv Shiksha Adbiyan, Midday Meal, and Health such as National Health Mission, Swachch Bharat Abhiyan etc. The change would adversely affect implementation of these schemes even at the existing level of coverage (which itself is inadequate) while the question of expansion of coverage and improvement in infrastructure and unit level increase in expenditure were unlikely to happen in many States. This was likely to be so particularly in respect of resource poor States where the coverage was lower, infrastructure deficient and which also had lower potential to generate increased revenue. This apprehension arose because of two reasons. One was the uncertainty about the quantum of net accrual of additional resources to each State post devolution and the other was whether it would be sufficient to fill the resource gap caused by reduced central share. The first apprehension was sustained by a RBI study based on 2015-16 Budget estimates which found that despite the increased share in central taxes by 0.5% of the GDP in 2015-16, the net impact of changed funding was a decline of 0.3% in central transfer of funds from the previous years (cited in Shetty, 2016). Further, Central Assistance and Special Central Assistance were reported to be subsumed in devolution implying that States would lose this amount as well which they received earlier in addition to normal plan assistance. Also, surcharges and cesses were not shared with the States. The increasing use of surcharge and cess as a taxing device in the central Budget itself was an unfair attempt to deprive the states of their legitimate share in the Central taxes and therefore eroded the spirit of federal structure. This did not exemplify the spirit of 'cooperative federalism' which was so eloquently being quoted as an example of greater democratic credentials of NDA government. The other concern was that the poor and marginalized sections of the society had low political clout in decision making at the State level. Faced with the competing demands for resources from other sectors of economy and more vocal and assertive interest groups, these schemes which largely benefited these sections were unlikely to receive the priority and the level of resources they deserved.

Yet another policy measure which was likely to affect expenditure in social sector was the announcement of the Government to remove the distinction between Plan and Non-Plan spending with effect from 2017-18. Non-Plan expenditure relates to any expenditure that does not fall within the Plan expenditure while the Plan expenditure relates to financing of development schemes approved under the Plan and the unfinanced tasks of the previous plan. Once a scheme / programme taken up in a Plan completes its duration, its maintenance cost and remaining expenditure in subsequent years becomes non-Plan expenditure. This distinction was rigorously maintained to ensure that there was sufficient money for taking up new development programmes. With the abolition of this distinction, there was likelihood of 'non-plan' expenditure increasing substantially leaving lesser resources for new development schemes or expansion of existing schemes. Besides, this decision would have an adverse impact on those planning mechanisms which involved pooling of resources from Plan allocations to ensure adequate flow of funds to certain marginalized groups who may otherwise fail to get their due share from development schemes when competing with 'advanced' groups. The most important of such mechanisms were the Scheduled Caste Sub-Plan and Tribal Sub-Plan which prescribed a specified percentage of plan funds flowing towards their development based on the percentage of their population. Since this mechanism only operated in respect of Plan expenditure, there was no indication of the new basis on which funds would be transferred to these two Sub-Plans. Would the combined expenditure (Plan & non-Plan) form this basis? There was apprehension that in working out an alternative basis for pooling of resources, this mechanism might get progressively diluted, with the likelihood of it getting eroded and eventually disappearing. This was so because this mechanism had emerged not from on any statutory requirement but only constituted a planning strategy pursued through executive orders. Further, this arrangement had never had a smooth sailing even when it was formally adhered to. A great deal of resistance was encountered from sectoral ministries in enforcing it. The SCs/STs were politically weak and lacked sufficient clout in decision making to ensure that their interests were not undermined in the new arrangement.

There was yet another development which created unease about its likely adverse impact on the expenditure in the social sector. This was the seriousness with which Government proposed to enforce distinction between Revenue and Capital expenditure. Expenditure is labeled as 'Capital' when it increases assets and reduces liabilities of the government and is non-recurring in nature. Revenue expenditure involves recurring nature of expenditure such as salaries of employees, food subsidy, procurement of medicines for hospitals etc. It is well known that revenue expenditure in social sector schemes is much larger than the capital expenditure. Central government had hinted that it would no more finance 'revenue' expenditure in centrally funded schemes transferred to the States and would only fund 'capital' expenditure. This would shift the entire burden of meeting revenue expenditure on to the States which would find it difficult to bear within the resources available to them. This could also adversely affect efficient implementation of schemes as State government would hesitate to provide for adequate staff and maintenance of infrastructure to run these schemes so as to avoid continuing liability. This was most likely to happen in respect of States which could not put in additional resources from their side due to a weak resource base and relatively low potential for increased taxation.

There was also apprehension that social sector expenditure might also get curtailed because of Government's policy to push Direct Benefit Transfer in terms of cash to the accounts of beneficiaries based on Aadhar identification notwithstanding the direction of the Supreme Court to the contrary. This was justified on the ground that it would eliminate leakage i.e., benefits going to ineligible beneficiaries since bio-metric prints of the person would authenticate his / her identity. This requirement has already been posing problems as there had been complaints of delays, authentication failures, connectively problems among others. In Jharkhand, for example, many MGNREGS cards were cancelled for the sake of achieving 100% Aadhar seeding. MGNREGS workers had been off loaded by rural banks because their business correspondents were unable to pay them due to poor connectivity. Accounts in banks opened through Aadhar number faced authentication issues. There was thus a serious apprehension that Aadhar would turn out to be yet another mode of exclusion of the genuinely poor just as the BPL list was in the earlier dispensation.

The most significant departure in development policy made by the current Government has been the abolition of the Planning Commission and the abandonment of the planning process. This was evident as there was no Thirteenth Plan in sight. Government was replacing the plan with a long term vision document. This had implications for social sector expenditure because Planning Commission acted as a monitor to ensure that sectoral expenditures were adhered to, kept an eye on diversion, non utilization and mis-utilization of funds. It also ensured that Sub-Plan mechanisms were enforced and Central ministries and States earmarked the required percentage of funds from plan schemes to this pool. But far more important was its role in minimizing regional inequalities which had increased with the shift to a market economy. With no agency of comparable stature to oversee the pattern of expenditure at the central & state level (Niti Ayog is entrusted with Policy and advisory role), the limited thrust in favour of social sector expenditure that was pursued through the planning process would get severely undermined. Worse, the abolition of the Planning Commission had also removed the only forum available to civil society groups to raise their concerns and participate, however marginally, in the policy making process on development issues. This government, in any case, did not attach any value to the civil society groups – the social activists, NGOS and CBO and their views. This left the field wide open to the corporates and intellectuals of neoliberal persuasion to have a dominant say in the public policy making process.

The Budget 2016-17 was marked by two dominant trends. One was the rigorous pursuit of fiscal consolidation and measures undertaken to attract investment, particularly foreign. The other was the shrinking commitment to Social Development manifested in transferring of many Central schemes to States and reducing Central share in funding them and underfunding those that it still retained with the Central Government. It was also pushing favorite neo-liberal agenda of progressively replacing essential services provided by the Government with cash transfer or off loading the responsibility to the private sector providers. In the latter case, it had not hesitation in trampling on even right based entitlements. Further, an elitist approach underlined the strategy of implementation of some of the crucial social sector schemes. These brief observations became evident with reference to Budget proposals 2016-17 in respect of major Social Sectors – Education, Health, Agriculture, Food Security, Rural Development.

Education

Education is the most important subsector of social sector basket where a statutory responsibility, bolstered by Supreme Court directions, underline the right of school going children to get access to education. Consistent with its overall approach of downsizing the involvement of Union Government in Social Sector, the budgetary allocation made a meager enhancement in allocation for School Education from Rs. 42187 cr. in 2015-16 (RE), to Rs. 43554 cr. in 2016-17 BE, showing an increase of Rs. 1367 cr (3.2%) and in Higher Education from Rs. 25399 cr (2015-16) RE to Rs. 28840 (2016-17) BE, accounting for an increase of Rs. 3441 cr. or around 13.5%. Between the two, the Higher Education fared marginally better than School Education but neither of them responded to the enormity of the problems each one of the two sub-sectors faces. In fact, Union Government's expenditure in the sector showed a decline as a percentage of GDP from 0.66% in 2012-13 and 0.55% in 2014-15 to 0.48 in 2016-17 (BE). Even as a percentage of Union Government's Expenditure, it was reduced from 4.7% in 2012-13 and 4.1% in 2014-15 to 3.7% in 2016-17 (BE) (CBGA, 2016). This was despite the fact that the norms of provisioning for school education are governed by RTE. The Programme which translates this statutory requirement into deliverables is SSA (Sarva Shiksha Abhiyan) which was allocated Rs. 22500 cr., a mere 2.2% increase over 2015-16 (BE) allocation of Rs. 22015 cr. which could not even absorb the impact of inflation. In fact, the allocation had been reduced by Rs. 1597 cr in comparison to the allocation made in 2014-15. Worse, 65% of this meager allocation was financed from Education Cess and only 29% from the Gross Budgetary Support. This violated the clarification given by the then the UPA Government while introducing this levy that the money from the collection would be an additive to the normal allocation for the Programme (CSD, 2016). This arrangement virtually reduced the overall financial commitment of the Union government to the sector. The low allocation was justified on the ground that Central Government's share in the programme had been reduced from 80% to 60% pursuant to higher devolution of resources to the States from the 14th Finance Commission. The reduced Central share increased the financial burden of States enormously as the States do not get any share in the collections from the cesses. This implied that even the existing programme implementation would suffer irreparably where states were unable to put in this amount. The problem was far graver because even if States were to contribute their required share of 40%(which was unlikely in respect of financially weak States) the overall resource commitment itself was inadequate given that only 8% of schools met all the required norms laid down by RTE and 83% schools had a single teacher and 18.3% of children in 6-14 age group were still out of school (CBGA, 2016). This was hardly a recipe for improving the quality of School Education which the Finance Minister had recognized as a major problem. Further, teachers training which was the most important factor in the improvement of quality of education witnessed a reduction in its allocation from Rs. 558 cr. to Rs. 510 cr. RTE is a central law and Union Government has a major responsibility for ensuring sufficiency of resources for its implementation. The continuing poor quality of education resulting from inadequate provision of resources is pushing more and more children to private schools and, in some areas, even closing down of schools on ground of lack of students. This was a clear enough indication, if any was needed, of subtle undermining of the right based entitlement.

The Budget also had an elitist approach to improve the quality of education (CSD,2016). This was evident in promoting islands of improved educational institutions amidst vast number of those with poor quality. This emerged from two major announcements. One was that 62 new Navodya Vidyalyas would be setup and the other was to make 20 universities (10 public & 10 private) institutions of excellence. This was a typical method of securing the best opportunities for the better off and cornering meager resources for them. This would further reinforce inequality in access to education, its quality and outcomes. The vast majority of students who would not be able to get entry into these good quality institutions would be doomed to fail in realizing their aspiration for good quality jobs when they had to compete with students educated in them. The 750 universities and 50,000 colleges which provided access to higher education for students from non-elite families would continue to suffer from paucity of resources to improve infrastructure, and faculty. The Budget provided little hope for them in enhancing the quality of education imparted in them.

The third major announcement was about setting up a Higher Education Financing Agency with a capital base of Rs. 1000 cr. to leverage funds from private sector. This reliance on private sector to discharge a responsibility which essentially was of that government had many adverse implications. First, private sector funding would be no charity. It would have strings attached to it. The private sector financier would determine selection of institutions to provide funds, the area of study it should focus on, selection of courses, their content and orientation suited to its requirement and fee structure. Altogether this arrangement would benefit a very few selected institutions – perhaps the 20 institutions of excellence referred to earlier. This would inevitably restrict access to institutions so financed to a select few who could afford it. The students coming from the 'Aam Admi' background would be condemned to poor quality of education and would have no chance to realize their aspirations.

Health

Health is the other significant social sector which has relevance for the lives of the Common Persons particularly the poor. The Budget allocation for the Ministry of Health and Family Welfare was increased from Rs. 33,831 cr. to 38,206 cr. which worked out to an increase of 13%. Though this increase was higher than what had been allocated during the last three years, as percentage of GDP, the allocation continued to remain in the range of 0.25%, and was lower than what was provided 2012-13 when it was 0.27%. (CBGA, 2016) But despite this relatively higher increase, the allocation remained woefully short of the reasonable requirement considering the infrastructural deficit and shortage of manpower in the public health institutions of the country. In fact, Union govt. failed to fulfill its commitment made in the 12th Five Year Plan of raising the total public expenditure on health, centre and state combined, to 2.5% of the GDP from its existing level of slightly more than 1%.

The Budget made three new announcements 1) a new health protection scheme for the poor and economically weak families to reduce their unforeseen out of pocket expenditure which would provide a health cover to them of Rs. 1 lakh per family and for senior citizens another 30,000/- 2) to open 3000 stores under Jan Aushdhi scheme to distribute generic drugs at affordable prices. 3) A national Dialysis Service Programme through PPP mode under National Health Mission to provide Dialysis Services in all district hospitals.

Among the schemes of the Health Ministry, National Health Mission (NHM) is its flagship programme. Earlier called the National Rural Health Mission which dealt with rural areas, NHM new covered rural as well as urban areas. This required substantial increase in the size of its earlier budgetary allocations, more so because urban areas did not even have the primary level health institutions similar to the Sub-Centres, PHCS and CHCs in the rural areas. But budgetary allocation witnessed reduction from Rs. 19,715 cr. in 2014-15 (actual) to Rs. 19037 cr. in 2016-17 BE. Public health facilities had over the years deteriorated due to crumbling infrastructure non-availability of essential drugs and shortage of service providers. The reduced allocation showed that the Government was not really interested in improving their services. Consistent with its aggressive neo-liberal reforms, it wanted to divert patients to the private sector. This intent became clear from a continuous rise in the allocation of Health Insurance Schemes (CGHS, RSBY and RSSY) from 7.3% of the Ministry's budget in 2014-15to 9.5% in 2016-17 (CSD, 2016). This undermined the public health system as bulk of the funds under insurance schemes would go to private sector hospitals on account of their dominance in the tertiary care which the insurance package catered to. As per NSSO 71st round nearly 70% ailments were treated in private hospitals. Thus, public resources were being increasingly transferred to private health sector for its growth and expansion at the cost of the public health system. Besides, undermining the public health system, this reliance on private sector to provide health care to patients was also inefficient use of resources because the average amount of treatment in private hospital as per NSSO 71st round, was four times that of public hospitals (CBGA, 2016). This huge outflow of resources to the private sector would have benefited a large number of people and with greater social accountability of service providers if it had been allocated to public sector health units for improving and expanding their infrastructure. The insurance route to health care had brought out other negative dimensions as well. The scheme package covered only hospitalization cost but did not include OPD expenses and ancillary expenses incurred by the patients in availing of hospitalization. While major health episodes requiring hospitalization were fewer, larger expenditure was incurred on outpatient care – consultation and drugs. Therefore, there was likely to be no major relief to the poor in cutting down their out of pocket expenditure. Even for serious illness, the amount was inadequate as the cost of a major procedure in a private hospital was unlikely to be covered by this amount. Also, all insurance schemes were targeted. The identification of target group had always posed problems with exclusion of the genuine poor and inclusion of the non-poor. Besides, given the unethical practices resorted to by private sector and no functional regulatory system in place, exposing the poor of the country to private sector hospital services posed greater risk to their health as well. Also, given the small allocation made compared to the magnitude of the problem, the coverage of beneficiaries in the health insurance schemes would be a very small percentage of 8 crore households.

The allocation for PMSSY (Pradhan Mantri Swasthy Suraksha Yojna) which was about setting up of AIIMS type of Super Specialty Hospitalscum-Teaching Institutes and Upgrading of State Government hospitals has been enhanced. Quite apart from low level of utilization of allocated amount in 2014-15 which could be on account of design problems, the larger question the scheme raised was about the misplaced priority of the Government which focused overwhelmingly on tertiary care and ignored primary and preventive health care. A sound public health perspective did not inform Government's thinking. A large majority of illness episodes could be addressed with effective preventive care and efficient primary health care. This focus on tertiary care was an off-shoot of formidable clout the private sector enjoys in health policy making which had a dominance in this segment and was keen on promoting it due to enormous profits that can be earned. It was not interested in preventive or primary health care. The increasing dependence on private sector for providing health care was also manifested in the proposed new scheme of National Dialysis Service Programme which would operate in 'ppp' mode.

The promise made of supply of essential drugs in public hospitals free of cost was given up. Even as a mechanism to supply medicines at regulated prices, the Jan Aushdhi Scheme started in 2008 had not been successful because only 164 such stores were opened and in the last 8 years of which only 87 (50%) were functional (CBGA, 2018). The scheme received an increase of Rs. 18 crore which could not cater to even half of the proposed 1000 centres. Besides the scheme suffered from major operational problems such as non-availability of medicines under generic names, doctors not prescribing generic drugs (particularly those in private health units) and patients not in a position to make their own decision in the matter. With pharmaceutical sector having been opened to 100% FDI, there was likelihood of MNCs taking over local generic drug producing companies. The danger of generic drugs too becoming more expensive therefore loomed large.

Agriculture

Agriculture is considered a major social sub sector of development due to the largest segment of man power dependent upon and employed in. Its development is crucial for their well being. Agriculture is also important for its crucial role in generating employment and income and despite its very low and diminishing contribution to GDP has a huge potential for poverty alleviation due to its employment elasticity. A small boost in investment in it can create more jobs in agriculture than in manufacturing. Ministry of Agriculture therefore was rightly targeted for attention in the Budget and was allocated Rs. 44,486 cr., compared to Rs. 35958 cr. in 2015-16 (RE), an increase of around 13.5%. But within the Ministry, the Department of agriculture and farmers' welfare seemed to have received a much higher share of increase of Rs. 35984 cr. from Rs. 15,809 cr. in 2015-16 (RE), an increase of 127%. A closer scrutiny, however, revealed that there was a bit a cleverness in this increase as Rs. 15000 cr. on Interest subvention for short term credit was shifted from Ministry of Finance to Ministry of Agriculture. The actual increase for Agriculture, therefore, was modest. Rather, as percentage of GDP, Agriculture's share continued to be at 0.30% which was in 2012-13 though it did increase from the level provided in 2015-16 (RE). As a percentage of Union government's expenditure, too, it increased to 2.25% from 2.01% in 2015-16 (RE) (CBGA, 2016). But the bulk of this increase was made for Crop Insurance Scheme (Rs. 5500 cr) where there was an upward revision from Rs. 2955 cr. (2015-16 RE). The other major announcements in the Budget included 1) Government's intention to double the income of farmers by 2022, enhancement of Rs. 500 cr for pulses production, Rs. 850 cr for four new projects in the Livestock Development sector and a dedicated long term irrigation fund in NABARD with an initial corpus of Rs. 20,000 cr. It was also proposed to levy a surcharge at 0.5% at all taxable services for exclusive benefit of the sector & farmers and another 7.5% surcharge on undisclosed income.

There was, however, no road map of how the Government would double the income of farmers. Agriculture has been under distress for a long time. The level of investment proposed in irrigation, crop insurance and interest subvention does not even begin to address the structural, developmental and environmental crisis in agriculture and lack of public investment besides several policies which contribute to it. Farmers are not wage employees whose salaries can be increased through an executive order. Their income comes from what they produce and sell, besides wages earned in non-agricultural work. Government did not even announce MSP based on 50% above cost which was promised in the BJP manifesto. The existing growth rate in agriculture was very low at less than 2% (Nayar, 2016) and far lower than that of general economy which was at 7-7.5%. Failure of three consecutive crops had reduced the growth rate of rural wages. 84% of the farms were small and marginal where average income was Rs. 2000/- pm while it was Rs. 10000/- or more for a middle class family (Nayar & Misra, 2016). Farmers' suicides continued unabated due to indebtedness and failure of crops. Even if the Government was lucky with the monsoon during the calendar year, it would require a growth rate of 14% - 15% per annum in farm Income each and every year until 2022 to double the income in five years (Jha et al – 2016). Agriculture sector had not even been able to achieve 4% rate of growth rate that the UPA government had aspired to achieve. Massive Public investment, addressing high input cost and lower output prices, restoration of environmental degradation and increase in non-farm employment was required to put agriculture on the path to recovery from existing depressing state.

While the stress on pulses production was a right step, the level of enhanced allocation at Rs. 500 cr for incentivizing it in 640 districts was too inadequate to yield any significant outcome. The provision of a meager Rs. 385 cr for soil health and fertility was too inadequate considering the magnitude of the problem. Enhancement of credit from 8.5 lakh crore to 9.00 lakh crore was unlikely to benefit the needy small and marginal farmers due not only to a large number being defaulters but also because bulk of this credit was cornered by agri-business and large farmers as conditions of eligibility to access this credit had been liberalized. Their dependence on money lenders would therefore continue The promised coverage of Rural electrification as an aid to boost rural economy had to contend with the gap between provision of connection and supply of electricity, high cost, unsustainable supply, breakdown in infrastructure and under utilization of generated power in some areas on account of high cost (CITU, 2016). The creation of an irrigation fund in NABARD was virtually a revival of AIBP scheme of UPA which did not produce the desired outcomes (Alagh, 2016). There were too may incomplete schemes languishing for want of resources and the area to be covered by assured irrigation was too huge for this meager level of resource input to address the enormity of the problem. Besides, policy intervention was required to address issues of water use efficiency, over extraction of ground water and revival and rejuvenation of traditional water bodies. Crop insurance scheme though better than its existing versions still did not provide comprehensive coverage of all crops against all forms of damage and at all stages of crop cycle. It also did not subsidize the entire premium besides providing assessment of crop damage Block / Taluk level rather than at village level and made area rather than individual as a unit of assessment. It covered neither comprehensive nor universal converge nor income and yield risks and exempted non-loan farmers from its operations. Besides, in the absence of updated land records, the benefits of even this proposed scheme would fail to reach the affected cultivator. In this sector too, the Budget pushed its aggressive neo-liberal agenda by providing for 100 foreign owned firms to market agriculture products, thereby exposing farmers to MNCs and creating distortion in the domestic market with shortages in one part of the country co-existing with exports in another and MNCs buying cheap from one part and selling at higher prices in another.

The decentralized procurement proposed in the Budget speech was already provided for in NFSA (National Food Security Act). But it was unlikely to materialize in the absence of storage infrastructure, a dedicated agency with working capital to operate and linking it with local production. Besides, there was apprehension that this proposal might be used to dismantle Food Corporation of India and eventually the Public District System by replacing it with cash transfers which is what the advocates of economic reforms have been pushing.

Rural Development

It had also been claimed by the Finance Minister that the budget would boost rural economy. The claim was supported on the ground of a) increase in the allocation of Ministry of Rural Development from Rs. 79228 cr. (2015-16) RE to Rs. 87765 cr. (2016-17). MGNREGS received a major chunk of this increase which had risen from Rs. 35,766 cr. (2015-16) RE – to Rs. 38,500 cr in 2016-17 BE. But MNREGS allocation as a percentage of expenditure on Rural Development, was reduced from 47.6% in 2015-16 (RE) to 44.7% in 2016-17 and as a percentage of total expenditure from 2.1% to 1.95%. Besides, this increase was too little given the fact that there was an unpaid wage liability Rs. 4000 cr (it was actually far more) and a little less of unpaid material Bill over Rs. 6000 cr. (Sainath, 2016) of the preceding year. The latter would eat up around 20-25% of the year's allocation. In fact, the enhanced allocation for MGNREGS had not even reached the level of Rs. 40,000 cr made in 2010-11. The outlay was, in fact, much less in real terms when inflation was taken into account. The number of days of employment had increased compared to the preceding year and might exceed the average of previous years. Due to persistent droughts in many areas, the demand for work had increased considerably and number of days of guaranteed employment had been raised to 150 days in these areas. Besides, the Budget speech also mentioned cluster facilitation approach to articulate the hidden demand for work from backward and drought prone areas and ensure construction of water storage structures and natural resources management. The meager increase in allocation therefore far from boosting the rural economy would slow it down if additional allocations are not made and wages are not paid in time. Also, the delay in release of allocation would stop further work execution and increase distress migration. All this would have required far greater increase in allocation for MGNREGS than what was given. This was amply borne out by recent Supreme Court directions to the Central Government.

NRLM which focuses on self employment was also allocated an increase of around Rs. 1500 cr over the last years RE. NRLM was the least provided of the four major programmes as a percentage of 12th Plan outlay. With the intensification of efforts for formation of Self-Help Groups to promote multiple livelihoods, NRLM implementation was also expected to improve with greater utilization of funds and consequently demand for fund was likely to increase. IAY was also given an increase of Rs. 5000 cr. Though welcome, the programme had huge unmet demand. Besides, the increase made in the unit cost of the schemes recently would prevent substantial enhanced coverage which was anticipated with higher allocation. PMGSY, which related to construction of rural roads, despite Government's emphasis on infrastructure development and even with an enhanced allocation of around Rs. 4000 cr, would end up receiving only 53% of the allocation as a percentage of 12th Plan outlay, lowest among major programmes of the Ministry.

The Budget also added five new schemes.

1. Development of 3000 Urban Clusters as Growth centres under Shyama Prasad Mukherji Mission

2. Electrification of 18452 villages in 1000 days under Dean Dayal Upadhyay Gram Jyoti Yojna and IPDS.

3. Digital literacy under which two schemes would be taken up 1) National Digital Literacy Mission with allocation of Rs. 16.8 cr. and 2) Digital Saaksharta Abhyan (DISHA) with Rs. 12.00 cr. as allocation to cover 6cr. households in three years

4. Modernization of Land Records for integrated land information Management system. Rs. 150 cr had been provided for this purpose.

5. Rashtriya Gram Swaraj Yojna for which Rs. 655 cr. had been provided.

None of these schemes would contribute significantly to accelerating growth in rural areas Development of Urban Clusters would require considerable investment in rural infrastructure in the Small and Medium towns, first for improving infrastructure - sanitation, drinking water, power supply, road connectivity, housing, transport, credit and storage which not only remained neglected but would get relegated further with emphasis on Smart Cities development. Additionally, a substantial part of this infrastructure would have to be provided in these 300 clusters to spur growth. Where was the money for undertaking this massive infrastructure development?

Rural Electrification of villages must confront the problem of many electrified villages getting no electricity, many villages with merely an electricity pole counting for electrification, dilapidated and damaged infrastructure, sustainability of supply and its cost. A reality check was first of all necessary regarding villages claimed to have been electrified, sustainability of power supply, power generation capacity lying idle due to high cost of supply before its contribution to the economic growth of area could be assessed.

Digital Literacy targets were unachievable with poor quality of school education and absence of assured electric supply. Modernization of land records scheme had been in operation for a very long time but with little improvement in the updating of land records. Its achievement wherever registered had been largely towards digitization of information in the existing land records. But this information itself was dated. It needed to be brought up-to-date. Mere computerization of information and technological interventions in mapping of revenue villages and landholdings therein could not lead to land records upgradation. Land records updating was a very labour intensive and time taking task which required substantial resources, both financial and manpower, as well as time which states were unable to provide.

Rashtriya Gram Swaraj Yojana was virtually the renaming of the old scheme for strengthening PRIs which had been abandoned. The crucial problem which stifles PRI functioning was lack of devolution of three 'F's - Functions, Functionaries and Finances on the operational side, and infrastructure, capacity building and supportive manpower on the structural side. Rs. 655 cr. provided under the scheme was too inadequate to cater to the infrastructure on such a large scale. Fourteenth Finance Committee had provided substantial funds for Panchayats which hopefully would improve infrastructure to some extent. As the details of the scheme had not been spelt out, it was difficult to say on what items would the allocated money in the Budget be spent.

Food Security
he Budget showed a decline from Rs. 1.39 lakh cr. (2015-16) RE to 1.34 lakh cr (2016-17) BE in food subsidy which was reflected in fall of expenditure

as a percentage of Union Budget as well as the GDP. The reduction seemed surprising since implementation of NFSA (National Food Security Act) would require increase rather than decline in allocation. Many States had not yet implemented NFSA. Once they did, the allocation would need substantial increase. Besides, the Budget ignored universalization of IGMSY (Maternity Welfare Scheme) and ICDS. FCI's unpaid Bills would further cut into the allocation. This created genuine apprehension about the lack of seriousness in implementing NFSA so as to meet the fiscal consolidation target. This was yet another instance of undermining right based entitlement.

Decentralized Procurement had been proposed for addressing the problem of rotting food grains resulting from lack of storage infrastructure and high cost of transportation of food grains. While NFSA has also suggested decentralized procurement to equitably spread the benefit of procurement across the production zones and boosting local production, there was apprehension that it might be used to dismantle FCI and eventually the PDS itself which had been and continues to be an eye sore to neo-liberal economists and international agencies. The provision for automation facilities and opening of ATMS in rural areas was a pointer towards shifting to cash transfer in place of PDS. If decentralized procurement was effected, without linking it to local production it would force the deficit states which overwhelmingly depended upon FCI for their PDS, to access their requirement from open market. This would push up cost of food grains. It would create a greater crisis in States which did not have a procurement agency. Some states neither had the storage infrastructure nor the working capital to undertake this shift and there was no preparation for local production either to meet the requirement. Besides, the move would affect peasantry in Punjab and Haryana most adversely which supplied a very large part of the food grains procured.

Both the UPA and NDA governments have pursued the path of increasing penetration of market in economy and provision of public services. Between the two, the former tempered this pursuit with some affirmative measures for the Poor such as right based entitlements and modest increase in social expenditure at least in its phase I. The latter, however, is undermining even these measures and aggressively pushing fiscal consolidation and replacing government provisioning of services with private sector provisioning and cash transfers. The analysis of Budget 2016-17 provided modest evidence to support this. But far more was happening on the public policy making front which would be covered in part II of this article.

References:

Alagh, Y.K. (2016). 'Let Them Eat Schemes', *Outlook*, March, 14, 2016

Sainath, P (2013). 'If this is Pro-Farmer', *Outlook*, March, 14, 2016

Patnaik, P. (2016). 'Budget 2016-17: Hype is All', *Peoples Democracy,* July 24, 2016

Centre for Indian Trade Unions (2016). 'Rich in Rhetoric, Poor in Substance' *People's Democracy*, February 28- March 05, 2016

Centre for Budget and Governance Accountability (2016). *Connecting the Dots: An Analysis of Union Budget 2016-*17, March, 2016

Council for Social Development (2016). Discussion on Union Budget 2016-17, *SFF* 1/2016

Shetty, SL (2016). 'Underutilised Fiscal Space: Maharashtra's Budget Post Fourteenth Finance Commission', *Economic and Political Weekly*, May 21, 2016

Nayar, Lola with R.K. Misra (2016). 'Has Modi Junked Gujarat Model', *Outlook*, March 14, 2016

Jha, Ajit Kumar, M.G. Arun and Shweta Punj (2016). 'Down the Country Road', *India Today*, March 14, 2016

CHANT OF THE MASKED PEOPLE

Nirmalangshu Mukherji

[A Slightly shorter version of the piece was published earlier in EPW. Since the anniversary of those events are approaching, it may be interesting to look at the original piece.]

Some significant events took place in recent months in the Jawahar Lal Nehru University (JNU) in Delhi. As the dust on these events is beginning to settle, reflective evaluations have started. According to one historian, these were 'tumultuous events that have convulsed the subcontinent' ('From Institution to Mechanism', *The Hindu*, 8 April). According to another, they signaled a 'coming Left-Ambedkarite revolution' as 'soaring chants' 'rang out on the streets' ('Appropriating Ambedkar', *The Hindu*, 21 April).

From a less charitable perspective, we will see that there indeed were chants by both masked and unmasked protestors; as the official unmasked chants 'soared', they drowned the masked ones, as if by design. In the process, the ruling reactionary regime got what it wanted.

The Arrests

So what happened? According to reports, on 9th February this year a small demonstration took place inside the JNU campus to commemorate the third death anniversary of Afzal Guru. Afzal Guru, a Kashmiri muslim, was hanged and buried inside the Tihar jail in New Delhi for his alleged involvement in the terrorist attack on the Indian parliament on 13 December, 2001. As the evening shadows lengthened, some young people reportedly made speeches and shouted slogans to protest Guru's hanging; allegedly, they also engaged in slogans and chants demanding freedom of Kashmir.

Specifically, it was alleged that, within the collection of young persons, some people masked their faces with cloth. It was also alleged that, during the demonstration, some people shouted slogans that wished the dismemberment of India; they also pledged the continuation of the struggle for freedom until the destruction of India. It is important to note that that is *all* that happened. No arms were displayed and no specific plans for turning these slogans into material action were mooted. At worst, it was a rather strong expression of indignation at perceived massive injustice in Kashmir.

Apparently, a rival student group in the campus protested about what they perceived to be "anti-national" slogans and speeches. As a clash was likely to happen, the Delhi police was informed. Subsequently, after preliminary investigation, three JNU students—Kanhaiya Kumar, Umar Khalid and Anirban Bhattacharya—were arrested. The JNU authorities also proceeded to take disciplinary action against 21 students including the ones just named.

Since the matter is under examination by the courts, in what follows I will not be concerned with the veracity of the reported facts, details about who was present during which part of the event, and who shouted which slogan etc. I will also not comment on the latest disciplinary actions enforced by the JNU authorities; this is a matter internal to the administration of JNU. I am concerned with the larger political significance of 9th February.

To proceed, let me note that the police action was located in a politico-historical context that has nothing to do with JNU per se, the community of students as a whole, the university system, the caste system and tragic suicide of Rohit Vemula in Hyderabad, teachings of Babasaheb Ambedkar, etc. In so far as *this* police action was concerned, it was *not* directed specifically to crush 'what JNU stands for', the 'alternative kind' of students, if any, it nurtures, and the idea of 'liberal education.' To think otherwise is to unduly glorify the intellect governing the Delhi police system.

The police action was specifically directed at what in fact was the case: public display of support for Kashmir and Afzal Guru. The site of JNU was merely incidental. For example, on the same day, a small demonstration to protest Guru's hanging was also organized in Jadavpur University in Kolkata, and the police wanted to take action. However, the vice chancellor of the university did not allow the police to enter the campus and a crisis was averted. As protests on Afzal's hanging refuse to die, it is conceivable that many such meetings took place across the country, especially in Kashmir, often in small public forums outside the university system.

More significantly, a very similar event took place in Delhi itself on the next day, 10th February, at the Press Club of India where people gathered to commemorate the hanging of Afzal Guru. Here as well there were songs, recitations, speeches, and much chanting and sloganeering for nearly three hours. Incidentally, the speakers seated on the dais were associated, not with JNU, but with Delhi University.

This meeting was formally reported to the Delhi police. The speakers were interrogated at length for days, and Dr. S. A. R. Geelani, a teacher in Delhi University, was arrested for conducting the meeting. More on Geelani later. Importantly, the entire focus of the interrogations was to seek information about connections of people in Delhi, such as Geelani, with the resistance in Kashmir. Since I happened to be one of the speakers, the police showed much initial interest in my work on both the parliament attack case and the maoists in India. Here was the juicy prospect of unearthing the shadowy 'mass-front' of a terror network linking maoists and militants in Kashmir with intellectual coordination from universities in Delhi under the very nose of the union home ministry. Unfortunately, the fervent prayers of the police remained unanswered.

Unlike the JNU arrests, Geelani's arrest was not interpreted as an attack on what University of Delhi stands for and the kind of teachers it nurtures. As we will see, the atrocious arrest of a university teacher on sedition charges—for organizing an open public meeting in a very prominent place with due permission—barely found mention in the months that followed. Even though the JNU and the Press Club events were concerned with identical issues, the former was relentlessly highlighted in the public domain while sustained efforts were made to sideline the latter. We need to understand why.

Public protest

The sketched perspective on the arrests—with Kashmir at the center— was largely missing from the very impressive public protests that ensued after the arrest of the JNU students. Consider for example, an otherwise fluent and representative recent article in *The Hindu* on the apparent rise of Ambedkarite politics in some campuses ('Appropriating Ambedkar', April 21). This is how the author, who appears to be a witness to the protests, describes the student movement in one rousing sentence:

Anyone who participated in the multiple marches, teach-ins and demonstrations that took place in Hyderabad, Delhi, Calcutta, Bombay and elsewhere throughout January, February and March, following Rohith Vemula's suicide and the arrest and subsequent release of JNU students Kanhaiya Kumar, Umar Khalid and Anirban Bhattacharya, will recall immediately the visually arresting sight of red and blue flags raised, waved and carried by thousands of citizens, and the soaring chants of a coming Left-Ambedkarite revolution that rang out on the streets, in the squares and on university campuses for the first three months of 2016.

The point to note is that the author mentions the arrest and release of three JNU students in the context of a "coming Left-Ambedkarite revolution" that apparently started with the dalit student Rohith Vemula's suicide in Hyderabad in January. The remark gives a distinct impression that the JNU students were arrested for their involvement in widespread protests on Vemula's suicide.

The author is not alone. Many writers and speakers have so depicted these events. For example, Kanhaiya Kumar, the president of the JNU student's union who was arrested along with two others, repeatedly asserted after his release that the JNU students were "targeted" by the government for protesting on Vemula's suicide and for sustained agitation—the occupy UGC movement—on the withdrawal of non-Net fellowships by the UGC. While making fiery speeches in the parliament, Mr. Sitaram Yechury, on more than one occasion, directly linked the arrest of the students with Vemula's suicide to illustrate the government's repressive policies towards the student community.

Neither the *Hindu* piece under discussion nor Kanhaiya Kumar nor Sitaram Yechury in parliament ever mentioned Geelani's name while commenting on the arrest of JNU students. It was interesting to observe the leader of a communist party, wedded to the ideas of justice and equality, maintaining a deafening silence on the appalling arrest of a university teacher while loudly protesting the arrest of JNU students for exactly the same 'crime'.

Geelani's case was also systematically ignored in the dozens of 'teach-in' lectures in the JNU campus that continued for many weeks apparently as a form of protest against the arrests of students. The lectures were organized in the evenings in the open area in front of the JNU administration block. The area was temporarily designated 'freedom square'. The topics discussed in these lectures included concepts of nationalism, theory of Aryan invasion, Gandhi on Swaraj, Tagore on humanism, Ambedkar's vision of an inclusive India, lessons from Nehru's Discovery of India, contribution of Bhagat Singh and others in the Indian freedom movement, history of fascism in Europe, linguistic diversity of India, history of the Hindu right, neoliberal world order, political economy of communalism, feminism and the caste system, and much else. There was much fanfare, radical chants, and clarion call from the freedom square to change the world. It reminded us of the legendary sixties, at Berkeley and San Francisco.

The dark Kashmir issue was mentioned exactly once, and the spirited speaker was hounded for her 'aberration' for weeks; the case of Afzal Guru was not mentioned at all to my knowledge.

It is also pertinent to note that the Delhi University Teacher's Association (DUTA), which is currently dominated by the Congress-Left forces, promptly issued a strong letter of protest after the arrest of the JNU student, Kanhaiya Kumar. S. A. R Geelani, a DUTA member, was arrested four days after Kumar. DUTA maintained a studied silence on the arrest of its own member for nearly a month before it issued a note of protest following persistent petitions from groups of DU teachers. Significantly, the JNU teacher's association, JNUTA, and JNU student association, JNUSU, issued statement after statement protesting the arrest of JNU students; they never mentioned the arrest of Geelani.

Except for a small group of students in JNU, a handful of democratic rights activists, and some teachers of Delhi University, Geelani's arrest was essentially ignored. It is difficult to miss the elaborate planning and careful management of the protests to keep the case of Geelani unmentioned and separate from those of JNU students. One report suggested that, despite demands from a small group of students, the executive body of JNUSU deliberately decided not to shout slogans for Geelani. The handful of brave students went on to carry a few posters and shout occasional slogans for Geelani anyway, especially during the third rally. The main 'soaring' chants, however, maintained systematic silence on Kashmir, Afzal, and Geelani. Interestingly, much of the mainstream media obeyed the restrictions.

Why did the otherwise strongly motivated left-liberal sections of the intelligentsia in Delhi prefer silence on Kashmir, Afzal Guru, and Geelani? Earlier, we asked why did the regime crack down severely on events commemorating Afzal Guru. We will see that the answer to the two questions is virtually the same, in effect.

Since the present government assumed power nearly two years ago, it has been clear that, armed with a formal majority in Parliament, its aim is an authoritarian government embedded in a strong state. There is no space here to elaborate on the complex, evolving topic. The basic reason is that this regime has been catapulted to power to serve an inherently unpopular economic agenda. To serve the interests of domestic big business, rich Indians abroad, and imperialist powers, the regime will be compelled to further escalate the existing obscene concentration of wealth and the atrocious inequality thereof. In a formal democratic order, this can only be done by dividing and effectively disenfranchising vast sections of people to prevent popular revolt. Hence the need for a strong state under the supreme command of one chosen individual.

The Home Minister of India, Rajnath Singh, and the president of the ruling Bharatiya Janata Party, Amit Shah, gave rather definitive indication of the intentions of the regime in public remarks around the events of 9th

February. In one public address, Singh said, Anti-national activities and forces won't be tolerated. Anyone raising anti-India slogan or questioning India's integrity won't be spared. Government will take tough measures.

It is well-known that, in the context of a formal democracy, authoritarian regimes initially introduce their project with the widest available public approval. As this government has already seen, overtly divisive communal and fundamentalist actions have a tendency to backfire.

Kashmir and Afzal Guru

In this context, the deeply problematic Kashmir issue, especially when it is raised in connection with terrorism, offers a unique opportunity to the suggested authoritarian project. In fact, the opportunity is maximized when the situation in 'terrorist-infested' Kashmir can be projected as an attack on the sovereignty and the constitutional framework of India. The attack on the Indian parliament and the subsequent conviction of Mohammad Afzal Guru as the sole surviving 'terrorist' accomplished that job for the entire 'nationalist' right wing sections of the population, especially the Sangh parivar. Therefore, it is no wonder that, on every December 13 (the day the parliament was attacked), the RSS and BJP used to raise the pitch demanding the execution of Afzal Guru. It is ironical though that it is the second UPA government that finally hanged Afzal just months before the general elections of 2014. Such was the importance of Afzal Guru for Indian electoral democracy.

The other, dissident side of the story is that, ever since the trial on the parliament attack case began, democratic opposition to the entire legal process kept growing. By the time Guru was hanged and buried inside the Tihar jail, a considerable dissident literature was widely available. In a powerful review of this literature, along with his own careful reading of the case, the eminent historian and legal expert A. G. Noorani wrote (Why Afzal Guru Matters, Frontline, May 17, 2013),

The execution was perpetrated for blatantly electoral ends. But the ferocity of the reaction in Kashmir shocked its perpetrators in the government and others in New Delhi who had egged it on, within and outside the Congress. It revealed the complete disconnect between the people of Kashmir and their rulers in New Delhi as well as the chasm between the brave human rights activists who pleaded for Afzal Guru's release and the smug ignorant ones who justified the execution, ironically in the name of the rule of law... The entire case must be read in this context and in the historical context of great miscarriages of justice...

This explains why Afzal Guru's death aroused the wrath it did. Unlike Maqbool Butt, he was not a *symbol.* He *personified* the lot of his people. They suffer at the hands of the very forces and the agencies as he did; until he was put to death. If acquitted, he would have spoken freely. He knew too much. The man had to be killed. It was a frame-up like the famous Birmingham Six and the Guildford Four. Only this time, there was no judicial redress.

Afzal's hanging signaled a disturbing divide in the visible, articulate, non-subaltern public domain. On the one hand, there is the vast 'nationalist' crowd for whom Afzal was an enemy of the state and his execution was a patriotic action. On the other, there is the curious mix of a very small group of 'brave human rights activists' and the miserable millions in the valley for whom Afzal's hanging 'personified the lot of his people' and signaled the collapse of real democratic order. The small but determined meetings of remembrance that have been taking place every year since 9 February 2013— mostly in Kashmir but elsewhere in the country as well—symbolized this divide.

It is reasonable to assume that the right-wing authoritarian regime currently in power is very aware of this divide. It knows that commemoration of Afzal's hanging is vastly unpopular with the sections of the population that fill the audience of the mainstream media. So, by taking 'tough measures' on these ceremonies, the regime can safely enforce its authority with popular approval while breaking the back of the dissident movement around Kashmir. The project is central to the communal agenda of the Sangh since an attack on the independent identity of Kashmir is ipso facto an attack on Islam in the jaundiced eyes of the parivar. The great opportunity is that, to emphasize, *this* communal task can be pursued with popular patriotic approval.

In fact, there was a significant precedence to this plan last year, also in JNU. Apparently, a small group of students invited none other than S.A.R Geelani himself to address a commemorative meeting on Afzal on 9 February 2015. To remind, along with Afzal, Geelani and two others were also charged with participation in the attack on the parliament. The notorious POTA court sentenced Geelani, Afzal and one other to death. After spending over a year in the death row, Geelani was finally released after the High Court acquitted him of all charges. Needless to say, Geelani was brutally tortured during the interrogation stage.

Thus, after Afzal's death, Dr. Geelani has emerged as the 'bearer' of the dark image comprising Kashmir, azadi, Islam, terrorism, and the attack on the parliament. That meeting last year was also attacked by a rival student group in JNU. We may presume that proper instructions were conveyed in advance this year for the concerned parties to take appropriate action. The threat of tough measures emanating from the highest authorities signaled the determination of the regime to make full use of the opportunity.

If the commemoration of the death of a 'terrorist convict' is an opportunity for the right-wing regime, it is a difficult problem for the mainstream left-liberal opposition. The mainstream left did not cover itself with glory during the entire political process leading to conviction and execution of Afzal Guru and the subsequent 'ferocity of the reaction in Kashmir.' To my knowledge, with notable individual exceptions, the mainstream left as a whole never gave any definite support either to the Kashmiri freedom struggle or to protest on the 'great miscarriage of justice' regarding Afzal Guru. This is because, within a statist framework, each of these causes tests the idea of democratic dissent at the extremities of the framework. These causes challenge the otherwise progressive left to face two sharp issues:

1. Do the people of Kashmir have a right to self-determination even if the Indian parliament had unanimously resolved in favour of inclusion of Kashmir within the union of India?

2. Is it legitimate to protest the judgment of the Supreme Court of India after all legal avenues have been duly exhausted and the President of India had given his seal of approval?

The dilemma is glaring. While affirmative answers to these questions appear to challenge the supremacy of the parliament and the Apex Court, negative answers appear to curtail the fundamental right of democratic dissent. Dilemmas often induce silence. The strategic statist silence worked well as long as Kashmir remained a distant problem on the other side of the Himalayas.

Masked Outsiders

Unfortunately, the Himalayan barrier was seriously breached with the arrest of the JNU students, especially that of the president of the student union who happened to be affiliated with the mainstream left. The situation was grave for the leftist teachers of JNU who were faced with the difficult task of adhering to the party-line on Kashmir while finding convincing arguments to defend their students in the public domain. Since the students were charged with 'anti-national' activities around the issue of Kashmir, it was difficult to continue to maintain silence on Kashmir.

The simultaneous arrest of Dr. Geelani on the same charges just escalated the problem for the mainstream left. As noted, Geelani is very much the face of Kashmir; he cannot be defended without sharing his cause. If Geelani's case was placed in the same political package with the students, the pernicious cause of Kashmir would have infected the task of defending the students as well. As one well-known teacher activist of Delhi told me frankly, "If we now get involved with Geelani's struggles, we will lose all our other battles."

The solution to this rather turbulent problem was to, first, delink Geelani from the students by simply sidelining Geelani's case in an otherwise charged public discourse. Second, a very impressive campaign was launched not to highlight injustice in Kashmir and people's democratic right to protest about it, but to convert the incidental factors of students and university education as the central issues. The simmering protests on Rohit Vemula's suicide in the University of Hyderabad were linked up with the arrest of JNU students to reach the wider perspective on university education. Third, once the "left-Ambedkarite" package was carefully formulated as the real issue regarding the arrest of the students, the 'party-line' was restored by separating the JNU students from direct 'anti-national' engagement with Kashmir.

Opinion about the 'anti-national' character of the event of 9 February varied. For the hardliners, the very meeting to commemorate Afzal was 'anti-national' and severe judicial punishment was called for. Others, mostly from the mainstream left-liberal forces, agreed that the meeting was wrong and distasteful, but it did not violate any law of the land. However, *everybody without exception* agreed that the two specific slogans about dismemberment and destruction of India were definitely 'anti-national' and some form of punishment was in order. With this universal agreement on the 'nationalist' limits of dissent, the core authoritarian project of the regime found full endorsement. In effect, the regime made sure that, outside the valley, people will find it difficult to hold memorial meetings on Afzal in public.

Even the leaders of the otherwise vigorous student movement agreed with the basic dictat of the regime. Kanhaiya Kumar, the president of JNUSU said: We are appalled at the way the entire incident is being used to malign JNU students. At the outset, we want to condemn the undemocratic slogans that were raised by some people on that day. It is important to note that the slogans were not raised by members of Left organisations or JNU students.

Elsewhere, Kumar stated that what happened on 9 February was most objectionable warranting judicial action (*"karwai honi chahiye"*). JNUSU vice-president Shehla Rashid said, We condemn the undemocratic slogans that were raised by some people on that day. In fact, when the sloganeering had been taking place, it was the Left-progressive organisations and students, including JNUSU office-bearers, who asked the organisers to stop the slogans, which were regressive.

The JNU community thus cannot be held responsible for the 'undemocratic slogans' heard on that day. At last thus the "Left-progressive" organisations found their fall guy. The universally condemnable slogans were *not* given by anyone from JNU; they were given by 'outsiders'. With timely help from the media, some videos of 9 February surfaced, showing several people covering their faces while shouting slogans. The insinuation is difficult to miss: *these* were the outsiders shouting *those* condemnable undemocratic slogans. As noted, the matter is under judicial review. Without judging the veracity of the suggestion, I will just hold on to it to proceed with the political argument.

Suppose, as darkly suggested in a number of reports on the incident, that these 'outsiders' were students from Kashmir affiliated to various institutions in Delhi. By designating them as 'outsiders', the JNU community extricated itself from the problem of identifying with their cause; in effect, the community turned its back on their judicial destiny. The entire weight of an increasingly authoritarian regime is to be borne by a dozen or so young Kashmiris wearing masks and chanting furious slogans, hoping someone will listen. Do we know who they are? Why do they need to put on masks in free, democratic India? What is their compulsion for screaming those disturbing slogans and risking their lives in the process?

It is reasonable to assume that they belong to the current generation of Kashmiris who have spent their entire lives amidst catastrophic violence in which the civilian death-toll is nearing 95,000 in three decades of gut-wrenching conflict. They have heard about, if not actually witnessed, rape and murder of friends and relations on a regular basis as over half a million soldiers of the Indian union, armed with AFSPA, ransack their lives. They are witness to unmarked mass graves where erstwhile 'missing persons' found their place. They are surrounded by thousands of women and children undergoing psychological collapse. They have surely taken part since childhood in endless protests, strikes, shut downs, and processions as another atrocity occurred somewhere in the neighbourhood. Perhaps they know of friends barely out of their teens who compulsively joined the ranks of militancy knowing full well that, by now, the 'shelf-life' of a militant is a year at most. Perhaps they have carried the bullet-ridden bodies of their friends while marching in shivering cold with hundreds of others, weeping and screaming at the marauding Indian state. On the other side of the Himalayas.

On 9 February, they assembled again to commemorate the memory of a fellow Kashmiri who "personified the lot of his people." They congregate because "they suffer at the hands of the very forces and the agencies as he did; until he was put to death." With the instinctive alertness of a prey, they put on masks as they always do in Kashmir, before they screamed again cursing the state that has ruined their land. On this solemn occasion though they had friends from this side of the Himalayas, a tiny group of brave idealistic students who rallied in solidarity. Hand in hand, they chanted the song of hope and freedom.

The hope was short-lived as the predatory state struck. After the confusion partially cleared, the Kashmiris suddenly realized that no one from democratic India was holding their hands anymore. As if that was not enough, they have now been marked, isolated, and abandoned to the wolves so that the preparations for a Left-Ambedkarite revolution can proceed unhindered in multiple colours.

Postscript:

It is another matter that the vicissitudes of electoral politics in Kashmir has its own compulsions that, for now, might have saved these masked people shouting 'undemocratic slogans' from further harm, notwithstanding the patriotic demand for punishment by democratic India.

KASHMIR: WHEN IGNORANCE BEGETS TRAGEDY AND FARCE

Gautam Navlakha

As anger simmers under the relative surface calm in Kashmir, a farce threatens to turn into tragedy. Union Home Minister Rajnath Singh said on the floor of the Parliament on 18 July that referendum as a concept is "outdated and irrelevant." It is noteworthy that he has unwittingly lent legitimacy to this concept by bringing it to Parliament. This concept has indeed gained in relevance in the 21st century and is viewed as a democratic way to untie tangled knots and resolve intractable problems. When a state has nothing to offer to a rebellious people, and the ensuing armed conflict will not cease without a radical political offer, the demand for referendum is enough to politically nurture a movement while war rages.

Facts on the Ground

Singh stated on the floor of Parliament that a committee will look into the issue of "pellet guns". However, the Central Reserve Police Force (CRPF) Director General K Durga Prasad said on 25 July that while he was sorry about the pellet injuries that had blinded Kashmiri youth, his force would continue using these guns. The pellet gun called *chara bandook* was used by British hunters in the 19th century. The pellets are made of metal (some are rubber coated) and are sprayed at high speeds of over 1,000 ft per second. The 12 bore gun used to spray them has a cartridge which carries 600 pellets. The Israelis used it on the Palestinians but stopped after they realised that the pellets cause fatal casualties. Indian forces in Jammu and Kashmir (J&K), however, continue to use it. Former Minister of Home Affairs P Chidambaram's statement that there should be "greater autonomy" to deal with a grave situation in J&K, within the constitutional framework as was promised in 1947, was ridiculed. His own Congress party distanced itself from the statement while the Bharatiya Janata Party (BJP) accused him of "compromising national security," the mother of all charges in present-day India. There were other official statements made in Srinagar that made it clear that the Government of India (GoI) will decide "who to talk to and who not to talk with" only after "peace and normalcy is restored." Singh's assertion that "we want to build an emotional bond between the centre and Kashmir" sounded almost contradictory since the GoI is busy engaging in a war to subjugate its own people.

Such a quixotic rush towards restoring authority has its share of black humour as could be seen when the authorities, out of spite, made the curfew more stringent just as the *azaadi* activists relaxed the bandh they had called. In order to show the "separatists" their place the government had no compunction about doling out collective punishment to people, as the British raj was wont to do in the past. As Kashmir burst into flames, rhetoric flourished, copious tears were shed for soldiers and innocent people, Pakistan was (and continues to be) slammed, and an all party confabulation ensued. Meetings were held, hospitals and homes of victims were visited, and assurances were given. Committees were constituted, and recommendations solicited, but nothing changed once order had been restored.

A close look at the ground reality will lead to the question: Who got killed and blinded? Out of the 50 killed, only one was a soldier who met an accidental death, the rest were all civilians: minors and adults, men and women. According to the official version, out of the 1,738 security force personnel only 132 were hospitalised and 1,606 suffered minor injuries in 566 incidents. In contrast, 49 civilians were killed, 3,000 injured and more than a hundred were maimed and blinded by pellet guns. In just one hospital (the Sri Maharaja Hari Singh Hospital in Srinagar) 167 civilians who suffered severe pellet injuries to their eyes were treated in 11 days. The head of ophthalmology there, Khurshid Alam was reported as saying that "most people had been hit either in their head or abdomen. They (the forces) are not shooting in their legs" (Jameel 2016).

The staggering death toll, unsolved crimes of rapes, massacres, enforced disappearances, and the orphans, widows, half-widows, and lakhs of people suffering from trauma and post traumatic stress disorder (PTSD) are issues that are pushed to the margins and simply do not become part of the public discourse in India. As for the Indian intelligentsia, the relentless attacks launched by the Rashtriya Swayamsevak Sangh (RSS) in nexus with the police, have made them careful and cautious. Let alone a referendum, even the communalisation of the military as a consequence of waging war against Kashmiri Muslims is not acknowledged. The soldiers are told that they are fighting Pakistan that has instigated trouble and wants to dismember India. The Pakistani and Kashmiri Muslims thus become indistinguishable on the ground and in the soldiers' minds. Our own people become the "enemy," along with providing the dominant excuse for counter-insurgency in J&K. It also is a major cause of stress and trauma among soldiers and officers of the armed forces.

The people's resistance is expressed in myriad ways: from armed militancy to unarmed resistance; aiding and abetting the struggle by providing relief and help during mass upsurge and man-made natural calamities, to creative expression in literature, art and music. Many Indians remain oblivious to the debate in Kashmir over women's rights even as they fight the Indian state and its record of sexual violence. Kashmiris possess more respect for civil liberties because that has been denied to them. Indians fail to realise how often and in how many different ways Kashmiri society has been forced to look within and rely on its own wits and resources in times of crises. This collective sense of self-reliance has made them resilient, fearless and confident. And thus, despite all the encumbrances, the protests have persisted.

Post 1947, India has witnessed any number of struggles relating to land and resources. And so has Jammu and Kashmir (J&K). The common thread in such struggles is not the same constitutional arrangement, as much as the manner in which every type of constitutional guarantee gets tweaked/amended/modified across India. Despite Schedules V and VI of the Indian Constitution, the Panchayat Extension to Scheduled Areas and the Forest Rights Act, the forest dwellers in India have witnessed brazen violation of their provisions. Adivasis are at the centre of the war being waged in the name of crushing the Maoist rebellion. In Nagaland despite Article 371 A, (a) iv guaranteeing land and its resources to the Naga people, the centre claimed the right to mineral resources. In Assam there is a struggle going on against privatisation of oil wells by the BJP-led state government. Thus, notwithstanding constitutional guarantees, laws, and assurances, the Indian state's functionaries never give up trying to push their claims as their sovereign prerogatives. Unlike elsewhere, land grab in J&K takes place in the name of development, for national security, that is, land for the 6,00,000 strong military personnel deployed there, for the comfort of Hindu pilgrims, fortified camps for migrants and so on.

This means that despite the constitutionally guaranteed "state subject-hood," land grabbing continues. When the Bhabha Atomic Research Centre issued a tender for construction of "staff quarters" in Gulmarg in May without any statutory permission and in defiance of the J&K High Court's order, it obviously believed that as a GoI entity, it was above the law. The role of the bureaucracy and the pro-Indian political formations in pushing the proposal for setting up Sainik colonies for all ex-soldiers, non-state subjects included, and families of those who died or served for three years in J&K (from 2011 to 2016) is noteworthy. Land for the Sainik colony was identified near the Old Srinagar airport at Humhama, but the number of applicants rose and the Rajya Sainik Board asked for more land. The buildings had meanwhile been constructed. Faced with public outrage the government backed down and the Army declared that the constructed buildings were for serving officers and their families.

However, papers and documents in the public domain indicate back-pedalling. The land policy to settle non-state ex-servicemen is an old project of the RSS to settle "nationalists," and to allow non-state subjects unhindered access to land for industry, real estate, mining, and fortified colonies for migrants. The state government is sold on the idea that all things being equal, the economy will make up for all the political losses. Economic policy is not an independent variable in a war situation when there is continued financial dependence on the centre. The current state finance minister was quoted as saying that India follows an "economically coercive federation" where all powers rest with the centre (Irfan 2015). Comparing J&K and the North East to the 12th man in a cricket team, he said they too are like this player with no "say in the match". The `80,000 crore "economic package" is outdated, an aggregate of all the promised projects, mostly central projects, and not an insignificant amount is meant for raising more armed police personnel or pacifying the electorate in Jammu (*Kashmir Reader* 2016).

The registered unemployed in the state number 2.2 lakh which when coupled with the unregistered, goes up to 6.5 lakh. The`80,000 crore "package" includes jobs for 3,000 migrant youth and 5,000 in the armed forces while the rest of the jobs in construction will see workers and supervisors from outside the J&K compete with locals. Besides, the legal immunity given to the military from the criminal court and the control of the J&K's representative government, all point to micro-management of J&K by the centre. The state government has no authority to withdraw pellet guns, since even policing is under the Union Ministry of Home Affairs.

Indigenous Militancy

Burhan Muzaffar Wani and his comrades were born and died in the phase of militancy which symbolises the watershed in politics in J&K; pre- and post-1989–90. Burhan personified the new generation of militants. He spoke for them. They did not trust "leaders" and knew that they had a short time to live. One of his last messages was to the Amarnath pilgrims, welcoming them, expressing respect for their faith and assuring them that they need not fear for their safety. In the midst of the current grief and anger, social media provides evidence of pilgrims being rescued from a burning bus, at risk to their own lives by Kashmiris. Even in 2008 in the midst of the *ragda* agitation, volunteers ensured that *langars* were organised and shelters provided to the *yatris*. Indeed the Nitish Sengupta Committee appointed by the government following the 1996 snowstorm in which more than 200 pilgrims lost their lives, recorded its appreciation (1996) of the role played by the *tatoowallahs* and the local villagers, most of them Muslims in rescuing the yatris at great risk to their own lives. The rescuers also included militants. Eyewitness accounts of the yatris say that the Border Security Force (BSF) did not come to their help. Yes, the militants are self-consciously Muslim, but to claim they are fanatics is a lie. Burhan's message was a repeat of messages issued by indigenous militants in the past, and was a clear signal that they respect the faith of the "other." Hatred for the faith of the other is the hallmark of a fanatic.

The distinction between indigenous and foreign militancy is the sharpest here. Remarkably, it is the azaadi leadership which is reaching out to Kashmiri Pandits, to come and discuss a concrete plan for return to their original home and hearth. Their opposition to fortified camps for migrants is well taken. Their appeal to the Kashmiri Pandits to return is well meant.

It is disconcerting, therefore, that India's civil society, with honourable exceptions, remains mired in "nationalist" dogma, communal or secular, unequivocally wedded to the nation state and its inviolability, and refuses to accept that the problem is primarily located in the Indian nation state project, defined by hatred for Pakistan and Muslim as the "other." Knowledge of communalism has not encouraged interrogation of the role played by Hindutva in exacerbating the Kashmir problem. There is suppression of facts about its patronisation in J&K by the military, civilian establishment and the state government: the training and arming of 29,000 village defence committee members drawn from the Hindutva fold in the Jammu region (Jammu and Kashmir Coalition of Civil Society 2013); appointment as a minister from the BJP's quota of an absconder from justice in a case of lynching of two persons (Sharma 2016); allowing the cohorts of the RSS in a "disturbed area" to receive arms training and brandish weapons (Navlakha 2015); the lynch mob form of agitation launched in Jammu in 2008 by right wing elements which was mollycoddled, whereas the non-violent agitation in the Valley was showered with bullets; imposing of an economic embargo, an act of war, for a month against Kashmir by Jammu agitators and which the troop of 6,00,000 could not prevent (Navlakha 2008). The list is long.

The Indian government has nothing of substance to offer the Kashmiris. Gulzarilal Nanda, as Union Home Minister and interim Prime Minister, had famously told the Lok Sabha on 4 December 1964 that Article 370 was a "shell" which was "emptied of its contents." When the Farooq Abdullah government submitted the state autonomy report in 2002 to the Atal Bihari Vajpayee government at the centre, it went straight into the dustbin. The three subcommittees set up by the United Progressive Alliance (UPA) government went much farther than any other committee in recent memory in their recommendations, which were summarily ignored. As for the interlocutors' report in 2012, it made itself inconsequential by peremptorily dismissing the idea of reverting to the pre-1953 status. They were convinced that the Kashmiris do not know what they mean by azaadi, so all that is needed is panchayati raj. So when the GoI has neither intent nor political will, to offer greater autonomy, and Kashmiris will not settle for anything less than azaadi, it simply means that other than armed confrontation there is no way out.

A fatal flaw of counter-insurgency (COIN) is that it also implies psychological warfare, for perception management. The authoritarian origins of this concept should be borne in mind. As part of COIN, the armed forces have to appear to be triumphing while at the same time keeping the cauldron of fear boiling among the rebellious population and fuelling insecurity among the Indian public to justify military suppression. As a result we move from triumphalism, of having defeated and suppressed the "separatists," to consternation when a mass upsurge takes place, blaming Pakistan for fomenting this. The union home ministry provided living proof of this by simultaneously lambasting Pakistan for "interference" and insisting that terrorism in J&K does not pose a threat! In any case, J&K has been under the administrative control of the GoI for nearly seven decades which has deployed more than 6,00,000 armed soldiers who enjoy legal immunity and possess enormous powers and in addition, civil liberties are suspended. So how come Pakistan finds it so easy to stoke fires of rebellion in Indian administered Kashmir? If elections and electoral turnouts are markers of people's choice, and not a compromise to make life less onerous, then how come the very same people join funerals of militants and gather at encounter sites?

Truth be told, Pakistan is able to "fish in troubled waters" because the Indian government has closed all avenues for democratic expression and has nothing to offer. The fact that the Lashkar or Jaish have reactivated themselves is because of the same reason that young people after 2008 and

2013 began to drift towards militancy after the bloody suppression they experienced. Omar Abdullah, wiser after the event, nailed the truth when he tweeted that Burhan Wani dead will galvanise local militancy. Note what took place at Tral on 9 July at Burhan's funeral. The town ringed by security forces and police camps could not prevent the more than 40,000 people from attending his funeral. Young volunteers manned all entry points and obstructed the movement of vehicles of security forces, as Hizbul Mujahideen militants gave their martyr a 21-gun salute. Heed also what has taken place since.

Battles Won, War Lost

In the conditions that operate in J&K there will be many who would take to arms and an even larger number that see value in armed resistance. So militancy will not ebb until there are prospects of a democratic process, and people will not back off from lending militancy support or invest in the non-violent process unless there is a concrete political offer. Look at any insurgency the world over and the message is clear, if one is desirous of learning lessons. There has to be a radical course correction. One can discuss the minimum turnout required for referendum, and put the goalpost at two-thirds majority for a momentous decision. But to reject the right of self-determination because we have so far refused to entertain this possibility is evidence that this 69-year-old republic has lost its creative imagination. When wars, military suppression, manipulation and machinations all have failed, and elections cannot hide the micro management of J&K by New Delhi, then the arc of history bends in favour of a democratic resolution, a solution we have shied away from. When radical Hindutva runs amok across the length and breadth of India, it is hypocritical to complain of radicalisation of the azaadi movement. It has not happened, notwithstanding febrile concoctions by Indian agencies and their cyphers, but it can happen if a democratic solution continues to be evaded, and Indians refuse to stand up in solidarity with the azaadi movement. When ignorance and obduracy become the reigning deities, history as farce can cause a bigger tragedy, which will singe us all.

References

Irfan, Hakeem (2015): "All Financial Powers with Centre: J&K FM Haseeb Drabu," *Economic Times,* 21 May.

Jameel, Yusuf (2016): "The 'Non-Lethal' Weapon that Maims and Blinds," *Asian Age*, 20 June.

JKCCS (2013): "Jammu and Kashmir Coalition of Civil Society Demands Disbanding of VDCs (Village Defence Committees) and Ikhwans in India Occupied Kashmir," 16 August.

— (2016): "Composition of VDCs Has Led to Communal Polarisation," January.

Kashmir Reader (2016): "Drabu Gives Break-up of PM's `80,000 cr Package," 18 June.

Navlakha, Gautam (2008): "Jammu and Kashmir: Winning a Battle Only to Lose the War?," *Economic & Political Weekly*, Vol 43, No 45, 8 November.

— (2015): "Hubris of Propaganda on Kashmir," *Economic & Political Weekly*, Vol 50, No 52, 26 December.

Sengupta, Nitish (1996): "Enquiry on Amarnath Yatra Tragedy Committee Report," Department of Kashmir Affairs, Government of India, December.

Sharma, Arun (2016): "BJP MLA Who Led Murder Accused to Minister's House Was Named in FIR," *Indian Express,* 15 March.

See more at: http://www.epw.in/journal/2016/33/commentary/kashmir-when-ignorance-begets-tragedy-and-farce.html#sthash.OTGymcjr.dpuf

BHARAT BANDH: MOST SUCCESSFUL GENERAL STRIKE EVER DESPITE DETENTIONS

For Khushiram, the 30-year-old ex-employee of Maruti Suzuki India Ltd. and a member of the Maruti Suzuki Provisional Committee, the day of all-India general strike that would see workers from all sectors come together, was spent in the Manesar police station.

Khushiram is one of the 546 workers who were terminated by the Maruti management after the 2012 agitation. He along with twelve other people, two of whom are current office bearers of the Maruti Suzuki Workers' Union while the others are currently Maruti employees, were picked up by the police at about 6 am in the morning. They were detained in the Manesar police station, which is in the Industrial Model Township (IMT) for about six hours.

All central major trade unions had called for a Bharat Bandh against the "anti-labour policies of the government". It's the 17th such strike that India has seen since the process of liberalisation was initiated in 1992.

Despite the detention of the Maruti workers and a number of nurses by Delhi Police, workers who were leading the strike in the Gurgaon-Manesar area claim this was the most successful strike ever. Satbeer Singh, member of the Centre of India Trade Unions, said that this was the largest, with almost 20 crore workers taking part in it. He and other trade unions claimed approximate 1,000 factories were on strike in the Gurgaon-Dharuhera-Bawal area in Haryana, with workers from factories like Maruti, HeroMotoCorp and Endurance participating.

Daily activity in Tamil Nadu was barely affected much, with transport services and educational institution functioning normally. Karnataka's capital Bengaluru saw the workers of the Bangalore Metropolitan Transport Corporation (BMTC) and Karnataka State Road Transport Corporation (KSRTC) join the strike, which threw a massive spanner in the public transport's works. Many schools and colleges remained closed as a precautionary measure. Kerala too had most of its public conveyance services off the roads. Conditions were seemingly normal in Maharashtra, but some rural areas, especially in Buldana district had 'rasta roko' (block roads).

West Bengal saw clashes between the striking workers and the party workers of the Trinamool Congress in different district districts. According to a report, the Mayor of Siliguri Municipal Corporation, Ashok

Bhattacharya, was arrested along with 15 other protestors and a North Bengal State Transport Corporation bus was vandalised in Cooch Behar. Otherwise, public transport remained largely unaffected. Further east in Tripura, there was no unrest, but the state went into complete shutdown. "The strike was total and successful. People from all walks of life spontaneously supported the strike to denounce the BJP-led central government's anti-people labour policies and demanded increase of wages," said Manik Dey, of the Tripura unit of Centre of Indian Trade Unions' (CITU).

Odisha had a strong call of strike coming from the All India Government Nurses Federation and about 2,000 nurses stayed away from work. Train services were disrupted in areas like Bhubaneswar, Cuttack, Sambalpur, Rayagada and Berhampur. In areas like Patna, Purnea, Muzaffarpur, Begusarai, Bhagalpur and Gopalganj of Bihar, banks remain closed and private and public sector employees faced major difficulty in reaching offices. The situation was similar in Tripura with buses off the road and colleges, government offices and banks shut.

The only big central trade union to not participate in this strike was the Bhartiya Mazdoor Sangh (BMS), an affiliate of the Rashtriya Swayamsevak Sangh (RSS). BMS had pulled out of the nationwide strike in April (it did the same the last time too).

Khushiram's experience indicates that in certain areas, there seems to have been an effort to ensure union leaders could not join the strike. He and the other twelve workers were released by the police after being charged with Section 151 (causing disturbance of public peace) and Section 107 (instigating others to do the same) of Indian Penal Code. Khushiram alleged the Haryana police went to neighbouring villages and forced those who were on strike to join work. ACP Dharambir of Manesar refuted these allegations. He told Newslaundry that the 13 workers were detained after the management from Maruti Suzuki complained against them.

As life returns to normal today, the Left will take satisfaction in the fact that in terms of numbers, this Bharat Bandh was a success, making its presence felt both on the ground as well as on social media. However, in terms of making an actual impact and securing the revisions that are in the Centre of Trade Unions's list of demands, the road ahead is long.

Source:
http://www.newslaundry.com/2016/09/03/bharatbandh-most-successful-general-strike-ever-despite-detentions/

DROUGHT 2014-15

Jaya Mehta

On 20th June 2016, the national daily Indian Express reported, 'Monsoon finally arrives in drought hit Marathwada. Ninety percent of Maharashtra is lashed with rain.' Three days later on 23rd June the Times of India reported, 'Insufficient rains slashes sowing activities.' The report gave details of minuscule sowing in the region. Marathwada is subdivided into two divisions Aurangabad and Latur. In Aurangabad division the major crops are Maize, Bajra and Jowar. Normally Maize is cultivated in 2251.8 hectares of land. Till date sowing has taken place only in 71.81 hectares, which is 3.2 percent of usual area. Bajra has been sown to the extent of 8.3 percent of usual area and Jowar to the extent of 1.4 percent of usual area. Similarly, in Latur division sowing has taken place only to the extent of 3.3 percent of the usual area under cereal crops.

Two years of scanty and erratic rains and hailstorms have ravaged rural Marathwada and Vidarbha regions creating conditions unimaginable sufferings for the people.

In Katchincholi village in Beed district women get up at 3 a.m. and go to the bone dry bed of Godavari River with as many pots as they can carry. They dig the gravel with their hands till a muddy pool of water appears. They scoop the water in their pots and then strain away the sludge and stones. This is how drinking water is procured in the village. A single pot takes around 2 hours to fill and three pots mean a woman spending 6 hours a day to get 'drinking water' for the family. (Times of India 25th March 2015).

Yogita Desai a class V student of Sabalkhed Village in Beed district fainted and died while fetching water from a handpump. The number of trips that she made in scorching heat proved fatal for the 12 years old. Another 11 years old boy fell down into the well while trying to get water. A 45 years old woman fainted and died standing in a queue to fetch water from a hand pump in Atola village in Latur district. (PTI April 21 2016)

In Latur, civic authorities stopped supplying water in the pipeline since February 2016. Water is reached through trains and supplied by tankers in Latur town. Crores of litres of water has been sent to Latur from long distances. This has indeed made big news in the country.

In Yevalevadi village of Beed district all the young men and women have left looking for harvesting work in sugarcane fields leaving the children and elderly behind. Hansa bai's two sons went away leaving one bagful of

Jowar for her and her husband to consume. When the Jowar was finished Hansa bai went looking for work in the parched neighbourhood fields of Jowar. If she found work she got Rs.100. It meant 8 to 9 hours of back bending harvesting work. Her greatest fear was the eventuality of falling ill. If she fell ill her husband would not be able to even accompany her to the hospital. (Times of India, 24th March 2016).

There are stories of farmers committing suicides and even their adolescent children committing suicides.

Sandeep Pendse was a 27 years old small farmer in Patoda taluka in Beed district. Sandeep had not got a single decent crop for last three years and had collected debt worth Rs. 1.2 lakhs. The cotton crop on his tiny field got destroyed by drought last year. This year he sowed Jowar and hoped that he would at least have sufficient grain to eat. Unfortunately, just before the crop was to be harvested, untimely rain destroyed it. Sandeep ended his life by hanging himself from a tree. His widow Shobha now has two small children and a large debt to take care of.

Mohini Bhise from Latur district, wanted to become an auxiliary nurse midwife. Her father could not afford the required donation and fees. Her marriage would have also cost him a lot of money which he could not afford. When she heard her parents discussing selling of their land she could tolerate it no more. She committed suicide. (Agriculture is injurious to health, Atul Deulgaonkar and Anjali Joshi in Economic and Political Weekly, 7th May 2016).

Times of India reported that just in the first three weeks of April, as many as 65 farmers committed suicides in Marathwada region. Since January, 2016 the number has totaled up to 338. The highest number of suicides is reported in Beed district (Times of India 28th April 2016).

Stories can continue and Marathwada is not alone. In the year 2015, as many as 302 districts in 11 major states were declared as drought hit. The affected states include Karnataka, Andhra Pradesh, Maharashtra, Madhya Pradesh, Uttar Pradesh, Odisha and others. The drought 2015 has covered the entire country.

May be 50 years later all these people will just become numbers in the history records. Considering that around 60 percent of Indian households depend on agriculture and allied activities for their livelihoods, such vast areas affected by declared and undeclared drought conditions spell disaster for thousands and thousands of men and women. It is estimated that as many as 300 million people are in dire state because of consecutive failure of monsoon for two years and erratic rains and hailstorms.

There are two aspects to the situation. One is the efficiency of immediate relief measures for the affected people in order to ensure their sustenance till normalcy returns. Second aspect relates to the measures which need to be taken up so that occurrence of such extreme situations can be avoided.

Immediate Relief measures

In 1996, the famous journalist P. Sainath wrote a book - 'Everybody Loves a Good Drought.' He described in detail how funds allocated for drought relief programmes are misappropriated by vested interests at different levels. The poor in rural areas call the drought relief programmes as 'chouthi fasal' (fourth crop), which they don't harvest. The exact account of disbursement and management of relief funds in different states and districts in the years 2014, 15 and 16 is a matter of comprehensive research, but comments are warranted at macro policy level with respect to the performance of central and state governments.

Repeated failure of crops means no income for the cultivators and no work for agricultural labour households. Therefore, from the time of colonial administrative rule, drought management has involved public works programme in the region to provide basic sustenance to households dependent on wage income. This has been the major relief initiative for agricultural labour households as well as marginal and small farmer households. In the years 2014, 15 and 16, specific extra programmes are not being thought of. The country already has MGNREG Act 2005, which is supposed to take care of such contingencies. The Act guarantees minimum 100 days of employment at minimum wage to every households that demands work. The employment is supposed to be provided within 15 days of asking. In case employment is not provided, the person is entitled to unemployment allowance. The role of MGNREG scheme as a drought relief measure was recognised by the central government and the promised employment in drought hit regions was increased from 100 days to 150 days.

MGNREGA has miserably failed in providing minimum employment security to drought affected households. In the financial year ending in March 2015, in all 15.2 million people in the 11 drought hit states got employment under MGNREG scheme. Average number of days for which an individual got employment ranged from 30 to 35. Only 2.8 lakh persons i.e. 1.8 percent of the total got employment for 150 days.

The official position is that the scheme is a demand driven scheme and when demand is registered, employment is provided. Figures tell us that in the year 2015, 17.8 million households registered themselves and demanded work and 85 percent of them got the employment. This is a distorted picture. Actual demand for work is much larger than the registered demand. Many of the workers do not want MGNREGA work because the wage given is less than the minimum wage and the payments are often delayed. Sometimes, poor workers have not received their dues for months and years. Secondly, many times when people go to register their demand for work, local administrative units refuse to make job cards, if they cannot provide the work.

The reason behind the lackadaisical performance of MGNREG scheme is the paucity of funds. The central budget has capped the allocation to the scheme which amounts to violating the Act. In the financial year 2015-6, the spending on the programme was only 0.26 percent of the GDP. The state governments accumulated a deficit of Rs. 12590 crores because central funds were short. (Indian Express 18th and 21st April 2016)

MGNREG scheme performance must improve drastically if drought affected people have to be given some livelihood security. The Central government must prioritize the scheme and provide funds as required by the state governments. It is poor people's right over the government money and any denial of this right makes a mockery of the 'democracy' that our leaders and elite boast about in the world.

In addition to giving employment the other major task relates to supplying subsidised foodgrain to affected people. National Food Security Act was passed in 2013. It includes mid-day-meal (MDM) system, Integrated Child Development Services (ICDS) and Public Distribution System (PDS). The Mid Day Meal and ICDS are to have universal coverage. The subsidised grain at Rs. 2 and 3 a kg under PDS is supposed to reach 75 percent of rural population and 50 percent of urban population.

Implementing the Act required huge infrastructural preparations starting from identifying the beneficiaries, giving them ration cards, digitising them and then linking these cards with Adhaar cards. This has to be supplemented by upgradation of physical infrastructure. Additional ration shops and additional transport and storage capacities were required. Obviously this has not been possible in most states in two years especially in view of the fact that the government at center changed in 2014.

From Bundelkhand to Andhra Pradesh and Maharashtra, the village people are forced to buy grains from open market where prices have gone sky high.

Annapurna Yojna has been operating nationwide since 2001. Under the scheme the destitute population aged 65 years and above is entitled to 10 kg of free grain every month. The grains are provided by the Center. Under the scheme Maharashtra identified 78400 beneficiaries and was getting 225 metric tons of grain from the Center. The Central government stopped supply of grain in March 2014 because of some administrative reshuffle. The supply of grain has not been resumed for 10 months despite the severe drought conditions. The state government could not provide the grain from its own sources and the elderly and poor and hungry population had no other recourse but to buy expensive grain from the market or to remain hungry on most days. (Times of India 22nd Jan 2015).

On 13th May 2016, the Supreme Court of India issued directive to the Central government and State governments that National Food Security Act and MGNREG Act should be implemented throughout the country without any delay. The Center should promptly transfer the required funds to the states. The court directed that in drought hit states no one will be denied subsidised ration even if the person concerned does not have the ration card. The state of Gujrat was specially pulled up second time by the court for not implementing National Food Security Act which was passed by the Parliament. (www.livemint.com).

Long term measures required to avoid the extreme situations

There is a general feeling that the monsoon pattern in the country has changed perceptibly and this may be the consequence of the climate change - issues relating to which are being negotiated at international level according to Kyoto protocol and Paris agreement.

On the other hand, people argue that a careful study of decadal and inter annual variation in rainfall does not give any definite evidence that the drought in Marathwada region can be related to climate change. Bringing in climate change in the discussion leads to diverting our attention away from the immediate socio political factors, which are directly responsible for the massive agrarian distress. In other words, to control erratic behaviour of rains may not within our reach but vulnerability to environmental contingency can definitely be taken care off. (see Economic and Political Weekly 7th May and 4th June 2016).

Better water management, crop management and soil management can indeed reduce the vulnerability of the peasant population to climatic contingencies. The model of agricultural development followed in the country since late 60s is primarily focused on yield improvements. Little attention has been paid to the natural resource context and environmental sustainability of production. As a result we succeeded in pushing up food grain production, but the production trajectory led to an intensified use of synthetic fertilizers and pesticides as well as severe depletion of water resources and soil quality.

The new restructured model of agricultural development must insist on judicious crop choice, discrete use of ground water and local initiatives at watershed management. Along with water conservation soil quality should be taken care of. Healthy soils with higher content of organic matter have better water retention capacity. Use of chemical fertilizers must be restrained.

All these environment friendly suggestions sound good but implementing them is not just a matter of policy initiative by the government. The crop choice and water management are questions related to inequitable distribution of resource base between rural and urban areas, between agriculture and industry, between regions and most importantly among those whose livelihoods are dependent on agriculture.

Indian economy is entrenched in a deep agrarian crisis for past two decades. The droughts and floods only exacerbate the situation. The land question is central to the agrarian crisis. The numbers of households who are dependent on land for their livelihood are far too many. The land available is insufficient and is depleting fast. According to NSSO data, the land available for household operational holdings has gone down from 125 million hectares in 1992-3 to 94.4 million hectares in 2012-13. There are 109 million operational holdings on this land area, which means an average holding of the size 0.86 hectares. Further, this land is distributed in most skewed manner. There are only 7 percent holdings which are more than 2 hectares in size. Ninety three percent holdings are small and marginal holdings. Whereas the 93 percent small and marginal holdings cover 53 percent of land area the 7 percent medium and large holdings cover 47 percent of land area. This uneven distribution of land gets sharpened because the control over other resource base like water, credit and access to market, maps on to the land ownership pattern.

According to the official land use statistics, 55 percent of the cultivated area does not have access to irrigation. Although situation varies from state to state, but the rain fed cultivation invariably belongs to small and marginal resource poor farmers. Moreover, irrigation has shifted from canals to tube wells, which means that rich farmers have control over ground water which extends far beyond the actual land that they posses.

In a free enterprise economy when the government is allowing foreign capital to invest in all sectors, how can the farmers be stopped from growing water guzzling sugar cane crop and using up the ground water. And even if the water can be saved and watershed programmes are undertaken, what is the mechanism of reaching water to the marginal farmers with farm size as small as half an acre or one third of an acre.

Proper water management is possible only in a situation where control over land and water is socialised and decisions are taken not on the basis individual profit concerns but on the basis of what is good for the society.

Unfortunately water management alone does not resolve the agrarian crisis. As many as 51 percent of rural households are agricultural labour households. They need assured employment at reasonable wage rate.

But how can one talk about social good and community benefits in agrarian sector and at the same time allow corporates and urban elite to accumulate private wealth without any restriction.

The tragedies like the one in Marathwada region need never be repeated in any civilised society. But if such large sections of people live on the margins and operate on extremely fragile livelihood equilibrium, then slightest of perturbation is bound to result in a catastrophe. The situation demands not just efficient relief measures and environment friendly policy initiative, but a radical restructuring of production relations. The restructuring cannot be limited to the agrarian sector; it has to encompass the entire economy.

Without this every initiative will reach an impasse and tragedies will continue as before.

WHITHER WAR OF AGGRESSION

Malem Ningthouja

These days, friends, it is very difficult to speak out truth. Certain version of truth or certain versions of misinformation is promoted while the genuine democratic concerns of the people who deserve justice have been suppressed /denied.

Over the years, particularly in the last few months, we have seen escalation of carnages in the sub-continent perpetrated by the men in uniform who are supposed to be the security guardians of the people.

The Indian foot troops, called soldiers, whether military or paramilitary or police or underpaid auxiliary contract agents like the SPOs, Salwa Judum or whatever forces they have given name to; mostly recruited from lower class for lump sum monthly salary, are being exposed to some kind of civil war fronts. I say again that this people, these peoples, foot soldiers are insecure. They are living with frustration. They are living with war hysteria in Kashmir, in Manipur, Arunachal Pradesh, Nagaland, Assam, Chhattisgarh, Jharkhand and other areas where structural oppression is being enforced deliberately with muscle powers. They are exposed. I am talking about the soldiers who are being exposed to the war front. The soldiers recruited from the lower ranks. I am speaking on behalf of them little bit, mentioning about their plight. They are there to obey the instructions of the rulers that live on their blood and labour for profit. These helpless foot soldiers, to defend themselves and to protect their salary and promotion, are being converted into an oppressive and killing machines. They are being indoctrinated with draconian laws to indulge in widespread carnage upon democratic forces, patriotic sections and the masses that are defending economic and democratic rights. They also suffer losses. And they also created lots of losses and destructions. And these soldiers, many of them are also crying due to pain and frustration. In the Special Economic Zones, they are crying.

At the same time the carnage inflicted Kashmir is crying. The subjugated and oppressed Northeast is crying. Oppressed and displaced masses in the Special Economic Zones are crying. Exploited labours are crying. Pauperised peasants are crying. There are only cries. Cries of suffering and cries for justice. I should say that, but one thing is very clear to us, the rulers that have designed these cries are not crying. They never cry. They enjoy the carnage. They enjoy the war. They glorify the war and share war booty among themselves.

And, of course, we are not here, to glorify them. Our gathering today is remarkable because we are here to condemn this carnage. We are here to oppose the war that is being waged in the name of the Indian nation, security and development. We are here to share with the pains and frustrations of the soldiers who have been misled into war of aggression on civilians. We are here to share the pains and cry of our people who are being subjected to a war condition that is being waged against their will. Our gathering is remarkable, because this is how we should begin our journey to build a powerful democratic force, to bring real development, peace and democracy in the subcontinent.

When it comes to Northeast regions, particularly Manipur and the surrounding regions, I should say that an extensive war front has been opened up under the policy banner of Look East Policy, which is now being rechristened as Act East Policy. Let me tell you friends. Look East Policy is not an absolutely foreign trade orientation. It has a lot more to do with ... Well, India's security and commercial interest with the South East Asian countries is remarkable, but Look East Policy is a hype created by the Indian State and its protagonists that covers up the actual geographical space and the mode of operations encompassing the North-eastern region. So LEP should be seen as an integrated whole where the Northeast is always involved. The *Northeast Vision 2020* published by the Indian State substantiate my point.

My argument is that Look East Policy has created a vast geographical hub comprising the entire Northeast into some kind of Special Economic Zone of absolute territorial control, economic exploitation, political subjugation and, of course, carnages in various forms. What becomes inherent with LEP is the visible increase of foreign capital intrusion and economic plunder by big market forces. All these become symptomatic which are to be seen in terms of infrastructural components of what I would like to call aggressive projects to control hydro-energy power, carbon reserves, precious stones, minerals, forest products and, of course, market and labour. The components that have been tremendously enforced include railways, dams, mines, and forests resources (extortive kind of farming) and all other infrastructure components related to roadways, trade related buildings and commercial hubs. All these have brought about destructive changes on landscape, in the cultural ecology of the people, in the demographic harmony among the people (which have also) created cultural insecurity and finally income disparity and underdevelopment.

This policy comes along with heavy militarisation, policing, proxy wars and suppression of democratic voices. Therefore, when one looks into LEP, we also have to relate it with militarisation and increasing amount of policing. It is against this backdrop that I try to locate Armed Forces Special Powers Act, National Security Act, Unlawful Activities Prevention Act, Seditious Act and all forms of other repressive laws. These laws became legal instruments that give constitutional validity to an oppressive policy and very aggressive developmental projects. These legal instruments provide the law enforcing forces to unleash very very distressful reign of terror with impunity, that, in the name of defending India's national security, development, and, of course, peace, or say, they call it law and order. It is against this backdrop that there is violation of democratic rights, economic inequality, denial of proportionate and sustainable development, obstructions to political peace and social justice. This has led to widespread culture of impunity and, you know that, cycle of violence by the law enforcing forces at the grass root become self-propellant.

Our speakers who have spoken before me have emphasised on the manner how the law enforcing forces have taken law into their own hands. The situation seems to be similar everywhere across the sub-continent wherever structural injustice and restive tendencies exist. On records, we already have 1528 documented instances of fake encounter. In January, this year, a killer cop confessed to me, before he made it public, that, he had killed 133 people. That individual had killed, that killer cop had killed 133 persons just as a game. Imagine! He was authorised to do so, informally, by the higher officials. In fact, this man was responsible for the July 23rd 2009 fake encounter in the heart of the capital in broad day-light. The matter was covered up by the Chief Minister of Manipur and the Home Department. However, *Tehelka* came up with photographic evidence of the situation and people resisted and the matter was exposed. After CBI inquiry, this man was suspended along with 7 other team mates. But then why would he confess now? This man began to feel insecure. He thought that he would be killed by superior cops as the case is nearing to an end. The thought that, he thought that confession could either save him or expose the whole modus operandi of secret killings being commanded over to him by superior forces. He thought that he had killed for the sake of the country but, later on, he had realised that he was just a pawn. When he was suspended no help has been coming from the government. No help has been coming from the higher officers. He had to live a very miserable livelihood. He realised that to save himself and to avenge for the crime that he committed, he confessed. The case is still pending in the high court.

What I would like to say is, like, the structural injustice and killing, fake encounters and sufferings, all forms of oppression go together. These are symptomatic of an aggressive and unjust war that are being perpetrated in the name of the country, in the name of nation, in the name of development and peace. And the war had to be halted if there had to be development, peace and democracy in the sub-continent.

I can only trust myself and the like-minded comrades who had been fighting for justice for democratic rights. I think, we have to build a powerful democratic forces on some common strategic and tactical agenda. Otherwise, we are all going to be losers.

Long live democratic struggle
Long live revolution
Red salute to the comrades

Thank you

Malem Ningthouja
Campaign for Peace & Democracy (Manipur)

Note:
The above text is the transcription of the seminar speech delivered (in Hindi) at the public seminar on the 26th of September 2016, Constitution Club, New Delhi. Organised by MATIDARI: Forum for People's Right to Land, Life and Dignity.

THE DREAM OF BEING IN THE DONBASS
Food for thought and impressions from reality[1]

Sergei Golovchenko[2]

This land in ancient times was called "Wild Field". Here were wandering warlike tribes: Scythians, Sarmatians, Ostgoths, Huns, Avars, Khazars, Pechenegs, Cumans.

The modern name of the region is associated with the names of the rivers Don and Seversky Donets, as well as with deposits of coal. The most powerful geological layers of coal are concentrated in the region with the city of Donetsk as its centre (with 1,5 million inhabitants), but also exist in four neighbouring areas. Thus, the name Donbass is an abbreviation for "Donets basin", and it is one of the largest coal regions not only in Europe but in the world.

However, its economic importance and development began not with coal, but with the extraction of salt: in the XVII century, when these lands were called Novorossiya.

This troubled and, in fact, abandoned the region was exposed to the raids of nomads, initially populated by the Cossacks, including the Ukrainian Orthodox Cossacks who fled from Catholic Poland. The eighteenth century was spent in many wars fought between Russia and Turkey. The victory of Russian arms led to more intensive settlement on the land by the Russian peasants and refugees from territories subservient to the Ottoman Empire. Among them were the Serbs, Greeks, Arnauts (Albanians), Moldovans, Armenians...

At the same time here were founded colonies of Germans. During the reign of Catherine II, who was of German nationality, they were generously awarded in the New Russia arable land on fertile black soil.

The first coal fields began to be developed here in the mid-nineteenth century. Soon after the abolition of serfdom in Russia capitalism began to develop. This led to the growth of industry in the Donbass, the construction of railways and major cities.

The larger role was played by foreign capital, dominated by French and Belgian companies. They controlled more than half of the total coal production. Before the First World War, in 1913, there were 1200 coal mines. Annual coal production was 25 million tonnes. But this figure is hardly indicative of the success of the mining industry in tsarist Russia. For comparison: at the same time in England, four thousand mines have produced 200 million tons of coal per year.

Soviet Stalin's industrialization doubled the number of mines in Donetsk and Luhansk – the two leading areas of Donbass. By the beginning of the Second World War, the Donbas was producing 85 million tons of coal for the country. The Soviet period of national history was a real "Golden Age" for Donbass. In 1920 half a million people lived here, in 1940, five million, in 1985 – already eight million.

It produced many eminent Soviet state and party leaders, major business leaders, outstanding scientists, famous generals, celebrities among intellectuals.

Thousands of local factories produced everything from typewriters to giant engineering designs for spaceports. Even after the destruction of the Soviet Union and a general decline in production, the share of the Donbass region (and this includes only two out of 24 Ukrainian regions) in the gross domestic product of Ukraine was 25%. In other words, Donbass fed many other regions of Ukraine, but in no way it was subsidized, despite all the cynical today's broadcast leaders of Kiev.

In the 1960-70-80s Donbass had a reputation as one of the most developed regions of the USSR with a very wealthy population. Miners ' wages reached 600-700-800 rubles a month. Wages in other industries, especially of workers and servants, were less: from 150 to 350 rubles. Was it a lot or a little? Let's take the prices of consumer goods, including luxury items and delicacies. Of course, they varied, but if rounded they looked like this:

Travel in public transport was 4-5 cents, a pound of bread – 15-20 cents, cinema tickets – 20-50 cents, school or student dinner – 30-40 cents, high quality chocolate (100 g) – 1 ruble, a kilo of meat - 1.5-2 rubles, a kilogram of sausage – 2-4 rubles, cotton chemise – 10 rubles, a three-week trade Union trip to a resort – 20 roubles, selected bottle of vodka (500 ml) – 4-5 rubles, a bottle of elite cognac (500 ml) – 25 rubles, a kilogram of black caviar – 40 rubles (in the store) and 65 rubles (in the restaurant), a pair of leather shoes – 40-50 rubles, gold rings (without gemstones) 40-100 rubles, men's wool suit – 120-180 rubles, bike – 60-90 rubles, scooter – 130-200 rubles. The cost of the motorcycle came to 1500 rubles. But there were also motorcycles for 500, and for 300 rubles. Cars like "Lada" cost from 5500 to 7500 rubles.

Monthly payment for utilities (electricity, gas, water, etc.) varied depending on the size of the property and the number of family members living in the apartment or in the cottage. Usually it was from a few rubles to ten or more.

Needless to say that housing was provided for free to Donbass people, like to all Soviet people. But abroad, few people know that men could also buy property in the USSR. This housing was called a cooperative. One-bedroom cooperative apartment cost on average 3500 rubles, three – bedroom-5000 rubles. Of course, the Donbass people enjoyed free medical care and free secondary and higher education. Local universities and colleges were training free of charge huge number of foreign students. The USSR paid them a stipend of 90 rubles a month.

In the Soviet era in the Donbass there was an intensive process of ethnogenesis. No real socio-cultural differences were there between, for example, descendants of Ukrainians and Russians, the second generation began to speak the same language and showed the same mental and behavioural patterns of life. There are more than a hundred nationalities, but there never were any ethnic conflicts.

It was clear that the population of Luhansk and Donetsk (it restored the rights of the old name of their homeland – NovoRossia), brought up on ideas of friendship and the high level of Soviet patriotism, do not want to endure neo-Nazi processions with portraits of Bandera and other Nazi executioners. The absolute majority did not want entry into Europe at the expense of breaking ties with Russia and was strongly against Ukraine's membership in NATO. The current regime in Kiev declared Bandera and his crony national heroes, although they were agents of the British, German and US secret service, the sworn enemies of the Ukrainians, Russians, all the Soviet people, who fought with the troops of the aggressors, and after the war to strengthen socialism.

Kiev radical nationalists, those servants of their Western masters, tried to force the Donbass to the worshiping of fascist idols and to accepting the subordination of Ukraine to NATO's interests. Only blinded and brainwashed Westerners, not to mention the deliberate liars, can name as "democratisation" what is the very real fascistization of Ukraine: a process that, starting in 2014, became complete.

What happened?

Full-scale armed conflict in the Donbass, originated in the same 2014, can be divided into five main stages. They cover the period up to the signing of agreements known as the Minsk-1 and Minsk-2.

The first stage. April – May 2014

The Ukrainian army and nationalist paramilitary forces entering the rebellious Donetsk and Lugansk region. They occupied the Northern districts of Luhansk region, the West and part of the southern districts of Donetsk region. The indigenous population is arming and forms a militia to repel invaders. Fierce battles for the city of Slavyansk begins, where 2 thousand badly armed militias repelled three assaults by 10 thousand Ukrainian troops who were technically highly equipped and were continually receiving supplies and reinforcements. Already then neo-Bandera followers showed and continued to show abnormal cruel treatment of captured rebels and civilians.

Second stage. June – July 2014

Ukrainian General offensive. The goal is to cut off the Luhansk and the Donetsk People's Republic (LPR and DPR) from Russia, to take the whole of the Russian-Ukrainian border. The attack came from two sides. However, Ukraine's armed forces are unable to establish control over the main roads and the heights of the Donetsk region. They remained unable to occupy land borders with the Russian Federation for the length of about 100 kilometers. There began to form "southern boiler", in which the major forces of the Kiev regime were locked.

The rebels were forced to retreat from Slavyansk and Kramatorsk. But the combined forces attacked in the area of Saur-graves, one of the strategic heights of the Donetsk ridge. As a result five thousand Ukrainian soldiers ended up surrounded in a "pot". Not less than three thousand of them were killed. Into the hands of the people's militia fell about 70 units of armoured vehicles, a lot of other weapons.

The third stage. July – August

The frenzied fascist junta in Kiev has mobilized and started another general offensive. Their troops attempted to cleave and to isolate LPR and DPR from each other to get back to the Russian border, to save the remnants of the "South boiler". Separately, the objective was aimed to capture the crash site and the wreckage of downed July 17 Malaysian Boeing. They wanted to cover up the traces of their own crime, to blame it on the People's Republic.

Militias were forced out of the cities of Severodonetsk, Lysychansk, Popasnoe. Heavy fighting followed around Shahtersk. But there the Ukrainian military suffered a crushing defeat. Its total loss in tanks, combat vehicles infantry, armored personnel carriers was 125 units. The militias have defended Shahtersk.

Ukrainian command regrouped forces and redirected their troops to the capture of Ilovaisk and Khartsyzsk, to completely block Donetsk. The battle for the city Ilovaysk lasted twenty days, ending the liberation of the city from neo-Bandera followers and surrounded enemy units in the four "cauldrons". With severe losses, on which the official Kiev is silent, the remnants of the enemy fled. However, judging by what their commanders blabbed, just under Ilovaisk alone they lost more than 1 thousand troops.

The fourth stage. August – September 2014
A massive counter-offensive was launched by the armed forces of Novo Russia.

The following territories were freed from the Ukrainian army and punitive battalions of paramilitaries: Saur-grave, Marinovka, Stepanovka, Ilovaysk, Kommunar, Zhdanivka, Dokuchaevsk, Starobeshevo, Kuteynikovo, Telmanovo, Novoazovsk, Shirokino and many other towns. The militia came to the coast of the Azov Sea. This is the territory of the DPR.

In the LR they got under control: Metalist, Lugansk airport, Gravelly, Novoselovka, Lutugino, Merry Hill, Jubilee, Rodakove, Slavyanoserbsk, Krasny Luch, Khoroshee, Zheltoye. The militia threw the Ukrainian invaders from Luhansk to the North, beyond the river Donets.

The fifth stage. September – December 2014
The September Minsk agreement was not kept by the Ukrainian side. The declared cease-fire existed only on paper and in the speeches of diplomats.

Donetsk militias led trench warfare, thwarting attempts by Kiev troops to advance a bit into the DPR. Continued mutual shelling, raids and sabotage groups fighting in key strategic locations (Donetsk airport and the outskirts of Mariupol, etc.).

Lugansk militia, in response to provocations by neo-Bandera followers, forcing them over the river Donets, squeezed out the Ukrainian troops, pushing them farther and farther from the city. Freed were Valuiskoye and Nizhneteploye. There were fights over the villages Luganskaya, Kolesnikovka, Old Aydar, Schastye...

Intense fighting rolled over the turn of calendar 2014 and continues until mid-February 2016. But February's Minsk agreement were also subsequently ignored by Kiev side, which was violating the ceasefire and killing civilians at every opportunity.

Conclusion

"Anti-terrorist operation" of Kiev authorities that was actually unleashed by them with the full support of the West, was in fact a civil war, and they failed completely. Arrogant puppet President Poroshenko claimed that to achieve victory it would take just a few days. And some of his commanders (apparently inspired by the West's sending thousands of mercenaries and its generous military and financial help) were even speaking of just a few hours.

Wanting to justify their shame and not realizing that an armed nation is invincible, these "warriors" wailed about "the Russian aggression". One can only laugh at their reference to what was supposedly "10-20-30 thousand Russian soldiers and officers invaded a defenceless Ukraine". I think that this figure will increase with the escalation of military-political hysteria and psychosis that prevails in Kiev and among its Western backers. After all, they announced that the United army of Novo Russia has one hundred thousand soldiers. If there was such prodigious number, the Donbass people would have long freed all of Ukraine from those fascists. Of course, if you count how many ordinary people – workers, peasants, intellectuals, students, pensioners – initially took up their hunting and trophy weapons, including cold arms, to protect themselves from banditry of armed forces of Ukraine, this figure will rise, indeed, to hundreds of thousands. Later, people's power supplied them real weapons of war, and it happened many times that Bandera occupants received serious blows from yesterday's miners who have swapped the miners tools for a machine gun.

At the same time, the people of Novo Russia dream of Russia sending at least one regiment of the regular Russian army, after which the criminals in Kiev would have only one option left: to immediately pack their bags. Approximately 90-strong grouping of Ukrainian troops thrown against the people, are powerless to cope with the greatly outnumbered by them military units of the DPR and LR. (Even the few volunteers who came from Russia and Europe to help the rebels, were mostly non-military people, significantly behind in terms of professionalism thugs: Yankees, officers of the armed forces of Poland and other Western mercenaries.

The armed conflict in Donbass has led to thousands dead, wounded and missing, to the masses of refugees, to the catastrophic destruction of industrial, agricultural and other infrastructure. People, especially children and the elderly, were dying of hunger, of an inability to obtain medical care. If not for the huge support from the Russian brothers, Donbass might have become a desert. Moreover, the Ukrainian chauvinists out loud, at the level of state leaders they say they want to make the area deserted in order to settle here their "elected, full-blooded Ukrainians."

According to the United Nations in the first year of the conflict the number of internally displaced persons (i.e. those who left to other regions of Ukraine) was half a million. The same number was granted asylum in other countries. But by now only the number of refugees on the Russian territory exceeds one million.

Official Ukrainian and foreign sources speak of roughly 5,000 killed in the conflict zone civil and military people. There is every reason to believe that this figure should be multiplied at least by ten: 50.000 – and it is only the number of the dead.

Russia sends in Donbass troops and convoys with humanitarian cargo. They are sent not only by the government but also by the authorities of many Russian cities and public organizations. Dozens of trucks with food, medicines, clothes were sent by the Communist Party of the Russian Federation.

As for the Ukrainian Communists, it should be noted that the seizure of power by the gang of Poroshenko strengthened their influence on the liberated territories. There is no place here for the "decommunisation", proclaimed by the Kiev regime and perpetrated on the rest of Ukraine by the hands of thugs. On the contrary. Is, so to speak, the Communisation that is taking place. On the one hand, it is humble. After all, the Communists do not have enough forces and means to lead a massive printed and other propaganda. On the other hand, it is huge. Because even those people who before were indifferent to the appeals of the Communists, now fully recognize the correctness of the ideas of Lenin and Stalin. The members of the different Communist organizations from the very beginning were actively involved in the struggle for the independence of Novo Russia. Thy created two teams, which are called "Communist brigades". One is in Donetsk and one is in Luhansk Republic. Neo- Bandera followers are afraid to attack their positions. The soldiers of these brigades are inspired by a belief in what is right and by the banners with portraits of Communist leaders. (Images of Lenin and Stalin in the liberated territories of Donbass can be seen everywhere.)

Over the years I visited more than once the territories of LPR and DPR. First impressions came from one of my trips with the journalists of TV company "Pelikan Production" and IGCP. The abbreviation means "Group of information on crimes against persons in Ukraine." The group was established by the Foundation of the "Actual historical research" (or

"Historical memory"), headed by an authoritative Russian expert and public figure A. R. Dyukov. Our films-reports after each visit to the rebels areas of Donbass are hosted on Youtube – under ID igcpua. This trip lasted 10 days. We visited the following cities and towns (in no particular order): Lugansk, Donetsk, Stakhanov, Ilovaysk, Shakhtersk, Thorez, Krasnodon, Lutugino, Irmino, Alchevsk, Bryanka, Novosvitlivka, Marinovka, Khryashchevatoe, Amvrosievka,and many others.

Our film "The War in the Donbass. Diary" includes scenes filmed in these settlements. That was the first feature-length documentary film about the civil war in Ukraine. People – the living and the dead, the buildings - whole and shattered, armoured vehicles - ready for the battle and torn to pieces, the roads -safe and sweep, sounds of musical concerts and of mortar-gun cannonade... All this is still before my eyes, ringing in the ears, to the heart. Where and how was it?

The City Pervomaisk

Almost 40,000 people lived here. Half of them fled at the onset of the Ukrainian gangs. They were shot by Ukrainian artillery. Some areas of the city were razed to the ground. The locals said that they buried about 700 civilians.

Khryashchevatoe

Working village near the South-Eastern outskirts of Luhansk. It was in the middle of the fighting, passed from hand to hand and is almost in ruins. LR militia eventually knocked out of Khryashchevatoe unfamous by their particular atrocities battalion "Aydar" and the Ukrainian airmobile brigade, deployed here from the city of Lviv

Lugansk airport

Was built in 1964 In the Soviet years up to 100 departures-arrivals were carried out here daily. It was connected by air lines with 70 cities in the country. In 2005-2006 it was reconstructed, which allowed to accept the Airbus A-320 and Boing 737.

In May 2014 the airport was taken under the control by the Ukrainian military and became a reference point for the shelling of residential areas of the city. From here they planned to break into the capital of LR.

On the 14th of June militia shot down Ukrainian military transport aircraft Il-76 on approach to airport, killing those on board - 40 paratroopers and nine crew members. The air supply of the occupation forces, concentrated near the city of Lugansk, was thwarted. And then it was cut off the main land routes of their supply.

In mid-August LR units went on the offensive and completely surrounded two thousand of the Ukrainian grouping in the area of the airport and Lutugino. They were cut it into pieces and by the first of September the Luhansk troops took the airport. Funeral team collected and buried more than three hundred corpses of the Ukrainian soldiers. Hundreds of dead among them were interred during the siege of the airport by the invaders themselves.

Ilovaysk

A large railway junction, the epicentre of fierce fighting in August 2014.

On the 29th of August, Russian President Vladimir Putin urged the militia to open a humanitarian corridor for surrounded the Ukrainian military to give them the opportunity to leave the area of fighting and to save their lives. The rebels agreed, adding that the encircled must get out of "boiler" without heavy weapons.

However, the Ukrainian army by orders from Kiev tried to break through the ring. Then the militsia opened heavy fire. According to information from enemy sources just a few dozen soldiers managed to get out of the encirclement. The others laid down their lives by the fault of Kiev bigots not wanting to admit defeat. To this day they deny their Ilovaisk defeat.

Despite the attention of the general public in Ukraine and abroad to these battles, the information about them by the Kiev regime was made classified and generally unavailable. But video recordings that illustrate the lies of the Kiev puppets and the brutal truth of the freedom fighters of Novo Russia, have become the best proof of both.

Donetsk

Iit is a metropolis with dense residential and industrial buildings, reaching a diameter of 40-55 km. According to the 2001 census, half of the citizens called themselves ethnic Russians. The native language was Russian for even greater number of people – about 90%. (A similar situation is in Luhansk and in Crimea, whose population in 2014, refused to obey the Nazis who have staged a coup in Kiev.) For ethnic Ukrainians, Greeks, Jews, Tatars, Armenians, Gypsies and other local Russian language never was and never will be a foreign language. But the Kiev junta has made great efforts to eradicate the Russian language, declaring it to be "foreign" and forcibly introducing English instead.

The city was subjected to artillery and air strikes, the attacks of the Ukrainian terrorists and saboteurs. But it survived and it lives – working, studying, building.

Kommunar

Settlement in the city of Makeyevka with population of 5000. It is known by the bloody events of the civil war period in Russia after the Great October Socialist revolution. The Whites executed here 45 communist prisoners and 70 unarmed local miners, who joined the Bolsheviks. (This event described in the famous novel by Mikhail Sholokhov "Quiet Flows the Don".)

It's been 97 years since that massacre. In August 2014, near the mine "Kommunarskaya" those who dream to pull Ukraine to Europe, to NATO, to fascist slavery are executing people again. After the executioners fled from the village, we were shown graves of civilians with signs of torture. There were many cases. In one of the pits we saw the body of a pregnant woman. In another pit militia discovered the headless body of a woman with bound hands. Near was the burial with five executed prisoners, fighters of DPR. The commander of the militia (nickname "Alabai") announced that here was a paramilitary unit consisting of approximately 500 people. They looted, drank, used drugs, and did not spare anyone.

From my diary, pieces that were not included in the film.

28.09. Arrived in **Lugansk**. Sunday. Evening. Empty streets. On the main street I counted only a dozen passers-by. In the park two old men sit on a bench. In one of them I recognize Nikolai Ignatievitch Gerasimov, the former Deputy Mayor. I ask him:

– How did you survive the shelling, bombing, blockade of Luhansk?

– Cheerfully. To fight I have not got the strength anymore. But at half past six in the morning with a few old men we went out daily for a physical walk. In spite of the enemies we walked under the bombs, and shells, and rockets of volley fire. Nobody bowed to the enemy, nobody fell to the ground. We try to set an example to the young. I dream to hold on to see the victory and the collapse of this whole Pro-American gang.

29.09. **Lugansk**. Morning. It is lively. Central market. Heavily damaged Mall. A middle-aged woman deals with the exchange of money from owner: ruble and hryvnia, hryvnia into rubles. She shares with us:

– When it became very creepy, I with the child went to relatives in Vinnytsia (i.e. Western Ukraine. – S. G.). Found a job. Placed my girl in kindergarten. Just two days she's been there. And on the third then I took Tanya home, we were walking down the street. On the corner their filthy yellow-blue flag was hanging. And suddenly my child was pointing a finger at it, and began screaming the Nazi salute: "Glory to Ukraine! Glory to the heroes!" Can you imagine? Only two days have passed, and this is what they have taught her... Well, I think, no, I will not allow them to maim my child. I gathered all our stuff and returned to Lugansk. Well, what about shelling?! But over there they would have turned my daughter into a Bandera follower. She would grow up and would cut to pieces all those who disagree with her, including me. Never mind them, I will not let them to take over my Tanya!

29.09. **Pervomaisk.** Severely beaten local man. He requests not to photograph it.
– What happened to you?
– I'm not a volunteer. I tried to drive to my mother in neighbouring Lisichansk (in enemy-occupied territory. – S. G.). After a truce was declared! At the Ukrainian checkpoint they asked: "How many roadblocks have you passed?"
I said:
– Two ours and two yours...
Instantly I got a kick into my face. They trampled boots on me until tired. My car was taken away. They took my money. Passport was burned. Well, at least I was not killed. I hobbled back to Pervomaisk. A truce... f*** such truce!

29.09. **Pervomaisk.** Cossacks stood on the protection of Donbass. An old man approached the commander of the Cossack brigade Pavel Dremov.
– Guys, give me some grenades.
– Why, father?
– I will throw them from the window when Bandera people will enter the city.
– They will not enter, father. While we are alive, they will not! – gravely declares Dremov, who was nicknamed the Cossack Che Guevara. (In December of 2015 Ukrainian bandits killed Dremov. But the enemy failed to break into the city. – S. G.).

30.09. Khryashchevatoe. Local farmer uncle Kolya says:

– I had five cows. Had a place to live, had what to live on. Now, no cows, no house...

Long and florid swearing follows. He lights cigarette and continues:

– But still the important thing is that we did not stay under Bandera. If Russia will hold out, we will again rebuild it, and again will have the cows, and I will work again...

01.10. Lugansk airport. Everything is broken. Demining is taking place. Our cameraman found a few packs of American honey, which was part of the Ukrainian soldiers ' rations.

– In the evening I will drink tea with it.

– Maybe you shouldn't. You never know what they could have laced it with... You may all of a sudden start shouting in your sleep: "Glory to Ukraine! Glory to the heroes!"

In short, we threw that honey away. To hell with it, together with its country- manufacturer!

01.10. Lugansk. One of the areas being raided. Militia LR captured a group of saboteurs. They got in a week ago. Were hiding in the gardens. And when they ran out of food and morale, they came to the shop and tried to sell to local drinkers a Kalashnikov for 500 hryvnia, roughly 25 USD. It is necessary, they say, for getting some money to get home – to the Lviv oblast... Now men will find out if they have any bloody crimes on their hands, and if so, they will be shot.

Nicely dressed up children with flowers and parents pass us by on the way to school. The 1ˢᵗ of October in the Novo Russia is the beginning of the school year.

02.10. I have been living and working in Moscow for a long time. But I was born in the Donbass. All my ancestors are buried on the local cemeteries. I passed in Lugansk the years of my boyhood and youth. My first job was in Donetsk regional newspaper "Komsomolets of Donbass". Now, to get from one city to another, it is necessary to zigzag around the place in order to avoid the enemy.

The taxi driver Sergey says

– Once I was stopped, and asked: "Is there electricity in Lugansk?". I replied "No." – "Is there water?". "No." "Is there a grub to eat?". – "It's all up". – And here they began to cheer: That's good!". Freaks...

03.10. **Lugansk**. Military staff of the LR. In June, the Ukrainian aviation tried to bomb it.

Vladislav Barseghian, a young volunteer, who had been a prisoner of the battalion "Aydar". He was exchanged. Hs hands are covered with scary cuts.

– They tortured me. Forced me to say that I am Chechen. (Many Chechens and other representatives of the North Caucasian peoples are enlisted in the militia of Novo Russia, and bravely proved themselves in this war. – S. G.). But I'm a local Armenian. I live in Lugansk. I only look like a Chechen. ...When they pushed needles under the nails, I managed to hold on. Did not even scream. I decided that I will endure, just like the members of Soviet underground group "Young Guard!" in Krasnodon endured during the Nazi occupation. But when they began to nail down something sharp between my fingers, right into the pain points... then, Yes, I screamed quite a bit...

I, a grown man, carefully take crippled hands of this boy and bring them to my lips. I'm not crazy, although from these pictures and stories one may well go off its hinges.

I want now that bastard Poroshenko's hand with which he signs his gangster decrees, will be tore off. I want his Ministers and generals to lose their legs (along with the balls!). To every Deputy from his party I wish that shrapnel will blow halves of their heads, and their half-heads should lie there, where now lie the bones of the fallen Donbass people. To Vice President Biden during his next visit to Kiev, I wish to choke on Ukrainian dumplings and to die from lack of medical care, of which by the grace of him and others like him? are deprived of thousands of residents of Donbass.

That's what I want!!!

04.10. **Donetsk**. The centre of the city. Lenin Square. A lot of people. The end of the working day and working week. Suddenly above our heads three loud bangs are heard. All look at the sky. Thus at the height of 1.5 km we see three neat white clouds. The deafening explosions are somehow not following. We found out about what happened, or rather, what could have happened. Only in the evening.

To the centre of Donetsk from the area of Kramatorsk three ballistic missiles "Tochka-U" were fired by the Ukrainian army. According to NATO classification, they are called "Scarab" or SS-21. In the non-nuclear option each missile carries at a distance of 120 km nearly 200 kg of explosives; the area of damage is up to three hectares. Before they always hit the target.

But today, they were successfully destroyed by the missile defence of the DPR's army.

– Look, what I want is not a pipe dream.

Endnotes:

[1] This article is exclusively for the magazine "Revolutionary Democracy".

[2] Sergey Golovchenko (1959) – Soviet and Russian documentary filmmaker, screenwriter, essayist. Graduated from the Institute of Countries of Asia and Africa in Moscow (in Chinese Philology), as well as from the journalism faculty of Moscow State University. Winner of national and international literary and film awards. Worked in newspapers, on television and radio. In the last 15 years, he shoots documentary films. He specializes on documentary journalism of an historical and political nature. They are a major contribution to the fight against neo-fascism.

Translated from the Russian by Irina Malenko

Syria

PARTY OF LABOUR OF IRAN (TOUFAN) INTERVIEW ON SYRIA

The English Facebook page of the Party of Labour of Iran (Toufan) has interviewed the comrade in charge of the office of the foreign relations of the Party, Comrade Jaafar Paknia, on the situation in Syria.

Q. Comrade Jaafar, thank you for the time you are spending with us for this interview. As you know, due to the Russian aerial bombardment and the destruction of the bases of Daesh (ISIS) and other terrorist groups, the balance of power has changed in Syria. The regime of Basher Assad has gone on the offensive and its forces have advanced significantly. The Turkish government of Erdogan has violated international norms and regulations and has frantically bombarded the bases of the Kobane Kurds and has declared its opposition to any autonomy for the Syrian Kurds. How do you evaluate these new developments in Syria?

A. The adventurist policy of Erdogan's government, a government that is sunk in the dream of the revival of "Great Ottoman Empire", and that shamelessly interferes in the internal affairs of the countries of the region has faced disgraceful defeat. This is clearly a sign of political shortsightedness of the present leadership of Turkey. By sending the Syrian refugees to Europe, Erdogan wanted to pressure the European governments to agree with his policy of toppling the legal and legitimate government of Assad and to pretend that only through NATO involvement in Syria and its support for terrorist organizations and eventually through the overthrow of the Syrian government it is possible to stop the influx of refugees to Europe. Erdogan's inhumane conspiracy has become a policy of instigation, war, and destruction in the region. This policy was rejected by the European governments, and consequently Turkey's shortsighted policy faced a dead end. Erdogan asked for three billion Euros from the European countries as blackmail to stop the influx of refugees to Europe.

The gains of the Syrian army against Daesh through Russian bombardment are increasing daily. These gains have encouraged the people in the Daesh-controlled regions to resist and to participate in the war against the terrorist organizations. ISIS has chosen the "flight" over "Heaven". These terrorists are returning to their homelands by the scores. The imperialist-trained Daesh and Jihadists have spread their terror campaigns to their motherlands. Though France has fallen victim to the terrorist operations, it has not stopped interfering in the affairs of the Middle Eastern countries. The Western imperialist countries that supported Daesh and other terror groups in killing 300 thousand Syrians will not escape these terror campaigns. Turkey itself will fall victim to Daesh's terror campaign soon.

The government of Erdogan that continues the criminal fascist suppression and bombardment of PKK and the Kurdish people is extremely frightened by the recent victories of the Syrian government over the terrorist groups, and it is asking Saudi Arabia and Qatar to jointly dispatch their armies to Syria to "fight" Daesh. What a joke! What a lie! These countries have been supporting, training, arming, and financing ISIS for the past 5 years. Even Barak Obama and NATO and EU officials are hesitant about the effectiveness of Erdogan's adventurist policies. The armed forces of Turkey enter Syria only for the purpose of destroying the democratic achievements of the Kobane Kurds and to fight against the Syrian army. This is obviously in violation of the sovereignty and territorial integrity of Syria.

Q. Some hold the opinion that Russian bombardment of Daesh has made the situation worse and has killed many civilians, that Russia's objective in its rivalry with the US imperialists is to preserve and strengthen its interest in Syria and the region, and that Russian interference in the Middle East is an imperialist act that should not be supported. What is your opinion on these issues?

A. Before we talk about the class nature of the Russian establishment, we must clarify the nature of the war that is being waged in Syria and the Middle East. We must analyze the reasons why the Western imperialists headed by the U.S. and their lackeys and allies in the region such as Saudi Arabia, Qatar, Turkey, etc. want to overthrow the legal government of Syria. Isn't this policy of aggression against Syria consistent with the doctrine of establishing the "Greater Middle East"? Isn't this the continuation of the policy of military aggression against Iraq, Afghanistan, Libya, etc? Isn't this policy in the interest of Zionism and world reaction? Do China and Russia desire to disintegrate Syria and split it into pieces?

It must be emphasized that Syria has political independence and therefore has the right to freely seek help from any force or country in order to preserve its national independence and territorial integrity. This policy of seeking assistance is not new in the struggle of the people of the world. In the war that is imposed upon Syria, the condemnation of the Western aggressors and their regional allies must occupy the first place. These aggressors are seeking the total destruction and disintegration of Syria. Furthermore, their objective is not limited to the overthrow of Assad's regime but to the suppression of Lebanon's resistance movement, aggression against Iran. And the dispatch of terrorist forces to the borders of Russia will come next. The U.S. strategy of "New World Order" is to weaken and remove the allies of China and Russia, to subdue these two imperialist rivals, and to impose its hegemony on the globe. The fact is that Eastern imperialists presently do not have the necessary military power or preparation to wage war on the Western united military forces of NATO led by the U.S. In the present condition, it is NATO that has military superiority and violates and threatens the independence, territorial integrity, and the rights of nations to self determination. Western imperialism, headed by the U.S., is the source of all present wars and is responsible for the flight of millions of people from their homelands in the Middle East, Horn of Africa, Yugoslavia, and Ukraine.

Russia and China vetoed the U.S. proposal in the UN Security Council and have expressed many times their opposition to the bombardment of Syria. This is a positive stand, as were the stands of Germany and France in opposition to the U.S. invasion of Iraq. It is clear that behind these stands and oppositions lie economic and political interests and motives. A political party, while clarifying the nature of the war and of the forces involved, must adopt its tactic. The independent state of Syria, as any independent state, can make use of the present world contradictions to preserve its independence; otherwise it will not overcome the aggression imposed on it. One may simplify a complicated political question and raise a general political slogan and put his mind at ease by declaring war on all forces involved and then watch the development of the events. This is not a responsible conduct and it is inconsistent with Marxism and Leninist tactics. Our Party emphasizes that we must defend the independence and territorial integrity of the countries that face imperialist military aggression. This defence is a defence for rights of nations to self determination by their own people.

We must add that Saudi Arabia, Qatar, and Turkey's opposition to Syria is over the export of natural gas from the region to Europe. Iran, Iraq, and Syria planned for a ten-billion dollar project for the construction of a pipeline to export Iran's natural gas to Europe starting in 2010. In 2012, a

Memorandum of Understanding was signed by these three countries. Two weeks later, armed clashes started in Syria. Armed terrorist groups were sent to Syria through its northern and southern borders. Qatar, Saudi Arabia, and Turkey utilized their means to overthrow the regime of Assad. Qatar now fights for a bigger share of market for its natural gas, and Saudi Arabia and Turkey want the gas pipelines to pass through their countries in order to become a broker for the export of Qatar's natural gas to Europe and to collect transit fees.

Q. Western media claim that Russian bombardments of Syria have killed many thousands of innocent people and that Russia is responsible for the continuation of the war and the migration of hundreds of thousands of residents. What are your views on these?

A. Western media lie about the events in Syria and also fabricate stories consistent with the official line of their governments. The Russian fighter jets bomb the bases and positions of Daesh and some other terrorist groups, and have significantly weakened Daesh's grips on the regions under their control. Russia displayed satellite pictures of stolen oil tankers going from Syria to Turkey. Daesh sells the stolen oil to Turkey at a low price, and Turkey offers it to the world at the market price. Russian jet fighters bombed many hundreds of these oil tankers.

Assad's victories over Daesh and over the conspiracies and plots of the Western imperialists are very bitter for Turkey, Saudi Arabia, the U.S., and the Western media. These conspirators try to disrupt and hinder the fight against the terrorists who have destroyed Syria. European countries that are vulnerable and are threatened by the terrorist actions want to stop their losses. They see that their policy of toppling the legal government of Assad has faced defeat and that their hopes are dashed though they, with the help from reactionary regimes of the region such as Kuwait, Qatar, Saudi Arabia, Turkey and Jordon made use of everything they could including the violation of the UN Charter and of the rights of nations to defeat Assad. Now they are interested in reduction of tension in the region. They see the reduction of tension in the region as useful to their interests and to the normalization of relation with Russia. The government of Erdogan that used Daesh of Arab, Turk, Turkmen, Chechen, Dagestan, and European nationalities to attack Syria now sees that the terrorist forces are on the run and are facing defeat followed by another defeat. Erdogan, with the hope of occupying and annexing northern Syria to Turkey, has invented a

Turkmen national minority in Syria that wants to join Turkey. Turkmen who are allies of Daesh and who behead Arabs and Kurds are Erdogan's brothers and friends and are defended as "non-terrorist" opposition. The Russian jets are making these terrorists martyrs for Erdogan. And of course, the jets that make these Turkmen martyrs have to be shut down by the non-terrorists provided that the U.S. has expressed its consent. With the defeat of Daesh, the Syrian Kurdish forces are gaining strength, and Erdogan is losing hope to split Syria. Obama and Erdogan play a sly and hypocritical role in the fight against Daesh.

In the present situation, Russians and Assad's army have no interest in bombarding the civilian regions. We should mention that long before the Russian military involvement in Syria, more than 150 thousand terrorists from 80 countries, financed by Saudi Arabia and Qatar and the U.S. and Europe, were mobilized to destroy and attack Syria. Now they are defeated and are on the run. The Western news media tries to instigate public opinion against the regime of Bashar Assad by engineering lies and distributing Photoshopped pictures.

Q. What is the future of the regime of President Assad? What stand the people are taking in this situation?

A. As I have mentioned several times, the U.S. objective is to overthrow the regime of Assad in the frame work of "humanitarian involvement". The U.S. imperialists and their allies want to divide Syria into four regions; a Sunni region in Damascus and its suburbs, the Druze region in Golan Heights, the Alavi region in Antakya region, and a Kurdish region in north eastern Syria. This would make Syria a weak, dependent, and fragmented country that serves the strategic interest of the U.S. and Israel and their allies. The silence of the so called human rights organizations on the violation of the rights of nations by the U.S. imperialists shows the hypocrisy of the fake human rights organizations.

It must be said that the overthrow of the regime of Bashar Assad by the hands of the Syrian people led by the working class and for the purpose of establishing freedom, social justice, and the preservation and deepening of independence of Syria would be a revolutionary act that serves the people of Syria and of the entire region. The toppling of the Syrian regime by the imperialist powers is neither in the interest of the Syrian people nor in the interest of the people of the region. Parties and organizations that have not learned from the experience of the occupations of Iraq, Libya,

Afghanistan, and others and that are still repeating the theories of "fight against all reactionary forces", and resolving "all social contradictions" at the same time understand neither tactics nor revolutionary politics. They are sunk in the Trotskyite quagmire of a "fight against two reactionary poles". These forces do not serve the people. On the contrary, they sabotage the national and liberation struggles of the people against imperialist aggression and invasion. It is the responsibility of the revolutionary and progressive forces to resolutely expose these deviated and decaying political currents that damage the movement under the name of "communist" and "left".

Today, the Western imperialists see that a significant section of Syrians, due to the destructive actions of the dark force of Daesh, have lined up behind Assad's regime and that not by any means will the Syrian people "rise up" against the "dictator". The U.S. imperialists and their allies are forced to talk about peace (!), but in practice they beat the war drums on all fronts.

STEP BY STEP MOVING TOWARDS A DICTATORSHIP

EMEP

The failed attempted military coup of 15 July, orchestrated by the so called 'Gülen Movement' – the pro-American Islamic organisation that shared power with the AKP government for 10 years – was called "a gift from God" by the Turkish President Tayyip Erdoðan.

The crushing of the coup was quickly followed by the declaration of a state of emergency (OHAL). OHAL enabled the government to take administrative and political decisions and to introduce regulatory legislation without the need for judicial and/or parliamentary approval.

Under the leadership of President Erdoðan, the AKP government issued emergency decrees (KHKs) one after another; leading to suspension and dismissal of tens of thousands of military and police officers, judges, prosecutors and civil servants. Almost 40,000 people, including academics and teachers were also arrested. The number of jailed journalists rose to a record high of 140. Meanwhile, 37 thousand petty criminals were released on the account that there was not enough space in prisons. Whereas the government initially claimed that dismissals and arrests were carried out only against coup plotters of the Gülen movement; soon it became clear that democrats and socialists were also targeted. Through only one decree, more than 10 thousand teachers, all members of Eðitim-Sen (Education and Science Workers Union), were laid off. A great majority of them were democrats, socialists and supporters of Kurdish national movement.

Following the attempted coup, overriding of rights and freedoms – traditionally deficient in Turkish political democracy – have increased; bourgeois law is at a standstill and has been replaced by arbitrary treatment of the executive/government. Replacing legislation with the state of emergency and rule by emergency decrees, and subordinating the judiciary to the executive through special courts and appointment of new judges and prosecutors; Erdoðan and AKP are trying to establish a fascist dictatorship regime of one-man, one-party.

The government issued unconstitutional and illicit decrees, while by law it only could issue ones that are constitutional and related to the events that lead to declaration of state of emergency. With the help of these decrees targeting the critics of AKP, demonstrations are banned, dissident newspapers, journals, radio stations and TV channels are shut down; their property and equipment are confiscated.

The municipalities led by HDP, third largest party in the parliament with 40 MPs and representing the Kurdish democratic movement, were raided by the police and more than 20 mayors arrested. Trustees were appointed to their posts without a public vote.

Finally, a total of ten HDP MPs – including the party co-chairs – were jailed. At the same time, 10 executives of the Cumhuriyet newspaper – founded 93 years ago with the establishment of Turkish Republic and politically aligned in recent years with social democracy – were also arrested.

Publications defending the revolutionary line of the working class – such as Hayatýn Sesi TV, Evrensel Kültür (a culture and art magazine), Özgürlük Dünyasý (a journal of political theory), Tiroj (bilingual Kurdish-Turkish cultural magazine) were among the television stations and publications closed down by the government.

Unconstitutionally, without breaking his association with AKP for nearly two years and consolidating all executive power in his hands, the de-facto president Erdoðan is trying to change the constitution in line with the aforementioned situation and pushing for a presidential system.

Furthermore, while insisting on a foreign policy based on expansionism and sectarian war, intimate with Islamist terrorist groups, the Erdoðan-led government is taking further steps. Over the last five years, it has supported radical Islamist gangs in Syria and their organisation, to overthrow the Assad regime. In a new attempt, Turkey launched a military operation in Northern Syria at the end of the summer, to back a few thousand Islamist terrorist militants it put forward initially. The intervention was under the pretext of fighting against ISIS, but its main target was Syrian Kurds. Turkey, along with Islamist gangs, controls/invades an area of almost 2000 km, stretching from the banks of the Euphrates river to the Kurdish canton of Afrin, including cities and towns such as Jarablus. Nowadays, the government pursues the propaganda of conquering al-Bab. However, a spike was put in Turkey's wheel due to US support for Syrian Democratic Forces – the backbone of whom is YPG – in the operation to liberate the "capital" of ISIS, Raqqa; and the support of Russia for the Assad regime, trying to capture al-Bab because of its strategic importance as a gate to Aleppo.

The AKP government, while fighting the PYD-YPG in Syria, is also in conflict with the Iraqi government due to its military presence in the Iraqi town of Bashiqa; Iraq is demanding the withdrawal of the Turkish forces.

The Turkish Air Force is regularly bombing Northern Iraq, claiming to attack PKK camps.

In the last year, Syria and Iraq policies of Turkey have increasingly changed; as well as relations with the US and the EU cooling, due to the Turkish belief that they supported the attempted coup of 15 July.

Following the agreement for Turkey to stop the migration from Syria, Iraq and Afghanistan and the EU to pay Turkey three billion Euros, as well as give Turkish citizens visa-free travel rights within the EU, both sides failed to keep their promises and the relationships between Turkey and the EU are strained. The AKP government is claiming that they'll wait two more months before cancelling the agreement and that they'll go to a referendum on EU membership due to its criticism of Turkey; EU, citing the imprisonment of journalists and the like, has started talking about halting discussions on Turkish membership.

Since its establishment, Turkey had close economic, trade and financial ties with the West and very strong military ties with the USA; as such it is undoubtedly very hard for Turkey as a NATO member to change its 'axis' or 'boss'. Nevertheless, President Erdoğan, having visited Pakistan recently, has stated "…why not? It will help Turkey feel at ease" on the issue of membership to the Shanghai Cooperation Organisation.

Besides the policies and steps taken by the AKP government, the Turkish economy is not going in the right direction either. The rate of growth has been falling for the last four years, the deficit and unemployment increasing. According to official figures unemployment is at 11% but the real figure is higher. The dollar has risen 10% against the Turkish Lira in the recent days; as if the Turkish Lira has devaluated and lost 10% of its value. The government is cutting the interest rate and increasing available credit in an attempt to stimulate the economy but stagnation has set in all sectors – primarily building and textile sectors. A capitalist crisis that is not limited to, and not necessarily starting in the financial sector is raising its "head" and this is the soft underbelly of the AKP.

Despite all bans and police oppression, strikes at workplace levels continue. The powers of the executive are ever increasing; students are demonstrating against the decision that university rectors will be appointed by the President. Solicitors and intellectuals are demonstrating to condemn the imprisonment of their peers. Opponents of AKP are trying to create new alliances. Unity for Democracy with its components of democratic, socialist, social-democrat and Kurdish national movements, including our party, is taking further steps to organise following a series of meetings.

New magazines are published in place of others.

Is the future of Turkey going to be a fascist dictatorship run by one man? Or the struggle for democracy and freedom will widen and strengthen to achieve new successes; the dimensions of the struggle and the level of organisation will determine this. Of course the international support and solidarity will have a great contribution to the outcome.

Labour Party (EMEP) Turkey
International Bureau

MODERN SOCIAL REFORMISM AND THE KKE

EMEP

The Europe[1] of today, despite its long-lost central position in the capitalist world, is still home to countries where both monopoly capitalism and the material pre-conditions for socialism[2] are most advanced. Faced with this reality, it is no surprise that the European peoples and workers' movements suffered the most from the many-faceted scars and the deepest effects of the temporary comprehensive defeat of the international working class. The specific asymmetry to note here is that in this region – where the material pre-conditions of socialism are most advanced and hence the most advanced sections of the only class that is able to carry out a social revolution (the working class) exist – the workers' movement is in an historically[3] least powerful, disorganized, most divided position and its trust in socialism is most shaken. This relative inverse proportional relationship between the objective and subjective conditions, caused by the historical defeat, has still not been overcome.[4]

Yes, this is despite the 2007-2009 economic crisis that shook Europe. It is clear that if the deep economic crisis – which began a period of deepening general depression under monopoly capitalism – had not coincided with this period of historical defeat, the development of the class struggle would have been different.

This crisis has also had an impact on the above-mentioned asymmetry. Not only did it expose the parasitic character and decay of monopoly capitalism[5] but it also led to new concerns among all classes and their political representatives that suffered socio-economic deterioration in their conditions. The crisis exposed the limits of the European workers' movement against the capitalist offensive, the serious frailty and weaknesses of those parties tasked with (or at least claiming to) organizing and leading that movement. This article will focus on two examples that highlight the typical ideological-political problems of the European workers' movement[6]. One of these is the increasingly evident modern social reformism within Syriza and the other is the emerging left doctrinarism and sectarianism within the Communist Party of Greece (KKE). Considering the general situation above, it is no coincidence that these two examples have come to a head in a country in which the crisis caused major social trauma.

MODERN SOCIAL REFORMISM
AND THE WORKERS' MOVEMENT

'*Die Wirtschaftswoche*'[7] [*The Economic Weekly*], the major media mouthpiece of German capital, presented its audience with a striking cover after the formation of the Syriza government: on the flowing red flag were three faces; '*the leader of the Podemos Movement*' in Spain, Pablo Iglesias was on the left; the new Prime Minister of Greece, Alexis Tsipras, was in the middle; and the new Finance Minister of Greece, Yanis Varoufakis, was on the right. The title was the chorus of The Internationale and the sub-title read: "The new left populists of Europe are poor, sexy and dangerous for our welfare!"

Any Marxist-Leninist who saw this cover would have laughed at first, since linking Syriza and Podemos to communism and the revolutionary workers' movement is laughable! This mouthpiece of German capital knew full-well that these juvenile '*socialists*' have nothing to do with revolutionary socialism. It seems that this magazine of capital could not resist – given the opportunity – ridiculing communism through these "*new left populists*". At the same time, it felt the need to warn that "anything they may spur people on to, one way or another, could threaten our welfare!"

We will return to the cause of this warning but first we must make something clear: how does modern social reformism[8] differ from the classical reformism that preceded it? What they have in common is clear: they deny the workers' revolution and workers' rule; they want to reform capitalism socially through public opinion and parliamentary means rather than through working class struggles; to make it more '*human*'; to replace '*savage capitalism*' with '*social and ecological capitalism*'; to achieve incremental social improvements through '*reforms*' based on capitalist relations, etc. In short, from an *ideological* perspective there is no difference between classical and modern reformism.

The most important difference between modern and classical reformism is its relationship with the working class – or the lack of it. Modern social reformism today is social reformism in the conditions of the historic defeat of the working class, the effects of which are still being felt. The classical one surfaced and found its political meaning in keeping a dynamic and revolutionary workers' movement within the bounds of capitalism, in order to curb the workers' movement and to turn it away from revolutionary action. When a serious revolutionary workers' movement develops in any country, without a doubt modern social reformism will also expand its role in this direction.

However, there is no serious revolutionary movement that embraces the bulk of its class today and modern social reformism has arisen and become strengthened despite this absence! In other words, to just say that social reformism is social reformism – that is, to look at the issue on a purely ideological basis – will prevent us from clearly grasping the reality of the problem.

If social reformism found the opportunity to develop in conditions where the workers – besides being revolutionary – could not act in unity as a class or repel the bourgeois offensives, then it should be noted that the real point of today's social reformism is not so much its reformism but its sociality. In other words, the ideological weaknesses of today's mass movements that are observed in many European countries and driven by socio-liberal reformist ideology should not prevent us from recognizing their social reality.

As is known, since the collapse of the Soviet Union and the Eastern bloc, international capital and especially European capital have carried out a widespread and relentless offensive against the working masses. In a fairly short period of time, the workers found out that the capitalism "that beat communism" did not bring the welfare and security that it claimed. Indeed, they lost many social, economic and democratic gains of the previous period. The big economic crisis deepened this offensive; the workers were made to pay the bill. Whatever the explanation by bourgeois and social liberal ideologues, the situation is that broad masses of workers, laborers and youth are protesting against this offensive, they are increasingly reacting against social and economic conditions and expressing their discontent against the status quo in different ways.

The toiling masses are increasingly opposing the attacks unleashed by capital and its governments, but what do they want? They put forward social, economic and political demands, such as the end of the offensive, of austerity policies and elimination of social rights; for new areas of work created and properly funded, especially for the youth, higher taxes on finance capital, better pay, an end to privatization, the limiting or abolition of subcontracting, the abolition of anti-worker changes in laws, equal pay, investment in health and education, the end of limitations on the right to strike, demonstrate and march, etc.[9]

Just as elections show the level of maturity of the workers, their demands show their political level. Of course not abstractly but in a specific period, conditions and situation. From this perspective, it is clear that these demands are generally defensive and focus on regaining lost rights. The character of these demands also shows a association between the workers' movement and social reformism.

Nevertheless, the social backbone of the modern social reformist movement is the labour aristocracy, the petty and (a limited number of) middle bourgeoisie and intellectuals.[10] The capitalist crisis and the increasing capitalist offensive (*'neoliberalism'*!) have caused disillusionment with capitalism itself and these strata are longing for a 'new' 'social capitalism' (*'social market economy'*), which is actually old (the *'social state'*!). Thus, while the bourgeoisie claims that socialism is a historical deviation, the modern social reformists claim that capitalism deviated from its essence!

From this perspective, today's social reformism represents a form of romanticism (from the *"return to principles"* of the French bourgeois revolution to the re-establishment of a *"social state"*!). Classic social reformism, on the other hand, was not romantic; despite being limited by the perspective of transforming capitalism through social reforms, it was forward-looking.

On the other hand, due to the historic defeat, the workers trust in socialism has been shaken and ideologically they are mainly influenced by social-liberal currents. Therefore, the two classes and strata, in the same state of mind due to their disillusionment and distrust (one with socialism and the other with capitalism) come together in 'social capitalism'. This association directly affects the working class in conditions where the struggle for socialism is seen as a dream; it pushes the working class towards modern social reformism, the form of which could be quite radical in relation to the crisis and the level of social shock it caused; it enables the working class to embrace a struggle along the line preached by social reformism in order to secure real and tangible improvements in its social and economic conditions.

Needless to say, unless the social and political reality of the European workers' movements summarized above is grasped, no revolutionary task can be carried out correctly and effectively. The more this is realized today, the clearer is the complexity and difficulty facing the communists in their duties to represent the workers' movement and the foresight, patience and flexibility demanded of them.

Let us return to the warning by *Wirtschaftswoche* about the 'dangerous' strengthening of modern social reformism, which in reality aims not to do away with capitalism but to re-establish the previous *'social state'* or *'social welfare society'*. This warning is an expression of the experiences of the monopoly bourgeoisie. Its ideologues are well aware of the many movements in history that started out with a certain social or political goal and ended with completely different aims or results. For this reason, they do not want to play with fire!

THE DAMAGE CAUSED
BY MODERN REVISIONISM

As Marxist-Leninists, we are aware that worthwhile social reforms are achieved by a revolutionary struggle of the working class and the masses. Besides, historically, reforms have always been a by-product of revolutionary struggles (while these measures and reforms are used to weaken and stunt the revolutionary struggle). "Without Social Democrats there would be no social reforms" (Bismarck). As such, without the October Revolution and the Soviet Union there would have been no 'social state'. The history of the European workers' movement is full of similar examples that support this thesis; thus this side of the problem is clear.

Another truth that is also clear is that the working class of today is separated from its history and historical experience. We are faced with a contradictory and specific situation: there is a serious discrepancy between the historical experience of the working class as a political class and the limited outlook of its current practical struggle. To see the real roots of this contradictory situation one needs to look at modern revisionism, which seized power at the 20th Congress of the Communist Party of Soviet Union, and the historical defeat that it brought about.

So that we do not lose track we will limit ourselves to stating this: modern revisionism turned working class revolutionary theory into a shallow and formal one; it blunted "*its revolutionary dialectics*"[11], seen by Lenin as "*decisive in Marxism*", and hence eliminated Marxism-Leninism as the guide to working class action. Under the dominance of modern revisionism, the workers' movement has never become a serious revolutionary movement, especially in Western Europe. There were numerous workers' struggles in Europe between the end of the 1960s and the early 1980s. But none of these struggles were directed – either by modern revisionism in the Soviet Union (and thus its fellow revisionist parties in Western Europe) or by Euro-communism – toward developing and organizing the working class or with a perspective and practice that would enable the working class to come to power. The more the revolutionary character of the working class was weakened, the more the workers became dominated by the liberal bourgeoisie through social liberalism. The collapse of the Soviet Union and the Eastern bloc was the icing on the cake, or rather a situation that was taking shape became politically clearer and the period of erosion of the revolutionary character of the working class was achieved...

So where does the KKE stand in this picture? Despite taking a positive stance in respect to the main ideological and political issues, such as its criticism of the 20th Congress and Khrushchev' revisionism[12], it still has not overcome the dismantling of the revolutionary core of Marxism-Leninism and primarily the damage revisionism has done to carrying out the role and duties of the communist parties towards the working class. Thus, the political, social and economic shocks in Greece, brought on by the worldwide economic crisis and the social erosion this caused, very quickly exposed the KKE's weaknesses. The shortcomings and mistakes of the KKE on the above-mentioned issues played a major role in its failure to fulfil its complex and difficult duty as a communist party in the conditions of the class struggle in Greece[13]. The friendly criticism of these weaknesses and mistakes are essential for the benefit of the Greek and European workers' movements.

We say 'friendly', because the criticisms made here are not related to the '*right opportunist*' criticism of the KKE[14]. Indeed, the KKE has for some time been involved in discussions with international groups that it is a member of. According to the KKE, there is a *"crisis in the international communist movement"*: *"the strengthening of opportunism is reflected in the ideological-political and organizational crisis of the international communist movement."*[15] The issues that *lead to splits* within the movement are widespread, from the character and stages of the revolution to concepts of parliamentarism, from approaches to capitalist crises to proletarian internationalism. For example, for the last two years this movement has failed to publish a joint declaration after their annual general conference.

Currently, the KKE made public its opinion on the discussions within the movement with a statement titled *"On some questions on the unity of the international communist movement"*. This and many other statements include many truths regarding openly right-wing theses (transforming the EU into a people's union; the illusions spread about China and Russia in relation to the BRICS countries; the *"socialist"* definition of Latin American *"progressive governments"*; support for *"21st century socialism"* and *"market socialism"* in China and Vietnam, etc.). (We should also mention that some of the KKE's evaluations coincide with ideas put forward by the International Conference of Marxist-Leninist Parties and Organizations – ICMLPO – which was borne from the struggle against modern revisionism, reorganizing itself with the Quito Declaration at a time when counter-revolution was rampant.) Despite these positive points, as will be seen below, the position of the KKE in terms of its responsibilities towards the working class, its duties and necessary tactics and alliances still retain doctrinaire and sectarian tendencies.

THE KKE LINE OF ALLIANCES
AND STRUGGLE

In the above-mentioned statement, the KKE draws attention to the line for the *alliances and struggles* it is carrying out in its own country. It states that it is *"placing emphasis"* on the *"regroupment of the labour movement and the reinforcement of the class orientation, on the strengthening of the class unity"*. Furthermore, the party's attempts to build a *"people's alliance, i.e. the alliance between the working class, the poor farmers, the small self-employed, women and young people from the working class families"* is emphasized. *"In the current conditions this alliance is expressed through the coordination of the struggle of the militant rallies* [organizations – translator's note]*: PAME in the working class, PASY in the farmers, PASEVE in the self-employed in urban centres, MAS in students, OGE in women"*.[16]

It might be thought that a real *people's* alliance has been established in Greece. Nevertheless, this is not the situation. The KKE claims that the *"people's alliance is a social alliance and has an anti-capitalist, anti-monopoly orientation."* But the reality is this: PAME, PASY, PASEVE, MAS and OGE are *combative units* established by and following the line of the KKE! As such they are naturally *"anti-capitalist and anti-monopoly"* units. In the KKE's words they are carrying out "vanguard, mass activities"! In short, this is not a *"social people's alliance"* in reality; rather it is an organizational unity between the union, farmer youth and women's organizations of the KKE and/or those that follow its line.

On the other hand, these *combative units*, in unity with the KKE, along their own *"anti-capitalist anti-monopoly"* line, are preparing for the revolution; the *"people's alliance"* *"will be reinforced in the daily struggle concerning all the problems of the people, it will adapt and prepare itself so as to play the leading role in the conditions of the revolutionary situation (which has an objective character and all parties must prepare themselves for it)"*. *"The KKE, the class oriented movement and the people's alliance are in the forefront of the struggle in Greece. They mobilize hundreds of thousands of working people, forces that come in conflict with the forces of capital, the parties and its governments, the imperialist*

European Union."

The KKE's concept of struggle must have been criticized in its international group, as the following is also included in the statement: *"The positions that try to incriminate the revolutionary struggle with the slander about sectarianism, downplaying the vanguard, mass activity of the KKE and PAME and the other militant rallies that struggle for specific goals concerning all the problems of the people against the monopolies and capitalism are causing damage to the communist movement."*

We cannot determine from this "statement" which bases and/or arguments the criticisms of *"sectarianism"* were based on. But we must point out that the KKE's *understanding of the class struggle has sectarian tendencies.* Carrying on the *"struggle for specific goals concerning all the problems of the people"* in the *"vanguard mass activity"* does not eliminate this sectarianism (recognized sectarian tendencies also claim that they are carrying out the struggle for specific goals concerning all the problems of the people). Besides, the real issue is not around which problems *'vanguard mass activities'* are carried out; the issue is the approach itself, the creation of *separate vanguard groups.* It is known that the KKE has created *separate vanguard groups* within the social movement; that in almost all activities it marches, mobilizes and organizes separately with these groups...

We shall continue. How can the KKE, a party that still has an important place in the Greek workers' movement, defend the creation of a vanguard group in the workers' movement in the name of Marxism-Leninism? This approach is based on two arguments:

1. *"The revolution in Greece will have a socialist character."* Those parties, movements, unions and mass organizations that do not follow the KKE or its line are considered reformist and/or bourgeois and belonging to the system (at least those that have a certain influence in the workers' movement). Because of the socialist character of the revolution, the alliances established must be "anti-capitalist and anti-monopoly". Hence, alliances should not be made with other groups; on the contrary, a *"social people's alliance"* will be built through winning workers to the *"vanguard, mass activities"* of the *combative units* under the control of the KKE.

2. The transition from capitalism to socialism has no *"intermediate stage"*: *"This is a big problem. The rationale of stages objectively (despite any intentions) entails the search of pro-people solutions on the terrain of capitalism on the grounds that the 'intermediate stage' will contribute to the maturation of the subjective factor and will operate as a bridge to*

socialism... This approach has not been confirmed anywhere and in any period. It is in contradiction with the lessons of the Great Socialist October Revolution in 1917. The worst thing is that the rationale of stages leads to the search of solutions for the management of the system e.g. of 'left-progressive or patriotic governments' that will (objectively) manage the interests of the monopolies which will continue to have the ownership over the means of production and the political power." According to the KKE: *"This choice fosters illusions; it does not contribute to the preparation of the labour movement for fierce class confrontations"* and on the contrary *"it condemns it to backwardness and makes it vulnerable to bourgeois ideology and politics, it entangles it in the web of parliamentary illusions."*

It is evident that the KKE has closed its eyes to the reality of the *"subjective factor"*! This can be seen in their statement that *"we will not put the class under a false flag!"* seen not only in the statement quoted above but in many of their other statements.[17]

Lenin's recommendation in facing such tendencies is to *"weigh the alignment of actual class forces and the incontrovertible facts as soberly and as accurately as possible"*[18] We need to do this because *in the conditions we are in,* where the effects of the historical defeat of the working class are still being seriously felt, where the working class' trust in socialism has been shaken, and furthermore when the bourgeois and social liberal outlook is dominant among the workers, the KKE is against this or that *"choice"* with the excuse that it will make the workers' movement *"vulnerable to bourgeois ideology and politics"* and *"entangle it in the web of parliamentary illusions".* Whom does the KKE have in mind when talking about these *"illusions"*? It cannot be the working masses, as they already are in the clutches of these *"illusions".* If the KKE looked at the reality of the workers' movement, it would realize that it has put the problem backwards; how can we redirect the workers entangled in these illusions onto a path where they can develop their own independent movement?

We will return to this question, which shows the most fundamental dimension of the complex and difficult tasks. We will also make two points regarding the argument about *"intermediate stages".*

1. Do *"intermediate stages"* mean what Khrushchev revisionism imposed on communist parties in the advanced capitalist countries: "a peaceful transition to socialism" through "anti-monopoly democracy"? It is clear that a programme that does away with socialist *revolution* from the

beginning, that absolutizes a theoretically possible but historically unique and temporary situation to replace revolution and that does not organize or prepare itself for a socialist revolution cannot be defended in the name of Marxism-Leninism. Hence an "*anti-monopoly democracy*" is wrong. In this approach the main issue is not a one-time possibility; on the contrary it is a diversion of the working class from the duty to organize and awaken the class as the one that will carry out the socialist revolution. So, if the KKE is against an *intermediate stage* that is not an "*intermediate stage*", then they are surely correct.

2. Nevertheless, this does not change their sectarian position. There is no need to ignore today's reality and to say that 'there won't be in the future' to reject this. There is no reason to reject all '*intermediate stages*'[19] saying: "Power will be either a bourgeois power or workers'-people's power; there cannot be any power which has an intermediate character".

Lenin, also basing himself on the experience of the October Revolution, says; "*History generally, and the history of revolutions in particular, is always richer in content, more varied, more many sided, more lively and 'subtle' than even the best parties and the most class-conscious vanguards of the most advanced classes imagine.*"[20] Intermediate stations and compromises are created "by "*historical developments*". And as Engels stated "*The German Communists are Communists because through all the intermediate stations and all compromises, created, not by them, but by the course of historical development, they clearly perceive and constantly pursue the final aim, viz., the abolition of classes and the creation of a society in which there will no longer be private ownership of land or of the means of production*".[21]

Nevertheless, leaving aside the fact that history does not make **absolute** statements; what is more important now is that this approach creates a big obstacle in terms duties of communists in the class struggle today. It is a obstacle because the 'one solution' approach narrows the horizons of the communists, reduces their work to a single dimension and renders them unable to see the rich varieties of the class struggle and make them a basis for the workers' movement. As long as the problems caused by modern revisionism in undermining Marxism-Leninism as a theory have not been overcome, the KKE – with its sectarian tendencies regarding the rising social-reformism and right-wing opportunism – is not only a party without a minimum program but, due to the lack of specific differences between strategy and tactics, is in a position in which its strategy does not need its tactics and its tactics do not differ from its strategy.

To clarify this, let us see what Elisseos Vagenas, a member of the KKE Central Committee and responsible for international relations, said in an interview with Evrensel newspaper just before the 2012 elections: *"the KKE does not fight today for any intermediate stage and therefore it has no minimum programme. Of course this does not mean that it has only a strategy and no tactics. The tactics of the KKE promote the need to rally the working people around goals of struggle, both for the defence of the workers', people's and democratic rights as well as for the satisfaction of the contemporary needs of the people. We have well-elaborated positions and goals of struggle for all the problems of the people, however, we openly declare that under the conditions of capitalism any achievements that the working people may gain will be temporary without the acquisition of the workers'-people's power."[22]*

There is no need to restate the concrete situation that the workers are in, but what is the logic behind saying that *"any achievements that the working people may gain will be temporary"* at a time when the workers' movement is in a historically weak position? Does this statement have any meaning at a time when all achievements have been lost? It is also not true that these gains are *absolutely* temporary. The achievements of today's working class could become the foundations of a revolutionary working class in the future. Isn't this what we should struggle for? Lenin talks about half-hearted and two-faced 'reforms' based on the current system and the transformation of these into *'bases'* of the workers' movement that is advancing to complete freedom of the proletariat.[23] Different gains and successes, turning them into bases – what will workers'-people's power rise on if not on such achievements – if it is to rise from the remnants of capitalism rather than from the dream of socialism or its specific human material?[24] What we should focus on today is not the temporariness of the reforms but the ways to achieve them, to use these to help the working class gain confidence, to turn them into bases for the complete freedom of the workers. When this has been achieved, the horizons of the movement would no longer be limited to partial successes and the workers'-people's power could become practicable as the only way to solve the concrete contradictions of today as opposed to just being a theoretical perspective.

Let us look at what has been claimed to be *"the tactics of the KKE"*: *"the need to rally the working people"*, the *"defence of its rights"* and *"the satisfaction of the contemporary needs"*. Is there anything here that could be a *concrete and identified 'tactic'*? It is clear that there is nothing specific in relation to the concrete situation before the elections of 2012, at a time when the country was active both socially and politically and when the party needed to develop an extremely flexible and even seemingly contradictory stance.

"*The programme defines the general and basic relations between the working class and other classes. Tactics define particular and temporary relations*" (Lenin).[25] It is a fact that the sectarian tendencies in the KKE's approach to the class struggle prevent the working class – which it claims to represent – from developing "*particular and temporary*" political relations that will improve its capacity to fight and to influence other classes. It is also a fact that the possibilities in that country, borne out of the severe conditions of crisis, have not been taken advantage of due to such shortcomings and weaknesses, and have been taken up by social-reformist and fascist forces.[26]

APPROACH TO THE WORKERS' MOVEMENT

In the last couple of years and especially in the last election, pressure on the KKE has built up due also to Syriza's rise and proposals of alliance, Unable to differentiate between ideology and politics[27], the KKE refused the proposal of alliance and Syriza, having won the elections, formed the government. The KKE stated that it will not be a party in power and that it will show no tolerance to Syriza…

It would of course have been wrong for the KKE to be a coalition partner in a government led by the social reformist Syriza. Engels' example, drawing attention to '*French social democrats*' taking seats in the progressive government formed after February of 1848, is well-known. The French social-democrats were wrong: "*As a minority in the government they voluntarily shared the blame for all the foul deeds and betrayals perpetrated by the majority of pure republicans against the workers; whilst the presence of these gentlemen in the government completely paralysed the revolutionary action of the working class which they claimed to represent*".[28]

Besides this, it *was* possible for the KKE to establish a platform that incorporated the urgent and pressing demands of the workers and people, join in a broad alliance with Syriza and other progressive forces around this platform, and make adherence to these demands a precondition for an alliance with Syriza. This was essential under the current level of consciousness and expectations of the workers' movements. This tactical move would of course not expect Syriza to follow a revolutionary line; on the contrary, it would have helped the workers to base their demands on Syriza on solid and real foundations. That way, if their demands were met it would be due to their own initiative and not seem like it was due to Syriza. Under the conditions of a broad progressive alliance, the support of the working masses would not have been left to Syriza. The KKE could have proven that it itself is the most reliable defender of the demands of the masses and the strongest force able to meet the urgent needs of the people. As a result, it could have used this position to break the prejudices among the masses of workers and people in general regarding the KKE and socialism.

Under the present conditions, in which the main contradiction of capitalism is manifested in many different ways, and class struggle – also due to the proletariat not being able to create its own independent movement – is taking place in amore mediated conditions, it is necessary for the party of the working class to *"move in zigzags, to retrace our steps"*[29] compared to previously. *"The whole point lies in knowing how to apply these tactics in order to raise, and not lower, the general level of proletarian class consciousness, revolutionary spirit, and ability to fight and win".*[30]

Unfortunately, the KKE did not focus on the workers, their level of consciousness and expectations, their perception of events and the change in their mood as much as it focused on the social reformist character of Syriza. Should we not always focus on these points, and especially in the current situation? The shift towards Syriza among the workers points not only to their *"illusions"* but also to the fact that a large section of the people are reluctant to put up with austerity policies, to their demands that capital take on the burden of the crisis and not only on the workers; and to their search for a political alternative to the mainstream political parties that would meet their burning needs and demands.

Is it not clear that *"workers'-people's power"* will not be possible without a serious shift in the outlook of a majority of the workers and that this shift will happen not only through propaganda but through the "political experience" of the masses? Isn't it a fact that most things that are clear and visible to the communists are still not clear to the masses, especially in these times when the effects of the historical defeat are still being felt? The differences of opinion between bourgeois politicians *"are quite minor and unimportant from the standpoint of pure, i.e., abstract Communism, i.e., Communism that has not yet matured to the stage of practical, mass, political action."* But *"from the standpoint of this practical action by the masses, these differences are very, very important"*[31].

Isn't it the duty of communists today "*soberly follow the actual state of class consciousness and preparedness of the whole class (not only of its Communist vanguard), of all the toiling masses (not only of their advanced elements)*"? Is it possible to know how to "*act as the party of the class, as the party of the masses. You must not sink to the level of the masses, to the level of the backward strata of the class. That is incontestable. You must tell them the bitter truth*". Of course it is possible and obligatory because of the need to defend and develop this dialectical relationship, which seems a 'contradiction'! As Lenin put it "*the whole task of the Communists is to be able to convince the backward elements, to work among them, and not to fence themselves off from them by artificial and childishly 'Left' slogans*"[32].

In short, the KKE's approach to the workers' movement shows two weaknesses: 1) ignoring the pedagogical factor, and 2) party fetishism.

1. Without a doubt, the political duties of a communist party cannot be reduced to pedagogy. If this is done, party politics would lose its broad reach and become superficial; furthermore, it would lose its far-seeing and guiding character. But this truth does not and should not render unnecessary "*an element of pedagogics*" in the political work of the party – especially targeting the workers and people. To ignore this would mean the denial of the need to educate the whole of the working class, to explain revolutionary theory to the most backwards elements of the movement and to convince them that party politics are correct; that their conscious needs to be raised through "*steadily and patiently*" building their trust and acknowledging their experiences. To forget this factor would be to turn scientific socialism into "*a dry dogma*", something learned "*only from books*"[33].

The General Secretary of the KKE, Dimitris Koutsoumpas, in a speech just before the election that brought Syriza to power, celebrating the 96th anniversary of the foundation of his party, said: "*The people must be freed from all the anti-people governments and their political line, they themselves must take power. The situation today – both in Greece and internationally – does not allow for any time to be wasted.*"[34] The results of the general election showed that the people did not understand this need! A necessity that is not fully understood can only be a theoretical necessity. So, the people do not yet understand that "*they themselves must take power.*" Hence, the General Secretary is here stating only *his* (party's) will. Was Lenin not right in saying "*the most dangerous mistake for revolutionaries*" is to "*have mistaken their desire, their political-*

ideological attitude, for objective reality"?[35]

Yes, but do the Greek people not understanding what Koutsoumpas says they *must* do remove the historical-theoretical truth of what has been said? No, it does not, but it does not go beyond the statement of an abstract truth that finds no response in the reality of workers' lives today. We ask now whether we are wrong in our analysis of the KKE as a party that still has to overcome the narrowness created by the turning of Marxism-Leninism into a formalistic theory by modern revisionism?

2. Marx and Engels, while explaining the difference between communists and the proletariat in the *Communist Manifesto*, used the following statements which are highly relevant today: The Communists *"have no interests separate and apart from those of the proletariat as a whole"*, and *"They do not set up any sectarian principles of their own, by which to shape and mould the proletarian movement.".* The Communists *"are distinguished from the other working class parties"* by the following characteristics: *"In the various stages of development which the struggle of the working class against the bourgeoisie has to pass through, they always and everywhere represent the interests of the movement as a whole"*, and *"theoretically, they have over the great mass of the proletariat the advantage of clearly understanding the line of march, the conditions, and the ultimate general results of the proletarian movement."* The aim of the communists is *"formation of the proletariat into a class, overthrow of the bourgeois supremacy, conquest of political power by the proletariat."* (It is clear that this order is not arbitrary!)

Considering the clear statements above regarding the relationship between the proletariat and the communists and the aims expressly formulated as the battle cry by the latter, it is no surprise that Marx and Engels *"expressly formulated the battle cry"* into the initial text of the First International: *"The emancipation of the working class must be achieved by the working class itself".*[36]

What is the need for reminding one and emphasizing? Because modern revisionism has also caused serious damage regarding the concept of the party. It is as if modern revisionism created a party fetishism, for obvious reasons. The essence of party fetishism is putting the party in place of the working class. Nevertheless, the party is not an *objective* in and of itself, *"the highest form of proletarian class organization"* (Lenin)[37]; it is their most advanced *means* of struggle. The party can neither take nor fill the place of the working class and thus it should not and cannot act with such a motive! Lenin points out that "*instead of frankly and directly calling upon the advanced workers to join the political struggle, the Social-Democrat points to the task of developing the working-class movement, of organising the class struggle of the proletariat*" just for this reason.[38]

The more a party disregards the level of consciousness of the workers, their presumptions, illusions and the need to convince them; the more a party overlooks the specific political experiences of the masses, the readiness of the working class and its movement to act around its ideology-politics-organisation; the less it learns from the practice of the masses, the more party fetishism will spread in that party.

If a party focuses on itself and its cadres instead of organising the workers' movement and raising its consciousness and organisation, if it **confuses** the unity of its cadres with a "*people's social alliance*", if it does not aim for the unity of the working class in practice, if it fails to make developing the unity of the workers' interests in daily struggle and the workers' united struggle an indispensable element of its tactical stance, if it replaces it with a separate group of '*vanguard, mass activists*' within the workers' movement; then, no matter what that party says in theory, it cannot act as the party of the whole of the working class, which results in its failing in its duties to the workers' movement.

If party fetishism is not overcome, after a point this will lead to the party's loss of meaning to the workers or be stuck in a doctrinaire swamp. One will find oneself in the position that Marx called "unintelligible": "*We do not confront the world in a doctrinaire way with a new principle: Here is the truth, kneel down before it! We develop new principles for the world out of the world's own principles. We do not say to the world: Cease your struggles, they are foolish; we will give you the true slogan of struggle. We merely show the world what it is really fighting for*".[39]

In drawing attention to the relation of the October Revolution to WWI, Lenin commented on the revolution having "*new features, or variations, resulting from the war itself*" and that those who cannot grasp Marx's ideas could not see this. "*They have seen capitalism and bourgeois democracy in Western Europe follow a definite path of development, and cannot conceive that this path can be taken as a model only mutatis mutandis, only with certain amendments (quite insignificant from the standpoint of the general development of world history).*" The October Revolution was bound to show new features, "*for the world has never seen such a war in such a situation.*" As a second point that needs to be understood, Lenin said: *"while the development of world history as a whole follows general laws it is by no means precluded, but, on the contrary, presumed, that certain periods of development may display peculiarities in either the form or the sequence of this development".*[40]

This attitude and these statements of Lenin are extremely significant for today's communists. This broad and deep perspective needs to be adopted.

We can express the specific nature of our situation as such: the matured contradictions have not yet found their matured responses. This surely points to a big contradiction. We should not run away from the contradictions of life; on the contrary, we should embrace these contradictions; we should investigate them in order to better understand social issues and class struggles and we should draw from them practical results that help advance the position of the working class. The inverse ratio between our action and inaction dictated by the conditions is not insurmountable.

We need to explain to the working masses the content of their action and enable them to reach a real understanding of their action and themselves. Paying attention to the specific nature of the conditions we are in is a precondition to carrying out our duties in a way that is correct and not merely formal. As long as we do not reduce our attention to just a theoretical one it can be seen that, especially on issues that seem to be contradictory (i.e. revolution – reform, alliances – independent politics, theory – practice, women's issue – class issue, etc.), a more developed theoretical understanding and tactical flexibility is essential. Otherwise, it will become impossible to avoid or escape shallow right- or left-wing trends.[41]

Thus, given the specific historical conditions, our first aim is the *"formation of the proletariat into a class"* as mentioned in the *Communist Manifesto*; to facilitate the working class *"acting as a class."* Just as Engels stated in his warnings against the Germans who ran off to America and showed a sectarian attitude to the American workers' movement: *"Our theory is not a dogma but the exposition of a process of evolution, and that process involves successive phases. To expect that the Americans will start with the full consciousness of the theory worked out in older industrial countries is to expect the impossible. What the Germans ought to do is to act up to their own theory — if they understand it, as we did in 1845 and 1848,— to go in for any real general working-class movement, accept its actual starting point as such, and work it gradually up to the theoretical level by pointing out how every mistake made, every reverse suffered, was a necessary consequence of mistaken theoretical views in the original programme: they ought, in the words of the Communist Manifesto: 'in the movement of the present to represent the future of the movement'.*"[42]

Who could have known that the international working class would suffer a temporary but comprehensive historical defeat and that these warnings would become relevant to both the workers themselves and to the communists?

April 2015

Endnotes:

* This article was published in Özgürlük Dünyasý [World of Freedom], the political journal of EMEP, in May 2015. Since then there have been important developments in Greece. First, SYRIZA signed an agreement with the Troika despite the "No" vote in the referendum. But SYRIZA also won the elections and became the major party again. Second, the KKE was criticized in this article for not moving to organize the alliance of large sections of the people on the basis of their urgent demands. But after the general elections on September 20, the General Secretary of the KKE, Dimitris Koutsoumpas, said: "The KKE will work for the struggle to reorganize, to strengthen the workers' and peoples' movement and to organize a broad people's alliance." After this statement, we hope that the KKE will change its position for a platform of revolutionary struggle and will move towards building a real united front of the workers and labourers. We will be happy if this hope becomes reality.

[1] Undoubtedly, contemporary capitalism cannot be understood while overlooking the US. That said, within the context of the subject matter of this article, the US needs to be analyzed in its own right, because it has unique qualities that require a detailed assessment. Addressing this requirement in this article would, however, broaden its purview.

[2] Throughout this article, socialism as a social formation will denote the elementary stage of communism.

[3] Ever since the working class intervened in the political struggle as *a class*.

[4] See: "Emek Partisi – Enternasyonal Komünizmin Tarihsel Anlamý"; Enternasyonal Yolunda 20 Yýl, p. 124, Evrensel Basým Yayýn. [Party of Labour – The Historical Significance of International Communism; 20 Years on the Path of the International, p. 124, Evrensel Publishing House]

[5] As shown – first and foremost – with countries like the US and Germany, the crisis has created new and differing perspectives and groups within the monopoly bourgeoisie. However, such developments are beyond the scope of this article.

[6] Europe, for reasons already mentioned, constitutes the advanced example. The emergent issues and trends on this continent and can also be seen in the working class movements in other countries and continents.

[7] See: 16 March 2015, issue no. 12.

[8] Modern social reformism constitutes a broad range of currents. It embodies ATTAC [Association for the Taxation of financial Transactions and Aid to Citizens], anti-globalisation currents, yellow trade unions, the representatives of the Evangelical and Catholic churches that oppose *"evil capitalism"*, the Party of the European Left, Neo-Keynesians, and intellectuals and economists who advocate *"radical democracy"* and *"democratic socialism"*. Within this wide-ranging movement, projectors of "socialism" (such as *"21st century socialism"*) abound.

[9] Undoubtedly, in other countries there are many and different demands, which are not mentioned above. The aim here is to paint an approximate and a general picture.

[10] The discontent and fear of these strata and groups find their political reflection not only in social reformism, but also in racist, social-nationalist and openly fascist movements in both Southern and Northern Europe. In areas where the monopolies have a strong hegemony this burgeoning discontent and fear can be found side-by-side.

[11] "Our Revolution (Apropos of N. Sukhanov's Notes)", in Lenin's *Collected Works*, Vol. 33, p. 476, Progress Publishers, Moscow. Unless otherwise specified, all the quotations are from published English translations (*translator's note*).

[12] A few years ago, the KKE put forward its analysis of capitalist restoration in the USSR. In this analysis, the following evaluations are important and positive: the 20th Congress as a turning point, and the critique of Khrushchev's revisionism in the realm of politics and economics (thus far, these evaluations have been the dividing points between different political traditions). That said, the KKE's analyses do contain pivotal drawbacks and shortcomings, an in-depth analysis of which can only be the subject matter of a separate article.

[13] From 2012 to 2015, there were 50 24-hour and 48-hour general strikes. See: Seyit Aldoðan, "Yunanistan Seçimleri ve SYRIZA hükümetini doðru ve yanlýþlarýýyla deðerlendirmek"; Özgürlük Dünyasý, ["Greek Elections and the SYRIZA Government, Evaluating What Is Correct

and Incorrect"; World of Freedom] No. 262, March 2015.

[14] For example, statements regarding SYRIZA being part of the government: the thesis of *"a peaceful and gradual transition to socialism"*, etc.

[15] http://inter.kke.gr/en/articles/Some-questions-on-the-unity-of-the-international-communist-movement/

[16] ibid. Unless specified otherwise, the below citations are from the above source.

[17] http://inter.kke.gr/tr/articles/KKE-Genel-Sekreteri-DimitrisKucubas-Snf-yabanc-bayrak-altna-sokmayacagz/
[KKE General Secretary Dimitris Koutsoumpas We will not leave the class under a foreign flag]

[18] "New Times and Old Mistakes in a New Guise"; Lenin *Collected Works*, Vol. 33.

[19] http://www.evrensel.net/haber/30719/halk-iktidari-disindaki-cozumler-sermayeye-yarar, in English at:
http://www.roudefiisschen.net/rf-e-Greece.html

[20] Lenin, *"Left-Wing" Communism, An Infantile Disorder*, p. 100, English edition, FLP Peking, 1970.

[21] Lenin citing Engels's "Program of the Blanquist Communards" (1874) in: *"Left-Wing" Communism*, p. 62.

[22] http://www.evrensel.net/haber/30719/halk-iktidari-disindaki-cozumler-sermayeye-yarar, in English at: http://www.roudefiisschen.net/rf-e-Greece.html

[23] "Conference of the Extended Editorial Board of 'Proletary'", In Lenin *Collected Works*, Vol. 15, p. 440.

[24] Lenin, *"Left-Wing" Communism*, pp. 40-41.

[25] Lenin, "Revision of the Agrarian Programme of the Workers' Party"; *Collected Works*, vol. 10, p. 178.

[26] Without a doubt, from this statement one cannot derive the conclusion that the modern social reformist and fascist movements have gained ground in Greece solely and essentially due to the shortcomings of the KKE. Such a conclusion would not only exaggerate the actual influence of the KKE but would also negate the role of all other factors arising from the crisis.

[27] A striking example of this is the KKE's political approach to the EU. The KKE, on the one hand, correctly conceives of the EU as a union of imperialists and, in contrast to right-wing opportunists, it claims that the EU cannot be transformed into an entity functioning in the interest of the masses. On the other hand, it links the question of leaving the EU and the Eurozone to the need for a workers'-people's power! This means that the KKE will not demand that Greece leave the EU without

a revolution taking place. At the same time, the KKE does not ally itself with forces that do not demand Greece leaving the EU. Yet, if the demand to leave the EU is conditioned on such power, then this particular demand should not be the prerequisite for taking part in alliances formed around and for the demands of the masses. The result? The KKE will not be in alliance with forces that do not uphold the power of the workers! Naturally, this implies that there will be no united struggle with forces that say *"No to the EU and the Eurozone"*.

[28] "The Future Italian Revolution and the Socialist Party," in Marx-Engels *Collected Works*, vol. 27, p. 437.

[29] Lenin, *"Left-Wing" Communism*, p. 67.

[30] ibid, pp. 52 & 72.

[31] ibid, p. 99.

[32] ibid, p. 46.

[33] Lenin, "On Confounding Politics with Pedagogics," *Collected Works*, Vol. 8, p. 464.

[34] Rizospastis (Greek Daily), January 11, 2015. In English at: http://inter.kke.gr/en/articles/A-powerful-KKE-is-a-pillar-of-support-for-the-people/

[35] Lenin, *"Left-Wing" Communism*, p. 51.

[36] Marx & Engels to August Bebel, Wilhelm Liebknecht, Wilhelm Bracke, and Others (Circular Letter) in: Marx-Engels, *Collected Works*, Vol. 45, p. 408.

[37] Lenin, *"Left-Wing" Communism*, p. 41.

[38] Lenin: "The Tasks of Russian Social-Democrats", *Collected Works*, Vol. 2, p. 338.

[39] Marx, Letter to Ruge, September, 1843, in *Collected Works*, Vol. 3, p. 144.

[40] "Our Revolution," in Lenin's *Collected Works*, Vol. 33, p. 477. Mutatis mutandis is a Medieval Latin phrase meaning "with things being changed" (*translator's note*).

[41] See: "Enternasyonal Komünizmin Tarihsel Anlamý" – Emek Partisi; Enternasyonal Yolunda 20 Yýl, p. 125, Evrensel Basým Yayýn. [Party of Labour – The Historical Significance of International Communism; 20 Years on the Path of the International, p. 125, Evrensel Publishing House]

[42] Engels, Letter to *F. Kelley–Wischnewetzky in New York*, December 28, 1886 in: Marx Engels *Collected Works*, Vol. 47, p. 541.

NUMSA AND THE CRISIS IN SOUTH AFRICA TODAY

What is the class basis of the current crisis in the South African state and in the ANC?

We, the National Union of Metalworkers of South Africa (NUMSA) are not surprised by the recent political events which have dominated our nation. At our 10th National Congress in December last year, we predicted that the crisis in the Black African Capitalist class is bound to worsen. We predicted that the White capitalist class, (Afrikaner and English capitalists), which have always been dominant, would find itself increasingly in conflict with the emerging Black and African capitalist class, as it seeks to grow and consolidate its power. What we are witnessing is a reflection of this fight in the ANC and in the ANC government. The reshuffle is a manifestation of this fight. This is nothing more than a fight amongst greedy capitalists, who are battling each other for control over government and its budget.

What are the origins of this crisis?

The present crisis has its origins in the negotiated settlement which led to the so-called democratic breakthrough in 1994. The essence of the negotiations was to protect white wealth and privileges and the interest of international capital. The negotiated settlement entrenched capitalism, in post 1994 South Africa, by guaranteeing capitalist property rights in the constitution. Furthermore, the negotiated settlement also delivered capitalist socio-economic policies to a post-Apartheid South Africa.

The right wing leadership of the ANC capitulated to both domestic and international capital, and in turn, capital gave the ANC a Black government with which to police African poverty, and create a Black and African Capitalist class. This guaranteed that the Black government would essentially be a Bantustan government, just like the homeland governments of the past, it is a government without economic sovereignty.

White capital retained control of treasury, SARS, and the Reserve bank. Effectively this guaranteed economic sovereignty of the White population and the white capitalist class. It is this white economic sovereignty which feeds white racism. So the ructions we have been seeing are simply a battle by the same capitalist elites, for the control of the key pillars of white domination – which include the treasury.

The ANC and the reshuffles

There is a national mobilization around the dismissals of the finance minister Pravin Gordhan and his deputy Mcebisi Jonas. Zuma and his faction, including the new finance minister, Malusi Gigaba, are digging in their heels. What does this mean for the working class?

Many members of the middle class and the elite have condemned President Jacob Zuma for reshuffling the cabinet and have expressed outrage at the firing, in particular, of Pravin Gordhan. They are mobilizing for Zuma to resign or be removed from the presidency of the country and the ANC.

In this crisis the working class is bound to be confused, misled, and made to support causes which are detrimental to their class interests. The fundamental questions are: *Which of these factions of the capitalist class should the working class side with?* And, *when Zuma has fallen, who will replace him?*

What is Zuma fighting for?

President Zuma is fighting to take treasury away from white capital and guaranteeing that those who prevent him from controlling treasury are removed from government. This reshuffle is a purge of Zuma's enemies in the state and in the leadership of the ANC. Zuma has positioned himself as the CEO of a group of the capitalist class dominated by the Guptas and other black and African capitalists in opposition to the entrenched white capitalist class.

What is Pravin fighting for?

During his tenure as finance minister Pravin Gordhan was a consistent defender of discredited neoliberal capitalist policies. He is a slave to ratings agencies which are the global capitalist policemen for the austerity measures, which inflict daily misery on the working class and the poor. The same national treasury, which Gordhan was leading, removed exchange controls, allowing trillions of rand, which we desperately need, to leave the country, both illegally and legally, and exposed it to financial speculators. South African companies were allowed to list outside the borders of this country rendering this country poor. Pravin's response to this drain of money from South Africa has been to offer amnesty to the criminals.

The Reserve Bank's mandate, under the supervision of the treasury, continues to be the pursuit of disastrous inflation targeting, instead of targeting jobs. Through this policy the reserve bank ensures that it protects the value of white wealth, and in particular, that of finance capital.

This government and treasury have also been an obstacle in addressing the land question. They opposed nationalisation of mines and the commanding heights of the economy and have not aggressively pushed for beneficiation to take place, so that local jobs can be created. Under their watch, State Owned Enterprises (SOE's) are mired in cronyism and corruption associated with tenders. These parastatals spend millions of their procurement spend placing orders in companies outside of South Africa, and in so doing they destroy the economy.

Zuma and Pravin Gordhan are guilty of anti-worker, anti-poor policies!

We want to set the record straight on the open war between Pravin Gordhan and Jacob Zuma. It is obvious that Zuma and his capitalist group including the Guptas intend to use the SOE's, National Treasury and all available state institutions and structures to advance their own economic interests against the interests of the white capitalist group.

Both of these groups belong to the same class – the capitalist class. They are our class enemies, as the working class. Both do not deserve our support. Both want to loot us, to oppress us, to exploit us. Both are responsible for our suffering! Both these groups are guilty of ignoring the poor and the working class. They did not mobilize or campaign on issues which affected workers, for example:

* The killing of mineworkers in Marikana and farm workers in De Doorns.

* They have done nothing to punish the banks for criminal and illicit trading under Apartheid and in the post-1994 South Africa.

* They have allowed construction firms and other monopolies to get away with a slap on the wrist for price fixing.

* They have allowed for private ownership of the South African Reserve Bank.

* They are guilty of making South Africa the most unequal society in the world through neo-liberal polices imposed on the working class.

* They are responsible for deepening levels of unemployment, poverty, inequality and corruption.

* They have not demanded that racist Hellen Zille must fall for her defence of colonialism.

The so-called Rating Agencies, whose interests do they serve?

Both the Zuma and Pravin capitalist groups worship rating agencies.

Using national treasury, over the past 23 years they have bent over backwards to satisfy the rating agencies, and as a result, South Africa has become the most unequal society on earth, over this period.

NUMSA views the ratings agencies and their downgrade of South Africa to junk status with the utmost contempt this deserves. These agencies are self-serving and politically motivated. They blackmail governments to pursue policies in the interest of domestic and international finance capital. They do not care about the suffering of the poor and the working class. They are cold and insensitive and usurp economic sovereignty of nation states on behalf of the interests of global finance capital. No self-respecting sovereign state should take these agencies seriously.

They have now downgraded South Africa to junk status, the sad irony is that 60% of the population are forced to live on the junk heap of society, eking out an existence with little or no income, and forced to live with the indignity of life without electricity, basic sanitation or the guarantee of a decent meal a day.

Any working class ratings agency would rate the current South Africa way below junk status, considering the level of poverty, unemployment and inequality.

How are the two factions of the Capitalist class deceiving the working class?

The white capitalist establishment is exploiting its domination of the media to paint Zuma and his group, and deservedly so, as crudely very corrupt. As if *they* are not also corrupt. The implication here is that they represent a clean version of capitalism, an impossible feat as every worker should know. All capitalists are corrupt.

In the past 23 years the White capitalist class has consistently blocked land expropriation without compensation; while it is less than 10% of the population, it owns and controls 95% of South African wealth. The white capitalist class dominates in the economy and in society. Effectively this means South Africa remains a white dominated country, just like it was under Apartheid. It is this which feeds the root of racism in South Africa.

The Black and African capitalist group is conning the working class into believing that they are fighting for 'radical economic transformation'. In reality they are fighting for their own personal radical economic transformation. Zuma wants to ensure that his family and friends benefit for generations to come.

In 2013 at our historical NUMSA Special National Congress we resolved that the tripartite Alliance has been captured and taken over by right-wing forces, which are hell bent on championing neo-liberalism in all its forms. As NUMSA we also noted that the ANC had become a rotten structure, riddled with factionalism and corruption and that it cannot not be saved. It was clear to us that the ANC does not have solutions for the poor and the working class.

The country will continue to descend into authoritarian rule as Zuma and his cronies wrestle with white monopoly capital. Both camps are capable of becoming very desperate to defend their interests and can lead this country into fascism and civil war.

For the last 23 years, on behalf of the entire South African capitalist class – white, black and African – the ANC through national treasury have implemented neo-liberal economic policies which have destroyed jobs, and deepened inequality and poverty in the country. This government, together with the South African Communist Party (SACP) have endorsed right-wing economic policies like GEAR and the NDP which have attacked the very existence of the poor and the working class in South Africa.

This government has refused to ban the exportation of scrap metal which has led to seven foundries closing, destroying thousands of jobs. Their legacy in the past two decades is scary. They have shed jobs massively across various sectors of the economy, and they are directly responsible for serious levels of de-industrialisation which the country won't recover from.

The ANC and its government have failed to implement the Freedom Charter, leaving 87% of the land in the hands of a tiny white population. Access to quality education remains the privilege of the few.

There is a state of hopelessness in the country among the black and African majority. This majority does not live a dignified life. At least 40% walk to work because they earn starvation wages because the ANC has failed to uproot the Apartheid structure of wages and income inequalities. This majority is dying every day because it cannot afford decent healthcare. Good quality healthcare is only accessible to the wealthy whilst the majority suffer and die in under-resourced, dilapidated hospitals, without health specialists and scary conditions.

The ANC has consistently attacked the poor and working class for over two decades

On behalf of the South African capitalist class – white, black and African – the ANC government has been implementing decisions that constitute a sustained attack on the poor and the working class of South Africa. Instead of banning labour brokers, which is a system which creates uncertainty in the lives of our workers and exposes them to all kinds of labour law abuses, the ANC government has opted to regulate this form of modern slavery. Their latest assault is on the constitutional right of workers to strike by imposing limitations on the right to strike.

NUMSA has been angered by the mindless decision taken by the ANC government to close down five Eskom power stations in Mpumalanga, in the name of radical economic transformation. The closure of these power stations will mean that at least 40,000 jobs will be lost, and that 40,000 families risk being destitute. This will no doubt exacerbate the crisis of unemployment that we face as a country.

NUMSA is not surprised by the ideological bankruptcy and cowardly behaviour of the SACP

We were the first to make the demand that Jacob Zuma should resign in 2013 at our Special National Congress. We called on President Jacob Zuma to resign with immediate effect because of his administration's pursuit of neo-liberal policies such as the NDP, e-tolls, labour brokers, Youth Wage subsidy amongst others.

The SACP, ANC and COSATU leadership responded very angrily to our perfectly moral demand. Because of our correct position, the SACP worked with some in the ANC leadership to destroy us. Meanwhile the yellow bellied COSATU leadership resolved that NUMSA should be dismissed from the federation, and they pulled the trigger which fired more than three hundred thousand workers from a federation they helped to build.

NUMSA notes that three years after dismissing us, the SACP are now convinced that Jacob Zuma must go. What has changed in the last three years? Where is the ideological clarity and the Marxist tools of analysis? For the sin of daring to call for a corrupt and pro-capitalist president Jacob Zuma to resign we were vilified to the point where, on the eve of our Special National Congress, the SACP issued an open letter to NUMSA delegates to remove the leadership!

Without any trace of shame or humiliation, today the leadership of the SACP finally agrees with the industrial proletariat that Jacob Zuma should go. However, typical of the petty bourgeois leadership of the SACP which is parasitic on the ANC, while they at first threatened to resign their Ministerial positions if Pravin Gordhan was removed they have since renegotiated their positions with Zuma! In true fashion of any unprincipled leadership, and like true cowards and opportunists, these yellow communists chickened out and dumped their threat, once their incomes were guaranteed.

What is the campaign to "defend the national treasury" all about?

As a Marxist-Leninist inspired trade union, if we are to embark on any campaign, we need to ask the question, *in whose class interests are we taking up this campaign? What is the interest of the working class in a campaign that defends today's national treasury? What are the interest of other class forces who are now coalescing around this campaign?*

Is it to protect the continuation of neo–liberal policies, meaning to protect the current status quo? If that is the case, it is a campaign which we cannot be part of, as it contradicts our Marxist-Leninist principles and the status quo is based on the exploitation of the working class.

It is particularly disturbing that the SACP wants to create the impression that if Pravin Gordhan stays, the plight of the working class will be addressed, without demanding that neo-liberal policies should be dumped and agitating for a revolutionary agenda. Unlike the discredited SACP, we have no desire to end up as the vanguard of white monopoly capital. We are ideologically clear about who we serve.

Just so that we are not accused of failing to see a potential revolutionary moment to defend democracy against a "soft coup" and dictatorship, we want to borrow from Lenin's correct analysis of DEMOCRACY. Lenin made the following important points about DEMOCRACY;

"We Social-Democrats always stand for democracy, not "in the name of capitalism," but itn he path for our movement, which clearing is impossible without the development of capitalism." In the name of clearing the path for our movement, which clearing is impossible without the development of Capitalism.

"Democracy for an insignificant minority, democracy for the rich – that is the democracy of capitalist society."

"But democracy is by no means a limit one may not overstep; it is only one of the stages in the course of development from feudalism to capitalism, and from capitalism to Communism."

"Whoever wants to reach socialism by any other path than that of political democracy will inevitably arrive at conclusions that are absurd and reactionary both in the economic and the political sense."

From this outlook it is crystal clear that democracy plays an important role but from a class perspective Lenin is clear under which conditions we struggle for democracy *but not in the name of capitalism.*

Our demands, our programme!
We demand the abolition of poverty, unemployment and inequalities in South Africa!

As NUMSA we will take the working class to the streets to make the following demands:
1. We demand the full and immediate implementation of the Freedom Charter!
2. We demand full employment, with the state as employer of last resort!
3. We demand a national living wage!
4. We demand a real national minimum wage, not the Ramaphosa painful joke!
4. We demand the abolition of the apartheid wage structure!
5. We demand a 40 hour working week!
6. We demand fully paid maternity leave!
7. We demand universal medical care and medial cover for everyone!
8. We demand decent and quality housing for all!
9. We demand that the expropriation of land without compensation!
10. We demand that the mines, banks and monopoly industry be placed under democratic worker control!
11. We demand beneficiation of our minerals in South Africa!
12. We demand industrialisation to meet the social and economic needs of South Africans.
13. We want free quality, decolonized education for ourselves and children.

We want Socialism, now!
We are confident that our fellow capitalist marchers will recoil from us when we pronounce on these demands!

Should the working class participate in the ongoing mobilisation against Zuma?
We hate corruption from anyone. We hate what the capitalists of all colours and from everywhere are doing to the working class and the poor in this country. The workers are free to participate in the marches, stay-aways and protests with their own independent posters and demands, as outlined above.

NUMSA, however, is not part of any of the political parties and organisations that are calling for mass protests against Zuma or for Pravin.

All NUMSA members and any other workers who will participate in the marches and protests and stay-aways must know that they are doing so as individuals, as is their democratic right.

What is to be done?

NUMSA will be preparing for the mother of all strikes over government's decision to shut down 5 Eskom power plants. We have lodged a Section 77 Notice to this effect. We will lodge a further Section 77 Notice to strike for the demands we list above.

NUMSA will bring the economy to its knees to remind the government and all the capitalists in this country where the real power lies – with the workers! We will not allow them to silence us by eroding our right to strike. We will fight them in the streets and in the courts. We will use all the tools legally available to us to protect jobs, protect our families, our communities and to protect our rights.

We are hard at work forging the working class political party, and we are completing preparations for the launch of our new, socialist, democratic, worker-controlled and militant federation. We are also revitalising our United Front.

As NUMSA we will continue raising socialist levels of consciousness in the working class and building a genuine revolutionary socialist working Workers Party.

NUMSA is clear that it's time to build a socialist independent federation with no ideological confusion, but to rally workers for the struggle for socialism and pursue a radical fight to end economic exploitation.

The working class needs to be liberated from thinking that emancipation can come from the current liberation alliance which promotes Zuma and neo-liberalists who will continue to massacre and butcher the working class with their regressive economic policies.

NUMSA cannot allow the working class to be used for advancing the interests of its enemy classes once again, to endorse a narrow neo-liberal agenda. The price for South Africa's freedom was the blood, sweat and tears of workers who risked life and limb for the liberation of the people of this country. We dare not fail. We must organise or starve!

Issued by Irvin Jim
General Secretary NUMSA

5 April, 2017

THE SECRET MISSION OF A.I. MIKOYAN TO CHINA

(January-February 1949)

A. Ledovsky

Introduction

At the core of this article is the publication of the note by Mikoyan on his mission to China in the early part of 1949. It was written in 1960 at a time when fissures had appeared between the CPSU and the CPC on a wide range of questions. The Mikoyan note reveals some of the differences of views between the two parties during the time of their co-ordination on the brink of the establishment of the Chinese government.

It is valuable to examine these divergences.

First, we may note that the CPSU (b) and Stalin did not accept the proposal of the CPC and Mao that while establishing the Chinese state that the dictatorship of the proletariat should be incepted on the lines of the Soviet Union and the Federal People's Republic of Yugoslavia which had been formed in 1946. It was the understanding of the Soviet leadership that the government coalition should include those oppositional forces representing the middle classes which were opposed to the Kuomintang. The CPC eventually came to agree with the Soviet view. This later became a marker of the Chinese revolution but Stalin and the CPSU (b) could not have anticipated that a situation would arise in the post-Stalin period that People's China would declare itself a dictatorship of the proletariat whilst preserving more or less indefinitely the representatives of the middle bourgeoisie in state power.

The CPSU (b) gave its opinion at the point of victory of the Chinese revolution when the Kuomintang proposed in early 1949 to cease the war and agree to a peace settlement. The CPSU (b) suggested that the CPC should support a peace settlement but not agree to international participation in negotiations for this. In this manner the CPC would be seen as a supporter of peace whilst preventing the intervention of the US in the matter. In later years the CPC and Mao were to claim that the Soviet Union and Stalin were not in favour of the victory of the Chinese revolution. The correspondence exchanged between Stalin and Mao on this question which has already been published in this journal show that the later claims of Mao were the opposite of the actual situation.[1]

Third, Mikoyan on behalf of the CPSU (b) leadership, suggested that the CPC take over the main centres such as Shanghai and Nanjing as this would weaken the position of Chiang Kai-shek and help create a proletarian cadre through struggles. Mao differed from this view saying the CPC was basically peasant party which would not be able to run these centres. It was held in the CPC leadership in this period, that while the party considered itself, as Marx had thought, the advanced group of the proletariat, it also represented the peasants, the petty bourgeois, and the middle class of the towns. In her discussion with Liu Shao-chi in 1947, Anna Louise Strong noted that the Chinese leader referred to the position of Karl Marx that the industrial workers were the only class which accepted communism and could bring it to fruition. This was the position in the western world but in China he argued there were only two or three million of such industrial workers. Alongside these sections Mao was training two-three million from other sections which were in fact perhaps more disciplined and devoted than the industrial workers.[2] It is in this context that we may see the statement of Mao to Mikoyan when he averred that the political consciousness of the Chinese peasantry was more advanced than that of the American workers and many of the British workers.

According to the account of Mikoyan the CPSU (b) in these exchanges took internationalist stands on the questions of Port Arthur and Sinkiang saying that these were considered to be areas which belonged to China. The note of Mikoyan on the Mongolian question is of special interest. Prior to the Chinese revolution the CPC accepted the right of nations to self-determination and sought to establish a free federation of nationalities. In his discussion with Edgar Snow of 23rd July 1936, Mao expressed the view that the relationship of the Soviet Union and the Mongolian People's Republic throughout had been one based on complete equality. Once the people's revolution would be successful in China the 'Outer Mongolian republic will automatically become a part of the Chinese federation, at its own will'.[3] In the discussion with Mao, Mikoyan, Stalin (through his intervention through telegrams) and the CPSU (b) reconciled the views of the Mongolian People's Republic and the CPC. Stalin considered that it was not advisable for the Mongolian People's Republic to unite with Inner Mongolia to establish a united Mongolia as this would limit a range of territory from China. Nor did he consider that after its long history of independence that the Mongolian People's Republic would agree to be incorporated into the new Chinese state as an autonomous unit. It was for the state of Outer Mongolia to take its position on this question. Matters did not conclude there as is clear from the famous discussion of Mao and the delegation of Japanese Socialists which took place in July, 1964. Mao reversed his positions of 1936 and 1949 and now argued that under the Yalta agreement that the Soviet Union 'under the pretext of guaranteeing the independence of Mongolia, had actually placed that country under its domination'.[4] The plebiscite in the Mongolian People's Republic of 1945 which favoured independence was not a factor of concern for the Chinese leader. Mao revealed that in 1954 when Khrushchev and Bulganin visited China the Chinese leadership had raised the Mongolian question 'but they refused to talk with us'.[5] The varying stands of Mao between 1936 and 1964 on the Mongolian question suggest that he fluctuated considerably on the questions of proletarian internationalism.

The talk of the Japanese Socialists and Mao Zedong had its repercussions in the relations of the CPC and the Party of Labour of Albania. Enver Hoxha noted in his political diary on August 22nd 1964 that the raising of territorial claims on the Soviet Union and the people's democracies was not regarded as tactic by the CPC but as a matter of principle. He considered that the 'claims of the Chinese have been built on a dangerous platform, to the point that they themselves have pretentions to Outer Mongolia'. Enver Hoxha considered that by raising the territorial questions the struggle against Khrushchevism was being diverted towards nationalist ends.[6] The Chinese were inciting nationalist passions in Japan, Rumania, Poland, Finland, China and the Soviet Union rather than confronting revisionism.

Quite extraordinary, finally, was the position of the CPC and Mao himself in the talks of January-February 1949 that they wished to receive directions and orders from the CPSU (b). Mikoyan rejected this demand and said that it was not possible for the Soviet party to rule over the Chinese party. The CPC was an independent party and the CPSU (b) could only restrict itself to rendering advice to the Chinese. Even though the views of Mao were shunned by Mikoyan they were repeated to Stalin by the Chinese delegation which visited the Soviet Union a few months later in June 1949. Stalin and the CPSU (b) leadership again rejected the views of Mao and the CPC that the Soviet party should give orders to the Chinese party saying that it was not permissible for the communist party of one state to submit to another although the parties did consult each other on issues and mutually help each other.[7]

Vijay Singh

As we know, after the defeat of the Kuomintang in the civil war in China and the communist government taking power in October 1949, in the USA began a sharp internal political struggle around the issue "Who has lost China?", that meant: because of whom and for what reason did the USA suffer a serious defeat in relation to China, that meant the loss of what seemed to have been the very solid position of domination by the US in this country by the time of the end of the Second World war.

In the "White Book on China", published by the US State Department in 1949, the Soviet Union was named as a main culprit of the defeat of Kuomintang and thus of the defeat of the US policy in China. At the IV session of the UN's General Assembly in 1949 the representative of the Kuomintang government, with the support of the USA, filed a complaint to the UNO about the Soviet Union, titled "Threat to the political independence and territorial integrity of China and to peace in the Far East, caused by the Soviet Union's violation of the Soviet-Chinese Peace and Friendship Treaty of 14th of August 1945 and also by the violation of the UN Charter by the Soviet Union". In this complaint Soviet Union and the Soviet military command were accused of the following:

1. that they created obstacles to the timely input of the Chinese government army into Manchuria and to the installation there of the power of the Central government;

2. that when the USSR withdrew its troops, it passed the power in Manchuria into the hands of Chinese communists, opened a free entrance for them to Manchuria from Northern China and helped them to create there the powerful armed forces of the CPC, having given to their disposal almost all weaponry and military equipment of the capitulated Japanese Kwantung army of almost 1 million men;

3. that the Soviet government secretly from the Chinese central government signed several agreements and contracts with the communist power in Manchuria about giving them material, technical and other assistance.

In the declarations of the Kuomintang and the US representatives it was pointed out that the actions of the USSR, Soviet help and support for the Chinese communists became the decisive factor that defined the results of the Chinese civil war towards the CPC victory.[8]

In the 1960s the propaganda campaign against the USSR was unfolded from exactly the opposite positions: Mao Zedong personally and his supporters began to criticize the policy of the USSR towards China and

Stalin personally. First in their closed and later also in their open speeches they put forward whole range of claims and accusations, the most important ones of which came down to accusing the USSR of supporting the Kuomintang during the anti-Japanese war and of not providing support to the CPC, that Stalin allegedly interfered into internal affairs of the CPC after 1945, "created obstacles for the Chinese revolution", "did not believe into its victory", "did not allow the Chinese revolution" etc. According to the logic of these theses that later were taken over by the Chinese historians and politologists, if only the USSR had not provided help to the government of Chiang Kai-shek in fighting the Japanese, but had provided support only exclusively to the CPC, if only the USSR had not signed the Treaty of Peace and Cooperation with the government of Chiang Kai-shek. If Stalin would have refrained from giving any advice to the CPC leadership about the strategy and tactics of the Chinese revolution, then the CPC would have achieved the victory in the civil war much earlier.

Under the influence of these speeches a turn took place in the description of the issues of the Soviet-Chinese relations, of the role of the USSR and Stalin in the victory of the CPC, of the relations between Mao Zedong and Stalin in the western historiography. Many western authors began to develop versions that the Soviet help to the CPC was quite insignificant and did not play any serious role in the results of the struggle between Kuomintang and the CPC. Some authors almost literally quoted Mao's versions of "obstacles" created by Stalin for the Chinese revolution, about his disbelief in the victory of the CPC over Kuomintang etc.

Mao Zedong has passed away long ago, but the versions created by him are still being repeated in the works of the Chinese authors and of the authors from other countries. In the last few years some theses of such versions appear also in some publications of the Russian authors. There are different reasons for it. In some cases this is caused by a voluntary or involuntary following of certain ideological views or requests, in some other cases – by the inertia of the old approaches and stereotypes of the "cold war". In the third case it is caused by the wish "to follow the trends" in criticizing the Soviet policies. But in all these cases the versions of relations between the VKP(b) and the CPC, between Stalin and Mao Zedong, are mainly speculative and are not based on the studying of the documentary sources of the utmost importance.

The opening of the archives in Russia in the last few years gives new opportunities for their usage by the researchers, allowing to move a good bit forward in studying of the events of this crucially important period of

Moscow's policy towards China, in working out of an objective evaluation of its influence on the course and the outcome of the events in China in the late 1940s-early 1950s.

In relation to this, especially interesting are the documents related to the secret mission of A.I. Mikoyan in January-February 1949 to a small place called Xibaipo in Northern China (where the Central Committee of the Communist Party of China was situated back then), the notes of his discussions with Mao Zedong and other members of the Politbureau of the CC of the CPC, the ciphered correspondence between Mikoyan and Moscow, and also between Stalin and Mao Zedong. We had the opportunity to familiarize ourselves with a range of such documents in the Archive of the President of the Russian Federation.

Briefly; about the background of this trip. According to the documents, it was organized instead of the planned but not realized trip at the end of December of 1949 of Mao Zedong to the Soviet Union. The issue of such a visit had already been raised already in the beginning of 1947. The initiative for this came from the Chinese side. Stalin agreed to the visit, but under condition of its full secrecy. In the telegram to the doctor who was responsible for the connection, A. Ya. Orlov[9], Stalin wrote on the 15th of June 1947: "Please pass on to Mao Zedong that the CC of the VKP(b) wishes that his visit to Moscow will be completely unannounced. If Mao Zedong agrees on that, we think that the best way to do this will be through Harbin. If necessary, we will send a plane. Please send by telegraph the results of your discussion with Mao Zedong and his wishes".[10] But two weeks later, on the 1st of July 1947, Stalin sent to Orlov a telegram with different contents. He wrote: "In connection with the upcoming (military) operations and because the absence of Mao Zedong can have a negative influence on operations, we think that it would be necessary to delay temporarily the visit of Mao Zedong."[11]

In the course of further correspondence the visit of Mao Zedong to Moscow was planned for mid-July 1948. But in his telegram of the 26th of April 1948 Mao Zedong reported: "I decided to travel to the Soviet Union earlier than it was planned. It is planned to depart in the first days from the district of Fuping (100 km to the north of Shijiazhuang) Hebei province, and under the cover by troops to cross the Beijing- Kalgan railroad. It is possible to arrive to Harbin by the first days or by mid-June. Then from Harbin – to you. I will ask for advice and directions from the comrades of the CC of VKP(b) on political, military, economic and other important matters...Besides that, if it will be possible, I would like to travel to the countries of Eastern and South Eastern Europe, in order to study the experience of the popular front and other forms of work." Mao planned to take along with him Zhang Bishi[12], Chen Yun[13] and also two secretaries and several other workers – cryptographers, radio operators etc. If you agree with this plan, then we will act accordingly. If you do not agree with this plan, then I will have only one way – to travel alone."[14] On the 29th of April Stalin replied: "Your letter from the 26th of April is received. You can take with you anybody and as many people as you wish. Both the Russian doctors should depart together with you. We agree with leaving one radio station in Harbin. We will discuss everything else when we will meet." [15]

But soon, on the 10th of May, Stalin sent a telegram, suggesting to Mao to delay his visit. "In connection with possible development of the events in the area of your positioning, in particular, in connection with the started offensive of the troops of *Fu* Zuoyi[16] to Suiyuan, thus in the direction of three areas through which you are planning to travel to us, we are worrying that your absence will influence the course of events, as well as about your safety during the journey.

Based on this, perhaps you should somewhat delay your journey to us. In case if you will decide not to delay your departure… we ask you to inform us when and where to we shall send the plane. We are awaiting your reply."[17] On the same day, the 10th of May, Mao Zedong replied: "Comrade Stalin, today I received your letter. I am very grateful to you. Under the current circumstances it would be wise to postpone my trip to you. …I need a short rest after which I can fly by plane. I will inform you of the aerodrome for the plane and the port after finding it out."[18]

On the 4th of July Mao Zedong informed Stalin: "My health condition, in comparison with two months ago, is much better. I have decided to visit you in the nearest future. There are three possible ways to travel: by air, by sea and by land. But in all cases we will have to pass through Harbin, because I need to have a conversation with a range of high-positioned comrades in Manchuria… We hope that the plane will arrive around the 25th of this month to Weisian … If you will decide to transport us by sea, we hope that the ship will arrive to the designated port by the end of this month…If both the air and the sea ways are impossible for our transportation, then we will depart in any case around the 15th of this month to the north." Mao Zedong informed that 20 people will travel with him and asked, in case of transportation by air, to send two planes.[19]

On the 14th of July in response to that telegram of Mao Zedong came a telegram from Stalin: "To TEREBIN. Please pass on to Mao Zedong the following: 'In connection with the beginning of the grain harvesting season all leading comrades from August on will travel around the country with inspections and will remain there until November. For this reason the CC of the VKP(b) is kindly asking comrade Mao Zedong to time his visit to Moscow towards the end of November, in order to have the opportunity to meet all the comrades from the leadership.'"[20]

In his telegram to Moscow on the 14th of July 1948 A. Ya. Orlov wrote that Mao Zedong asked to send the following reply: "Comrade Stalin. Agree with your opinion, explained in your telegram dated July the 14th. Let's delay my trip to you till the end of October-beginning of November."[21] Reporting about the contents and his impressions of the talk with Mao Zedong that took place during passing on to him of the mentioned Stalin's telegram, A. Ya. Orlov wrote that Mao Zedong did not take seriously the references to the preoccupation of the Soviet leaders with grain harvesting. "Is it really so, - he said, - that they give such big importance to the harvesting of the grain in the USSR that the leading members of the CC of the party are attending to it?" Orlov wrote: "As far as I know Mao Zedong, for more than six years, his smile and words "hao, hao... - good, good" while he was listening to the translation of the telegram did not mean at all that he was content with the telegram. It was clearly obvious while looking at him. I personally think that Mao Zedong personally expected that in the worst case he would be refused a plane or a boat. But even this was unlikely for him, because the plane was offered by Moscow. He was certain that he will travel right away. Probably, the trip became necessary for himself. He was waiting for the reply with such great impatience...The suitcases of Mao Zedong were packed, even leather shoes were bought (he, like all people here, wears cloth slippers), a woollen coat was sewn. The issue not only of the trip itself, but even of its date was already decided for him. The only question that was remaining was which way to use. He now looks calm on the outside, polite and attentive, courteous purely in Chinese way. But it is hard to see his true soul. Zhang Bishi looks as if he did not expect a delay. Melnikov[22] told me that on the 15th of July Mao Zedong asked him the same question about the grain harvesting."[23]

In his telegram to Moscow dated the 28th of August 1948, A. Ya. Orlov reported about his new conversation with Mao Zedong, in which they have discussed the issues that Mao Zedong would like to discuss with Stalin.

"Mao Zedong said that if in 1947 he was not in a hurry with his trip to Moscow, then now, in 1948, the situation has changed, and he would like to visit Moscow as soon as possible. He would like to talk there about many things, to ask for advice about several issues, and for help with some, in the frame of what's possible.

The issues which Mao Zedong has intention to discuss in Moscow, are:

1. About relations with the small democratic parties and groups (with democratic figures). About the organizing of the Political Consultative Council.

2. About the uniting of the revolutionary forces of the East and about connections between the communist parties of the East (and others).

3. About the strategic plan of fighting against the USA and Chiang Kai-shek.

4. About the restoration and the creation of industry in China, including (and especially) military, mining, the infrastructure: railroads and motorways. To tell there what do we (the CPC) need.

5. About a silver loan of 30 million US dollars.

6. About policy in relation to the establishment of diplomatic relations with England and France.

7. On a range of other important issues.

Summarizing the above, Mao Zedong stressed: "We have to make an agreement so that our political course would be fully in line with that of the USSR."[24]

In his telegram to Moscow dates 28th of September 1948 Mao Zedong wrote: "On a range of issues it has to be reported personally to the CC of the VKP(b) and to the main leadership. In order to receive instructions, I am intending to arrive to Moscow in accordance with the timeline indicated in the previous telegram. For now, reporting in general lines all of the above, I am kindly asking you to pass it on to the CC of the VKP(b) and to the comrade main leadership. I hope sincerely that they will issue instructions for us."[25]

In a telegram sent on the 21st of November 1948 Mao Zedong, referring to a small illness and also to being busy with issues linked to the operations at the war fronts, asked to postpone the time of his visit to Moscow to the end of December 1948.[26] But during the discussion of this issue in the Politbureau of the CC of the VKP(b) on the 14th of January 1949[27] it was decided to postpone once again the visit of Mao Zedong to Moscow and to send A.I. Mikoyan to China instead. He was given the tasks to hold discussions with Mao Zedong and other Politbureau members, to express the opinion of the Soviet leadership on the issues raised by them to Moscow, to report to the Politbureau of the CC of the VKP(b) requests and wishes of the CC of the CPC.

The main contents of his negotiations with Mao Zedong and other members of the CC of the CPC, A.I. Mikoyan set out in his Note introduced to the Presidium of the CC of the CPSU on the 22nd of September 1960, that is published here below. In this Note are also included some previously unknown materials of the correspondence between Moscow and the CC of the CPC, between Stalin and Mao Zedong for the period of 1947-1949. Judging by the direct quotations, A. I. Mikoyan had those documents at his disposal when he was preparing his Note. But at the same time, the Note includes only a portion of the large amount of information contained in the telegrams and notifications of discussions with the leaders of the CPC, that have covered a broad circle of issues of internal and international policies, Soviet-Chinese relations etc. By their amount and importance, they could have concluded a separate documentary publication (and deserve it).

The note published below which is offered to our readers includes: - the full text of the above mentioned Note of A.I. Mikoyan, as well as grouped mainly by subject, large extractions from the documents, dated January-February 1949.

In all the published documents the geographical and personal names are given in their contemporary version.

Note of A.I. Mikoyan to the Presidium of the CC of the CPSU about visit to China in January-February 1949.

Is due to be returned to the CC of the CPSU (General Department, 1st section) N P2375

Is issued to the members of the Presidium of the CC of the CPSU and to the candidate members of the Presidium of the CC of the CPSU

Completely Secret
SPECIAL FILE

CC of the CPSU

In connection with the differences which have appeared between the Communist Party of China and communist parties of other countries and the forthcoming discussion of these differences I find it necessary to send to the members of the Presidium and to the candidate members of the Presidium of the CC in order to familiarize them with the texts of reports, passed on by me in January-February 1949 during my visit to China, and also with the instructions of the CC that were sent to me in the same period.

These reports were sent ciphered from Xibaipo, where the Revolutionary Committee[28] and the CC of the Communist Party of China were then situated and are given without any changes or omissions, in a exact copy. Two Soviet army doctors were accompanying Mao Zedong at that time – Terebin (who died later in the USSR in a plane crash) and Melnikov, who were treating Mao and his family. They had a radio station and performed communication functions.

I also consider it necessary to touch upon some circumstances related to my trip and the course of the negotiations.

In 1947-1948 an exchange of opinions was taking place between our CC and Mao Zedong about his visit to Moscow. He had never been to Moscow before, and our invitation was issued to him already back in June 1947, we expressed readiness to receive him for discussing the issues of the Chinese revolution, issues that the CPC would have to deal with after the military victory, including Soviet-Chinese issues.

But the dates of the trip were postponed many times because of the difficulties in communication in connection with the remoteness of the places where Mao Zedong was staying, because of his illness, because of the complications in the battlefields of the Chinese revolutionary army and because of other reasons.

By the end of 1948 the battle actions of the Chinese communists were developing swiftly and in a favourable direction. In Northern China decisive battles were taking place. The Chinese revolutionary army that had received the weaponry of the 700,000-men strong Japanese Kwantung army, which was fully passed by us to China, was moving towards the centre of China, in the direction of Beijing.

On the 14th of January 1949 during a meeting of the Politbureau of the CC, while discussing the reply to Mao Zedong's request about the timing of his visit to Moscow Stalin expressed the opinion that the arrival of Mao Zedong at that particular time was not really expedient. He was in the position of a guerrilla commander and even though he was planning to travel incognito, the news of his departure from China would definitely leak. His trip undoubtedly would be seen in the West as a visit to Moscow for receiving instruction from the Soviet communist party, and he would have been branded "an agent of Moscow". This would have caused damage to the reputation of the CPC and would have been used by the imperialists and the Chiang Kai-shek clique against the Chinese communists.

In the meanwhile, soon the official revolutionary government of China could be formed, led by Mao Zedong. Then he would get the opportunity of a visit not incognito, but as the official head of the government, in order to conduct the negotiations with a neighbouring country. This, to the opposite, would raise the prestige and the reputation of the Chinese revolutionary government and would have a big international importance.

Even though such a delay of Mao Zedong's trip to the USSR, was delaying the discussion of pressing issues, but this negative side could be balanced with a business journey to China of one of the members of the Politbureau of our CC.

At that time everything was already prepared for the arrival of Mao Zedong. The Politbureau, having discussed this issue, approved Stalin's proposal and he immediately dictated a telegram to Mao Zedong which said:

"Still, we insist that you will temporary postpone your journey to Moscow, because your stay in China is very necessary at present. If you wish, we can immediately dispatch to you a responsible member of the Politbureau to Harbin or to another place for discussing the issues that are of interest to us."

Mao Zedong responded that he had decided to delay his trip to Msocow and that they welcomed the dispatching of a Politbureau member to China, at the same time he expressed a wish for his arrival to take place in late January or early February and not in Harbin, but in the place where they were situated.

Stalin made the offer to me to travel to China.

In order to minimize the difficulties during negotiations in China and to be better prepared, to exclude unnecessary dispatches to Moscow, I drafted a list of possible questions that the Chinese could ask us, thought about possible answers and discussed them with Stalin and other Politbureau members.

By that time we defined two issues that were questionable and which had a difference in approach of our CC and of the CC of the CPC.

I . About the disagreement of our CC with the point of view of the CPC who thought that after the victory of the Chinese revolution all parties, except the CPC, should disappear out of political life. In Mao Zedong's telegram dated November 30th 1947 it was stated: "In the period of the final victory of the Chinese revolution, following the example of the USSR and Yugoslavia, all political parties, except for the CPC, will have to leave the political arena, which will strengthen significantly the Chinese revolution."

In the responding telegram of our CC, signed by Stalin on April 20th 1948, about this it was written in particular the following: "We do not agree with this. We think that various oppositional political parties in China who represent the middle classes and oppose the Kuomintang clique, will still exist for a long time, and that the Chinese communist party will have to involve them to cooperate against the Chinese reactionaries and the imperialist states, while keeping its hegemony, and thus the leading role. It is possible that some representatives of those parties will have to be allowed to enter the Chinese people's democratic government, and that this government will have to be declared a coalition, in order to broaden the support for this government among the population and to isolate the imperialists and their Kuomintang agents."

As we know, in accordance with this advice the CPC has changed its policy towards the bourgeois parties.

II. About the attitude towards the offer of Nanjing government to the Soviet government to become a mediator between the Nanjing government and the CPC on the issue of ceasing the war and signing peace.

On the 9th of January 1949 a note from the Nanjing government was received which offered to the government of the USSR (as well as of France, England and the US) to take upon itself mediation between the Nanjing government and the CPC on the issue of ceasing the war and signing peace.

In the telegram to Mao Zedong our CC conveyed:

"We think to respond in such manner. The Soviet government always supported and continues to support the ending of war and establishment of peace, but before agreeing to mediation, we would like to know if the other side (the Chinese communist party) has agreed to accept the mediation of the Soviet Union. For this reason the Soviet side would like to make sure that the other side – the Chinese communist party – would have been informed about the peace initiative of the Chinese government and that the agreement of the other side for the mediation by the USSR would be requested. This is how we would like to respond and we are asking you to inform us if you agree. If you do not agree, please give us a hint of a more suitable answer.

We also think that your response, if they will request it, should be like this: the Chinese communist party always supported peace in China, because it was not the party, but the Nanjing government that has started this civil war, and it is this government who should bear the responsibility for it. The Chinese communist party supports peace negotiations with the Kuomintang, but without the participation of those war criminals who had unleashed this civil war in China. The Chinese communist party supports direct negotiations with Kuomintang, without any foreign mediators."

To this telegram of 10th of January Stalin added the following explanatory remark on January the 11th 1949:

"As it is clear from the above, our draft of your response to Kuomintang is aimed at a breakdown of peace negotiations. It is obvious that Kuomintang will not agree to peace negotiations without the involvement of foreign mediators, especially without the mediation of the USA. It is also clear that Kuomintang will not want negotiations without the participation of Chiang Kai-shek and other war criminals. That is why we count on the Kuomintang refusing negotiations under the conditions offered by the Chinese communist party. As a result of this it will be clear that the CPC agrees to peace negotiations, and because of this it cannot be blamed in wanting to continue the civil war. In this situation the Kuomintang will look like the guilty party in the breakdown of the negotiations. In this way the "peace" manoeuvre of the Kuomintang people and the US will not work, and you will be able to continue the victorious liberation war. We are awaiting your reply"

On January the 12th Mao Zedong sent his reply, which said that the Soviet government should respond to the request of the Nanjing government in the following way: "The USSR government has always wanted and wants to see a peaceful, democratic and united China. But what is the way to reach peace, democracy and unity in China, that is a matter for the people of China to decide themselves. The USSR government, basing itself on the principle of non-interference into the internal affairs of other states, finds it unacceptable to participate in mediation between the two sides in the civil war of China...

Only the USSR has a high reputation among the people of China, that is why the USSR in response to the note of the Nanjing government will take such a position as you have offered in your message dated 10th of January, that will lead to a situation in which the USA, England and France might think that participation in mediation is necessary, and that will give Kuomintang an excuse to insult us as militantly minded elements. And the broad popular masses who are unhappy with Kuomintang and are placing their hopes on a speedy victory of the People's Liberation Army, will be in despair...

Now we are keen to reject with all directness the deception of "peace" by the Kuomintang, because now, based on the fact that the class balance in China has already changed drastically, and international public opinion is also not on the side of the Nanjing government; and the PLA can already in the summer cross the Yangtze river and launch an offensive on Nanjing...

As if we will never again have to undertake a circumventing political manoeuvre. At present there is more harm than good in undertaking such a political manoeuvre."

A response to this was signed by Stalin in a telegram dated 14th of January 1949 which said:

"How can we respond to such a manoeuvre by those in Nanjing and the USA. There can be two replies. The first variation is to reject openly and directly the peace proposals of those in Nanjing and by doing so to declare the necessity of continuation of the civil war. But what would that mean? That means in the first place that you will put on the table your main trump card and that you will give into the hands of Kuomintang such an important weapon as the banner of peace. Secondly, it will mean that you will help your enemies in China and abroad to look down at the communist party as a supporter of the continuation of war and to praise Kuomintang as a supporter of peace. Thirdly, that will mean that you will give the US an opportunity to work on public opinion in Europe and America in such a direction that peace with the communist party is impossible, because it does not want peace, that the only way to reach peace in China is to organize an armed intervention, of the type that was undertaken against Russia for 4 years, from 1918 till 1921..."

Further the second, flexible variation of a response was outlined, in the spirit of already mentioned, in the first Soviet telegram proposals. On the same day, January the 14th, Mao, referring to the receipt of additional message dated 11th of January, as described above, declared in his telegram that "we are completely united with you in the main course (breakdown of negotiations with Kuomintang, continuation of the revolutionary war till the end)", and also reported that on this day they have published 8 conditions for agreeing to begin peace negotiations with Kuomintang. In connection with this it was reported to Mao Zedong that from his last telegram "it is obvious that there is a mutual understanding between us on the issue of the peace proposals of the Nanjing people, and that the CP of China has already started its "peace campaign". That means that the issue is closed."[29]

I went to China under the fake surname of Andreev and this is how I was signing the telegrams, addressing them to the fake name of Filippov.[30] It was done at the initiative of Stalin, in case if the information about my stay in China would leak from there.

I flew to China on the 26th of January, arrived there on the 30th of January and stayed there until February the 8th 1949. Together with me were in China: the former minister of transport Kovalev[31], who was proposed to be appointed our representative at the CC of the CPC at that time, and interpreter, employee of the apparatus of the CC, also surnamed Kovalev.[32]

We flew out of Port Arthur early in the morning, before dawn, and by dawn we arrived to the former Japanese military airport near Shijiazhuang. We were greeted by the commander Zhu De[33], member of Politbureau Zhang Bishi and interpreter Shi Zhe[34]. From there we went by car, a trophy Dodge, approximately 160-179 Km to the base of the CC of the party and the revolutionary committee, Xibaipo, that was situated in a gorge.

For the first two days Mao Zedong informed us of the history of the Chinese revolution and of the fractional struggle that had taken place inside the Chinese communist party. Later, during following meetings, he also came back to these issues of the history of the CPC, spoke a lot about how hard was it for him to fight against the left and the right deviation in the party, how the party was broken and the army was destroyed because of the actions of Wang Ming[35] who was supported by Comintern, how later they managed to correct the mistakes, how the fractionalists were destroying the cadres of the Chinese communists, and that he barely managed to survive himself, he has been arrested, thrown out of party, they wanted to dispose of him. But from that time when Wang Ming and Li Lisan were unmasked, Mao Zedong, according to him, works well with his comrades, has put an end to the destruction of the communist cadres. He was and remains the supporter of tolerance within the party, he thinks that men should not be thrown out of the CC when they have different opinions, they should not be repressed.

Take Wang Ming, for example, said Mao Zedong, he played a bad part, but we have left him in the CC, he is at the disposal of the CC, even though he practically does not do any work. He spoke in great detail about the errors of Wang Ming, probably he wanted to test our opinion about him, and if we would attempt to support him or to listen to his advice. I knew about the differences between Mao Zedong and Wang Ming and I did not support these conversations. We had agreed already in Moscow that I will not meet Wang Ming, and he was not present during my conversations with Mao and he did not make any attempt to meet me.

Some issues discussed with Mao Zedong and other members of the CC of the CPC are worthy of attention.

I. To my question when Mao Zedong thinks it possible to take over the main industrial centres – Nanjing, Shanghai etc, he said that he is not in a hurry to do this. He said, for example, that "it would take us another 1-2 years to become in the position to take China over completely, politically and economically", he hinted that the war cannot be over before this. He also expressed the thought that they avoid taking over big cities, but aim for taking over agricultural areas. For example, they do not want to take Shanghai. They say it is a big city and the Chinese CP has no cadres. The Communist Party consists mainly of peasants; in Shanghai the communist organization is weak. Also, Shanghai lives on imported raw materials and fuel. And if they will take Shanghai over, there will be no fuel imports, the industry will collapse, there will be unemployment, all of this will make people's lives worse; the CPC has to prepare cadres, they already had started working on it, and in time, when the cadres will be ready, they will take over Shanghai and Nanjing. Based on the position of our CC, worked out already back in Moscow, I argued with him, and tried to explain to him that the sooner they will take the big cities, the better, that the cadres will develop with the struggle. Sooner or later the issue of fuel and food supplies for Shanghai will rise in any case. But the takeover of Shanghai will seriously weaken Chiang Kai-shek, and will give a proletarian base to the communists.

II. Mao Zedong did not give the necessary importance to the proletarian layer in the composition of the party and the attention of the CPC towards the cities and the working class was weaker than that towards the peasants. This position was based on the old times, when the party and the army acted in the mountains, far away from the working centres. Times have changed, but the attitude towards the workers remained the same.

From my notes it is clear, for instance, that Mao Zedong proudly stressed that the communist party has total influence in the countryside where it has no competition. Chiang Kai-shek has helped communists in this by his policy towards the peasants. In the cities it was different. Here among the students the communist party has big influence, but among the working class the position of the Kuomintang was stronger than that of the communist party. For example, in Shanghai after the victory over Japan the influence of the communist party covered 200,000 out of 500,000 workers, the rest followed Kuomintang.

It is also worth to mention such a remark of Mao Zedong as "Chinese peasants have more political consciousness than all American and many British workers."

III. Based on the instructions of the CC, I attempted to convince Mao Zedong not to delay the formation of the revolutionary government, to create it quickly, based on a coalition that will be profitable. For instance, after taking over of Shanghai or Nanjing one could announce immediately the formation of the new revolutionary government. This would be useful also in international relations: after that the communists could act already not as guerrillas, but as a government, and that would make it easier to fight Chiang Kai-shek in the future.

Mao Zedong was of the opinion that there is no need to hurry with formation of the government, he even said that it is better for them to remain without government. Because if there will be a government, there will be a coalition, and that means, they will have to be responsible towards other parties for what they do, and that would cause complications. For now they acted as a "revolutionary committee"[36], independent of the parties, even though they continued to maintain ties with them. This, according to Mao Zedong, was helping to clear the country of counter-revolutionary elements. He was stubborn on this issue, and claimed that the government should be formed not immediately after taking of Nanjing (it was supposed to happen in April), but only in June or July. But I insisted that extra delay with formation of the government will weaken the forces of the revolution.

As we know, the government was formed on the 30st of September.

IV. About Port Arthur. Mao Zedong said that he had been visited by one woman – a bourgeois politician who raised the issue that when China will have a revolutionary government it will make no sense for the Soviet Union to keep the navy military base in Port Arthur and that it will be a great thing for China to get that base back.

Mao Zedong said that, in his opinion, it is a wrong position, that the woman did not understand politics, that there are communists both in Soviet Union and in China, but that does not exclude, but allows the USSR to keep their military base in Port Arthur. That is why they, the Chinese communists support this base to remain. American imperialism sits in China for exploitation, but Soviet Union sits in Port Arthur for defending China against Japanese imperialism. When China will become sufficiently strong to defend itself against Japanese aggression, then USSR itself will have no need in a base in Port Arthur.

Our CC and Stalin had a different position: there is no need to have a base there, if the government in China will be a communist one. I outlined this position to the Chinese comrades. Having received my report about the Chinese position on this issue, Stalin wrote in a telegram to Mao Zedong on the 5th of February 1949:

"...With the takeover of power by the Chinese communists the situation will change drastically. The Soviet government has taken a decision to denounce this unequal treaty and to withdraw our troops from Port Arthur as soon as peace with Japan will be signed and thus the American troops will leave Japan. But if the Communist Party of China will consider it desirable to withdraw the Soviet troops from the Port Arthur region immediately, then Soviet Union will be ready to fulfil this wish of the CPC."

Mao Zedong insisted on his version, but it was obvious that he had some tactical reasons of his own which he did not share with us.

V. About Xinjiang. This is also an important issue. Mao Zedong had suspicions about our intentions in Xinjiang. He mentioned that in the Iliysk district of Xinjiang there was an independence movement that does not obey the Urumqi government and that there is a communist party there. He told us that when in 1945 he has met Bai Chongxi (31) in Changchun, he told him that in Iliysk district the rebels have artillery, tanks and planes of Soviet make.

I told him clearly that we do not support the independence of the Xinjiang nationalities and even more so, we have no ambitions in relation to Xinjiang's territory, being of the opinion that Xinjiang is and should be a part of China.

Mao Zedong made a suggestion to build a railway between China and the USSR through Xinjiang. Zhang Bishi offered, as a variation, to build such railway through Mongolia. Later, when this issue was discussed in Moscow, Stalin supported the building of such a railway through

Mongolia because it would be shorter and the construction would be cheaper, and then later on to build another road through Xinjiang.

VI. About Mongolia. Mao Zedong asked out of his own initiative what is our attitude towards the issue of reunification of Outer (32) and Inner Mongolia (33). I told him that we do not support such unification as this would lead to the substantial diminishing of China's territory. Mao Zedong said that he thinks that Outer and Inner Mongolia could unite and become part of the Chinese Republic. To this, I answered him that this is impossible because the Mongolian Popular Republic enjoys independence already for a long time. After the victory over Japan the Chinese government also recognised the independence of Outer Mongolia. The MPR has its own army, its own culture, develops its economy and culture fast, it already tasted independence for some time and is unlikely to ever give it up voluntarily. If it ever unites with Inner Mongolia, undoubtedly as a result it will become a united independent Mongolia. Zhang Bishi who was present during this conversation, remarked that in Inner Mongolia there are 3 millions of population and in Outer Mongolia only one. In connection with this information from me Stalin sent me a telegram to familiarize Mao Zedong with it, which said:

"The leaders of Outer Mongolia support the unification of all Mongolian regions of China with Outer Mongolia under the banner of an independent Mongolian state. The Soviet government speaks out against this plan, because that would mean the breaking off from China of a range of regions, even though this plan does not endanger the interests of the USSR. We do not think that Outer Mongolia would agree to give up its independence in favour of its autonomy within the Chinese state, even if all Mongolian regions will be united as an autonomous unit. Naturally, it is up to Outer Mongolia itself to decide this."

After having familiarized himself with this telegram Mao Zedong said that he will consider its contents, and that "of course, they do not support the Great Han chauvinist line and thus will not raise the issue of Mongolian unification".

VII. About the recognition of the future revolutionary government by other countries. Mao Zedong had two variations on this issue: the first one, for the USSR as first and other foreign countries would recognize the new government of China immediately. The second variation that obviously enjoyed the preference of Mao Zedong himself, consisted of not trying to achieve the immediate recognition of the new government, and if a foreign government will announce such intention to recognize it, not rejecting it, but not agreeing to it immediately either, and continuing such tactics for approximately one year. The advantages of this second variation, according to the Chinese, was that the new government did not need to have its hands tied and could easily pressurise all things foreign in China, without having to take into consideration the protest of the foreign governments.

***

Mao Zedong was saying all the time that they, the CC of the CPC, are awaiting directions and leadership from our CC. I answered him that the CC of our party cannot intervene in the activities of the CC of the Communist Party of China, it cannot issue any directives, it cannot rule the Chinese communist party. Each of our parties is independent, we can give only advice, when we are asked about it, but cannot issue orders.

Mao Zedong insisted, declared that he is awaiting orders and leadership from our CC, because they still do not have enough experience, he deliberately diminished his own role, his own importance as a leader, and as the party's theoretician, by saying that he is just a pupil of Stalin, that he does not give importance to his own theoretical works, because he did not add anything new to Marxism etc.

I think that this is the Eastern way to demonstrate modesty, but it does not correspond with his real importance or with what he thinks of himself.

As a confirmation of this I can give some extracts from our conversations with Mao Zedong that had taken place at that time. Already during our first conversation he said: "I am asking you to take into consideration that China is much behind Russia, we are weak Marxists and are making many mistakes, and if you measure our work by Russia's standards, then it will appear that we have nothing."

I answered that such words are probably a sign of modesty of the leaders of the CC of CPC, but that it is difficult to agree with them. It would be impossible to lead the civil war in China for 20 years and to conclude it with such a victory if they were weak Marxists. As for errors, all actively working parties make them. Our party too, makes mistakes, but it is steadfastly holding up the principle of mercilessly analysing its own mistakes in order not to repeat them and to learn a lesson from them.

Mao Zedong added that they make mistakes *in good faith* and correct them in good faith too, giving an example. In 1946 the CC of the CPC committed an error in the realisation of the land reform (34). When they began to analyse it, it appeared that already back in 1933 he had written correctly about the land reform (35), but that they forgotten about it by 1946. If they had read this work again in 1946, they would not have committed those errors. They reprinted in 1946 what was written about the land reform in 1933 and openly told the farmers about their error, having taken all the responsibility for it, because the leadership bears responsibility for the errors of the lower rank workers, even though the leadership itself has not committed those errors.

I noted that one cannot agree with Mao Zedong's statement that if we use Russian criteria for the Chinese revolution, then it will appear that they have nothing.

First of all, Chinese revolution is a great historic event, secondly, it would be incorrect to use Russian criteria without taking into consideration that reality in which the revolution in China is taking place.

As if to confirm that, Mao Zedong said that the CPC in 1936 in the Soviet regions has shown dogmatism, by copying the Soviet methods, and that lead to a serious defeat.

Further Mao Zedong stated that "one of the big tasks of the CPC is the Marxist education of cadres. In the past they thought it necessary for the cadres to read all the Marxist literature. But now they came to the conclusion that it is impossible, because cadres are getting their education and at the same time they are doing big practical work. That is why they decided to make it compulsory for their cadres to read 12 Marxist works. Having named these works (The Communist Manifesto, Socialism: Utopian and Scientific (36), State and Revolution, Questions of Leninism and others), he did not name even one Chinese communist work.

I then asked Mao Zedong, if he considers it correct that in the list of 12 books for the party education of cadres of the CPC there is not even one work of the leaders of the CPC that covers in theory the experience of the Chinese revolution.

Mao Zedong answered that he as the leader of the party, has not added anything new to Marxism-Leninism and cannot place himself next to Marx, Engels, Lenin and Stalin.

Raising a glass for the health of comrade Stalin, he stressed that at the base of today's victories of the Chinese revolution is the teaching of Lenin and Stalin and that Stalin is the teacher not just for the nations of the USSR, but also for the Chinese people and the peoples of the whole world.

About himself Mao Zedong said that he is a pupil of Stalin and does not think that his own theoretical works are important, that they just realise the teaching of Marxism-Leninism in practice, without adding anything new to it.

Moreover, he personally had sent a strict telegram to local party cells, forbidding them to name him together with the names of Marx, Engels, Lenin and Stalin (37), even though he had to argue about it with his closest comrades.

I answered that this is a statement of modesty of Mao Zedong, but one cannot agree with it. Marxism-Leninism is being used in China not mechanically, but based on taking into consideration the peculiarities, the Chinese conditions. The Chinese revolution has its own way, that gives it the outlook of an anti-imperialist revolution. That is why the studying of the experience of the CPC cannot be but theoretically valuable, cannot but enrich the Marxist science. How can it also be denied that the generalisation of the Chinese experience has theoretical value for the revolutionary movement of the Asian countries? Of course, it cannot be.

Mao Zedong remarked that in their party a strong stress on Chinese peculiarities was made by the followers of Wang Ming in order to fight against the party line. (38)

To this, I answered that usually the nationalist elements use the historical peculiarities of their countries in order to turn the party into the way of bourgeois degeneration, but Marxists take them into consideration in order to lead the revolution in a Marxist-Leninist way, and Mao Zedong did not argue with that.

In my telegram of 5th of February 1946 I informed you that during one of the conversations Mao Zedong "stressed that during the studying of the issue of the character of the Chinese revolution he based himself on the quotations from comrade Stalin, dated 1927, and on his later works about the character of the Chinese revolution.

Mao Zedong said that the most valuable for him were the remarks of comrade Stalin that the Chinese revolution is a part of the world revolution, and also the criticism of the nationalism of Simic (39) from Yugoslavia.

Mao Zedong stressed several times that he is a pupil of comrade Stalin and that he maintains the pro-Soviet orientation".

***

During the last conversation, that took place on the 7th of February, Mao Zedong expressed satisfaction with the completed discussion of the most important issues and warmly thanked Stalin for his care for the Chinese revolution.

When I arrived in Vladivostok, Poskrebyshev phoned there and on behalf of Stalin informed me that the Politbureau is very pleased with my work in China. Every day men read and discussed my telegrams in the Politbureau. Stalin asked me to come to Moscow as quickly as possible and to tell about everything in more details.

Having arrived in Moscow, I found out that Stalin and other members of Politbureau were really glad and considered that I have fulfilled my mission properly.

I am adding texts of my telegrams from Xibaipo and the replies received by me from Moscow.

To be continued

A. Mikoyan.
APRF

Archive of the President of the Russian federation, Fond 3, Opis 65, Delo 606, Listy 1-17. (Machine typed text, copy)

Footnotes:

1. 'Continue Your Glorious War of Liberation'. The Correspondence of J.V. Stalin and Mao Zedong, January 1949 in *Revolutionary Democracy*, Vol. III, No. 2, September 1997.

2. Anna Louise Strong, 'The Thought of Mao Tse-tung', *Amerasia*, New York, Vol. IX, No. 6, June 1947, pp. 162.

3. Edgar Snow, *Red Star over China*, Harmondsworth, 1973, p. 505.

4. Mao Tse-tung's 'Talk with Japanese Socialists' in the booklet *In Connection with Mao Tse-tung's Talk with a Group of Japanese Socialists*, Novosti Press Agency Publishing House, Moscow, 1964. pp 17-20. This is also available in a different translation in Franz Schurmann and Orville Schell, Ed., *China Readings 3 - Communist China* Harmondsworth, 1968, pp. 368-370.

5. Ibid. p. 20.

6. Enver Hoxha, *Reflections on China*, Vol. I, Tirana, 1979, p. 75.

7. From the Speech at the Reception for the Chinese Delegation (27th June 1949). J.V. Stalin in *Revolutionary Democracy*, Vol. XX, No. 2, September, 2014.

8. See about it in more details A.M. Ledovsky Chinese policy of the US and the Soviet diplomacy. Moscow, 1985, pp.191-217.

9. A. Ya. Orlov in 1949 was using a codename "Terebin" for coded correspondence.

10. Archive of the President of the Russian Federation (further - AP RF), F.39, Op.1, a.31, L.23.

11 Idem, L.24.

12 Zhen Bishi (1904-1950) - at that time a member of Politbureau and of the secretariat of the CC of the CPC.

13 Chen Yun (1904-) - at that time member of Politbureau and of the North Eastern Bureau of the CC of the CPC.

14. APRF, F.39, Op.1. Doc.31, L.30-31.

15. Idem, L.32.

16. Fu Tsin (1895-1974) - one of the generals of the Kuomintang army, at the time commander of the group of troops in Northern China.

17. AP RF, F.39, Op.1. Doc.31, L.33.

18. Idem, L.34.

19. Idem, L.35-36.

20. Idem, L.37.

21. Idem, L.38.

22. Melnikov- 2nd Soviet doctor and adviser from Moscow. Real name and years of his life are unknown.

23. AP RF, F.39, Op.1. Doc.31, L.40.

24. Idem, L.41.

25. Idem, L.42.

26. Idem, L.44.

27. See note by A. Mikoyan.

28. Apparently, it means Military Council of the CC of the CPC.

29. See also S.L. Tikhvinsky. Correspondence of Stalin and Mao Zedong in January 1949, "New and Newest history", Moscow, 1994, No. 4-5, pp. 132-140. [This is available in English as 'Continue Your Glorious War of Liberation' Correspondence of J.V. Stalin with Mao Zedong in January 1949, Revolutionary Democracy, Vol. 3, no 2, pp. 123-135.]

30. Philippov- code name used by Stalin in those years in coded correspondence.

31. I.V. Kovalev (1901-1993) - in 1948-1949 leader of the group of Soviet specialists in economic issues, representative of the CC of the VKP(b) at the CC of the CPC.

32. Ye. F. Kovalev (1907-) - at that time senior official of the CC of the VKP(b).

33. Zhu De (1886-1976) - at that time member of Politbureau and of the secretariat of the CC of the CPC, main commander of the People's Liberation Army.

34. Sh Zhe (1914-) - at that time senior official of the CC of the CPC.

35. Wang Ming (Chen Shaoyu) (1904-1974) - at that time member of the CC of the CPC, vice chairman of the Political and Judicial Committee.

36. Li Lisan (1899-1967) - at that time member of the CC of the CPC, vice chairman of the All China Trade Union Federation.

37. It is a reference to the Treaty about friendship and union signed in Moscow on 14th of August 1945 by the representatives of the governments of the USSR and the Republic of China. Simultaneously were signed the Agreement about the Chinese Changchun Railroad, that was including the mutual use of that railroad, about Port Arthur, which included an agreement on the mutual use of its military maritime base, with the USSR being responsible for its defence, about Dalny which prescribed turning it into an open harbour, free and open for trade and usage by ships of all countries, with the USSR being given to rent part of the harbour and some warehouses. The Treaty was annulled by the Soviet side due to signing of Treaty of friendship, union and mutual cooperation between the USSR and the PRC on the 14th of February 1950.

38. Bai Chongxi (1893-1966) - well known person in the Kuomintang government at that time.

39. Reference to Mongolian Popular Republic.

40. At that time – the regions inhabited by Mongolians in the Northern and North-Eastern China.

41. Reference to the leftist twist in the realisation of the agrarian policies of the CPC in 1946-1947.

42. Reference to Mao Zedong's work "How to Differentiate the Classes in the Rural Areas", October 1933, See Mao Zedong, Selected Works, Moscow, 1952, vol. 1, pp. 229-234. This work, along with some others, was republished by the CPC in the late 1940s.

43. Reference to The Communist Manifesto, Socialism: Utopian and Scientific.

44. Document is not published.

45. In reality at that time and later in the CPC documents and in the PRC history books Wang Ming was accused of dogmatism, blind copying of the Soviet experience, in not understanding of the necessity to take into consideration the peculiarities of China and the Chinese revolution.

46. Simic, Stanoe – minister of foreign affairs of Yugoslavia at that time.

Source:: Issues of the Far East", no. 2, 1995, pp.96-111.

Translated from the Russian by Irina Malenko

CONCERNING THE SITUATION IN JAPAN
(January 8, 1950)

J. V. Stalin

The CPSU (b) after the Second World War was requested by a number of communist parties, including the CPI, to help clarify programmatic questions in their countries. This Cominform article by Stalin[1] played an important part in guiding the Communist Party of Japan much in the same way as the Cominform article of January 27th later in the month had in criticising the 'Trotskyist-Titoist' line of socialist revolution supported by the Ranadive leadership of the CPI[2]. The article of Stalin focussed on the situation in Japan where the US had occupied the country. Equally important was the criticism of the views of Stalin on the political line of Nosaka who had suggested that the American occupation troops were playing a progressive role in Japan which would facilitate the 'peaceful advance to socialism' in the country. The views of Stalin in the matter are of importance as they show forcefully the critical views of the Soviet leader on the possibilities of the peacible, national, parliamentary path to socialism. Representatives of the CPSU (b) - Stalin, Molotov, Malenkov and Grigorian – met the leadership of the Communist Party of Japan- the General Secretary K. Tokuda, S. Nosaka, R. Nishizawa and S. Hakamada - in the Spring and Summer of 1951 in three meetings and discussed further the programmatic perspectives of the party. (In the third meeting the ambassador of People's China, Wang Jiaxiang, and his translator were also present.) An account of these exchanges has been given by the interpreter at this meeting, N. B. Adyrkhayev.[3] A memoir also exists by Satomi Hakamada, who was in a minority in these discussions.[4] During the course of the first meeting Stalin noted that the situation in the Japanese communist party was much the same as the CPI which had gone to pieces. The draft of the new party programme was prepared in Moscow by the Japanese leaders. The New Programme was published in the journal 'Bolshevik' in November,1951.[5]

After the failure of the predatory plans of the American imperialists in China and Korea, the State Department and U. S. militarists focussed their main attention on Japan as the principal base for military ventures against the Soviet Union and the democratic movement in the countries of Asia.

Above all, they try, by means of various groundless pretexts, to delay the signing of a peace treaty with Japan, and, in this way, to legalise a long term stay of the American army there.

With the help of their army and Japanese reaction, the American invaders seek to suppress the democratic movement, to smash the Communist Party and trade unions and to become the real masters of Japan. Even now Japan's entire political and economic life is directed by the American militarists. Japanese economy is completely subordinated to the U. S. monopolies and is placed at the service of the aggressive plans of American imperialism. The Americans, carrying out widespread construction work on air and naval bases on Japanese territory, expanding the munitions industry, and re-arming the Japanese militarists, are turning the country into a base for military ventures.

In an interview with a correspondent of the London "Daily Mail" on March 2nd 1949, McArthur declared outright that the U. S. had long since regarded Japan at a new springboard and were engaged in considerable work in this respect.

On Okinawa, he went on, "I have laid out 25 airfields, capable of ensuring 3,500 flights daily by our heaviest bombers... The Pacific is now an Anglo-Saxon lake."

In this way the political and economic situation of Japan is completely determined by the aggressive policy of the United States and by the actions of the American occupation authorities arising therefrom.

Pursuing a policy of reviving Japanese imperialism and militarisation of the country, the American authorities in Japan, with the help of Japanese reaction, are waging a ceaseless onslaught against the interests of the working people, destroying democratic organisations and practising on a wide scale the policy of sending spies and provocateurs into the trade unions and organisations of the Communist Party.

Having seized the main Japanese monopolies, the American capitalists control some 85 per cent of Japan's economy. Nor are the Japanese capitalists lagging behind. Nearly 40 per cent of the 1949 budget appropriations were allocated to subsidise the big monopolies. Taxes paid by this group of Japanese capitalists account for a mere 3.6 per cent of the revenue, while taxes paid by the population account for 73 per cent of the revenue. In this way the working people of Japan are doubly exploited. And despite the demagogy with which the American imperialists try to screen themselves, the colonising and militarist nature of their actions in Japan is obvious.

The American journal "Pacific News-Week" frankly declared that the main object of the new plan of the United States is to turn Japan into a military-industrial anti-Soviet bastion. The Japanese newspaper "Mainitsi Simbun" likewise expressed its satisfaction that "Japan is now in the front line of the struggle against Communism".

Despite the fact that American policy in Japan flagrantly contradicts the Potsdam decisions concerning the democratisation and demilitarisation of Japan and is a policy of an all-out offensive against the economic and political rights of the Japanese people, the Japanese Government gives full support to the American colonising plans. Hence, the reviving of militarist Japan and the suppression of the democratic movement has long been the common aim and basis of the bloc of Japanese reactionaries with American imperialists.

Apart from the common aims, each of the partners of the bloc is trying to realise his own plans. Japanese reaction is utilising United States' interest in Japan as an ally to bolster its political influence in the country, while the American imperialists are using the Japanese reactionaries as a tool with the help of which it will be easier to smash the democratic organisations and establish complete political and economic domination in Japan, to turn the country into a base for military ventures and the Japanese people into cannon fodder.

In these conditions it is imperative for the working people of Japan to have a clear programme of action.

The organisations of the Communist Party, the trade unions and all democratic forces in the country should rally the working people, daily expose the colonising plans of the foreign imperialists in Japan and the treacherous, anti-people's role of Japanese reaction. They should wage a resolute struggle for the independence of Japan, for the establishment of a democratic and peace-loving Japan, for the immediate conclusion of a just peace treaty, for the speedy withdrawal of American troops from Japan and to ensure lasting peace between the peoples.

The leaders of the working people and people's patriots of Japan should realise that Japan can arise and become a great, independent power only if she renounces imperialism and imperialist alliances, if she takes the path of democracy and Socialism, if she follows the line of peaceful development and the strengthening of peace between peoples. Either Japan takes this path—which will be her salvation—or she does not, and then she will be forced to become a miserable tool in the hands of world imperialism, deprived of freedom and independence and doomed to stagnation.

But, as the facts show, the statements of certain leaders of the Communist Party of Japan are not directed towards the successful carrying out of these important tasks. They do not understand this programme and give wrong orientation to the working people of Japan in the complex situation that has arisen in the country.

Thus, for instance, Nosaka (Okano), one of the leading figures in the Communist Party of Japan, analysing Japan's external and internal political situation, endeavoured to prove that all the necessary conditions are at hand in post-war Japan for effecting the peaceful transition to Socialism, even under conditions of the occupation regime, and further alleged that this "is the naturalisation of Marxism-Leninism on Japanese soil". (Nosaka, Report to Second Conference of the Communist Party of Japan, January 1947).

As for the occupation army, this army, in the opinion of Nosaka, far from hindering the aims of the Japanese Communist Party will, on the contrary, in pursuing its mission, facilitate the democratisation of Japan.

"The stay of Allied troops is aimed at disarming Japan and. at the same time, at liberating the people from a totalitarian policy, at making Japan a democratic country. In occupying Japan, the Allied troops have no intention of turning our country into a colony."

According to Nosaka, the Communist Party of Japan can, even under conditions of the occupation regime, lead the working class to power:

"The possibility has arisen", Nosaka declared, "that proletarian parties, by winning a majority in Parliament, might be able to form their own government and take political power into their hands by destroying the bureaucratic apparatus and its forces. In other words, the possibility has arisen of winning power by parliamentary, democratic methods".

In June 1949, Nosaka again emphatically claimed in his report to the Plenum of the Central Committee of the Communist Party of Japan, that the establishment of a people's democratic government under conditions of an occupation regime is without question, quite possible.

"The occupation troops will be withdrawn the moment such a government is established".

Thus, Nosaka went so far as to utter the bourgeois platitude that, even with American occupation troops in the country, it is possible for Japan peacefully to go over direct to Socialism. Nosaka had expressed such views earlier. For instance, in the draft manifesto of the Communist Party prepared by him, and later in an article printed in the bourgeois newspaper "Mainitsi Simbun" in May 1946, Nosaka claimed: "With the support of the majority of the people arid relying on the efforts of the people themselves, the Party intends, by peaceful, democratic means, to develop the social system into a more perfected system compared with capitalism, namely, into a Socialist system".

Nosaka's viewpoint, that the American occupation troops in Japan are, allegedly, playing a progressive role, that they are helping in the "peaceful revolution" along the path of Japan's development towards Socialism, misleads the Japanese people and helps the foreign imperialists to turn Japan into a colonial appendage of foreign imperialism, into a new centre of war in the East.

Nosaka's attempt to invent a "new" theory, the "naturalisation" of Marxism-Leninism in Japanese conditions, as he puts it, the theory to the effect that after World War Two the conditions were created in Japan, and this under the undivided domination of foreign imperialist authorities, for the peaceful development of Japan into a Socialist country—all this "naturalisation" of Marxism Leninism is nothing more than a Japanese variation of the anti-Marxist and anti-Socialist "theory" of the peaceful growing over of reaction to democracy, of imperialism into Socialism, a "theory" which was exposed long ago and which is alien to the working class.

Nosaka's "theory" is the theory of embellishing the imperialist occupation of Japan, the theory of boosting American imperialism and. consequently, a theory of deception of the popular masses in Japan.

As we see, Nosaka's "theory" has nothing whatever in common with Marxism-Leninism. Actually, Nosaka's theory" is an anti-democratic, anti-Socialist theory. It serves only the imperialist occupiers in Japan and the enemies of the independence of Japan. Consequently, the Nosaka "theory" is, simultaneously, an anti-patriotic, anti-Japanese theory.

OBSERVER

From:
For a Lasting Peace, For a People's Democracy
January 8, 1950.

Endnotes:
[1]. The authorship of Stalin of this article on the situation of Japan is confirmed by the former Cominform worker Alexey Vladimirovich Romanov in his article: "Nashumevshiye stranitsy Kholodnoy voyny" / "Kholodnaya voyna: Sem' let na peredovoy (zapiski zhurnalista-mezhdunarodnika)".

http://alumni.mgimo.ru/page/adaptive/id43711/blog/264634/?ssoRedirect=true&ssoRedirect=true

2. 'Mighty Advance of the National Liberation Struggle in the Colonial and Dependent Countries, *For a Lasting Peace, For a People's Democracy*, 27th January 1950.

3. Adyrkhayev, N. 'Vstrecha Stalina s Yaponskimi Kommunistami, in Problemy dal'nego vostoka No. 2, 1990, pp.140-44.

4. Excerpts from a chapter, "The fateful meeting at Kuntsevo," in Satomi Hakamada's *Watahino sengoshi*, (My Postwar History), Asahi, Tokyo, 1978, 93-102. (Translation in seven pages from the Japanese by David Wolff).

5. 'Blizhayeshie trebovania Kommunistticheskoye Partii Yaponii', Novaia Programma', Bol'shevik No. 22, Noyabr', 1951, pp.57-63. The English edition of this is available in the section on People's Democracy in Japan in the Archival Materials section of the website of the journal Revolutionary Democracy:

www.revolutionarydemocracy.org

WEBLINKS

The updated articles, the Stalin Archive, Archival Materials and international links of Revolutionary Democracy may be viewed on the website of the journal at:

www.revolutionarydemocracy.org

FOR THE MOTHERLAND! FOR STALIN!
From the history of political protests in the USSR

Lavrentiy Gurdzhiyev

Currently, the majority of Soviet and foreign communists, and generally the Left, have finally established themselves in the opinion that since the mid-1950s, the revisionist and opportunist line prevailed in the Soviet Union and the world socialist camp. At the XX Congress of the CPSU emerged the schism between the genuinely Soviet and secretly anti-Soviet periods of the history of the USSR. During the so-called Perestroika – it was already openly anti-Soviet and anti-communist. The ideological and practical basis of the revisionists and opportunists all these years was an ominous and disguised synonym for anti-communism - anti-Stalinism, sometimes lurid, sometimes muffled, but never-changing.

The actions of overt and, otherwise, covert counterrevolutionary forces within the Soviet and world communist movements have been thoroughly investigated by historians, economists, and publicists of different countries, and are fairly well known to the progressive public. What is much less studied are the evidences of inner-Party and popular resistance to the outbreak of the Khrushchev counter-revolution.

For a long time, there was an opinion that the members of the party unanimously supported the decisions of the XX and the subsequent congresses of the CPSU. This is not the case. Dissenters were in the minority, but a minority of a fair number. In some primary party organizations - up to 40% of the composition. Anti-Stalinism did not have a full support even in the most subordinate and disciplined structures - in the army party organizations. For the sake of justice, I note that the essence of the anti-socialist reforms that the Khrushchevites were passing was not noticed by many people because of the treacherous Marxist-Leninist rhetoric that concealed the pro-capitalist degeneration of the country. Nevertheless, outrage in the party and among the people sometimes acquired explosive nature.

It should be recognized that in a number of concrete speeches there was an anti-Soviet component. However, most often it was a spontaneous splash of the people's anger specifically against the violation of Soviet rules and norms by the government. Such protests could not but connect with the name of Stalin, whose image in the eyes of a large number of Soviet people embodied socialist legality, despite all the "exposures" of Khrushchev.

One of the little-known mass protests in support of Stalinism was half-century old event that took place in the Azerbaijani city of Sumgait. Anticipating its description, I would like to raise an important issue.

Professional liars connect the concept of "illegal repressions" in the USSR only with the name of Stalin, while giving Khrushchev merit for the rehabilitation of unjustly affected ones. What nonsense! Khrushchev, while heading the Moscow regional and city party organizations for five years in the 1930's, unleashed the real terror against communists and non-partisans, whose victims, according to the most conservative estimates, were over 50,000 people. Stalin hastened to calm the zealous Khrushchev and in 1938 sent him to Ukraine.

Here, as the first secretary of the Central Committee of the Communist Party of the republic, Khrushchev again led it to the leaders in terms of the percentage of the repressed. His bloodthirsty telegram to Stalin has been preserved. In it, Khrushchev, if not as a psychopath, then, as an undoubted sociopath, resents the fact that Moscow, after a thorough check, approves only 2-3 thousand out of 17-18 thousand monthly sentences pronounced by Ukrainian authorities.

Again, who cooled the pathological zeal of this "humanist" with his hands covered in blood up to elbows? Stalin. Who was the first rehabilitator of victims of despotism and under whose leadership in the late thirties the first mass rehabilitation took place? Of the 1.2 million prisoners in the 180 million country, about 350,000 acquitted persons on political and criminal cases were released. Their innocence was proved unlike a significant number of those criminals who were indiscriminately rehabilitated in the years of Khrushchevism and Gorbachevism. Repressions of the Stalin era are in reality an inevitable, predictable class struggle in the harshest conditions of the imperialist encirclement. Moreover, this is the suffering and death of an insignificant minority, which caused suffering and death to the vast majority. This is the doom of those who brought death to the people. Stalin's repressions were directed exclusively against anti-Soviet and anti-communist elements who fought against socialism, often with weapons in their hands. Sometimes, the innocent suffered from them - this was the result of ordinary judicial and investigative errors. Occasionally, the number of innocent people suddenly increased sharply - this was the result of intrigues of not yet unmasked enemies of the people. Most importantly and undoubtedly, on the whole, they were a boon to the progressive development of the country and the entire anti-capitalist humanity.

Bourgeois and pseudo-left propaganda keeps quiet about the repression of Khrushchev's executioners. They are silent about Khrushchev's elimination and harassment of leaders and rank-and-file, whose ideological orientations were unacceptable for the opportunist and his loyal servants who broke through to power. Khrushchev expelled 70% of the members of the Stalin Central Committee from the top party leadership in the 1950's. Subsequently, distrustful and vindictive, he changed the composition of the Central Committee by another 50%. He changed the composition of the Central Committees of the Communist Parties of the republics, as well as regional parties, city and district party committees by the same amount multiple times. This was how the vengeance, the beating of cadres, the creation of a sycophant valetry and planting a primitive cult of a primitive personality were done.

Fabrication of criminal and political cases and defamation in press, public moral executions of honest people and their secret murders are indispensable attributes of the repression of the Khrushchev period. The maximum prison terms were given to ordinary citizens for chatter, which Stalin did not pay attention to or punished on the administrative line. People in Tbilisi, Temirtau, Biysk, Novocherkassk and a dozen cities of the country received bullets in response to rallies, gatherings and processions as soon as they protested against the policy that was increasingly anti-popular in Khrushchev's time.

But what is more important is this. Post-Stalinist repressions are characterized by half-heartedness toward anti-Soviets, anti-communists. Instead, they were – consciously and instinctively! - tough against the Stalinists, who even then represented, and now represent an unprecedented example of devotion to Soviet power and the communist ideals. Unlike bourgeois dissidents, the repressed Stalinists did not whimper and appeal to foreigners for help, did not write libels against our reality. They did not write memoirs about the libel spilled on them, or about tortures administered by Khrushchev's jailers, about their personal broken fate, for they did not want to throw even the slightest shadow on our state. The state which is no longer there, but to which, as Bolsheviks, as Leninist-Stalinists, they remained forever faithful.

Today they are passing the baton of this fidelity to the growing post-Soviet generation. After all, among this generation - to the alarm and even panic of the domestic bourgeoisie - a great interest is being ripened in the content and forms of life in the Stalin era, which today's young men and women give a predominantly positive assessment.

I emphasize that the state security organs of the USSR were able to immediately stop the subversive work of pro-capitalist dissidents and their close ties with the West. But, contrary to the widespread myths, they did it sluggishly, and sometimes reluctantly. For during the post-Stalin period, they gradually turned from a reliable and just instrument of the dictatorship of proletariat into a rusty instrument of petty-bourgeois politicking. As a result, instead of sending dissidents to the uncomfortable logging camp, they were expelled to hospitable USA and Europe, where they were deployed in all their anti-Soviet fullness and prowess, causing us even more harm than when they were inside the country. Moreover, there is not a single fact that shows that Stalinists, who were arrested for unlawful actions but of different content, would be repressed in this way. A Stalinist could be thrown in jail, but never was he sent to the People's Republic of China or the People's Republic of Albania, i.e. to the states that actively condemned criminal de-Stalinization.

Khrushchev's lie about Stalin provoked the first major anti-government unrest in 1956. It covered almost the whole of Georgia, especially the capital of the republic - Tbilisi. Former front-line soldiers, leaders of production and honoured cultural figures, communists, members of the Komsomol and non-party people, workers, engineers and teachers, men, women and children came to the streets. Many put on orders and medals. Those people were unfoundedly attributed to be motivated by nationalistic sentiments.

But then, the Georgian youth, brought up in the spirit of Stalinism, raised the following slogan, among others: "The Socialist Fatherland is in Danger!" Tbilisi demonstrators, without any hesitations, were shot. In hindsight they were accused of counterrevolutionary activities. They searched but never found a trace of foreign involvement.

In 1989, in the same Tbilisi, young people, inflamed by the feverish atmosphere of Perestroika, were shouting: "Down with Socialism, Down with the Soviet Union, Down with the Communists!" After waiting, they were dispersed, but no one fired at them. Gorbachev's power did not even try to accuse them of counter-revolution, although the counter-revolutionary nature exposed itself openly, as a parade. And the foreign special services left their traces in such a way that it was not even necessary to look for them. These were the fruits of upbringing in the spirit of anti-Stalinism.

The scenery and the formal plot remained the same: the capital of Georgia, the manifestation of protest. But how strikingly different were the protestors! After a little more than thirty years, not only did generations and the eventual occasion changed, but so did the charges of social poles. The byproduct of de-Stalinization and bourgeoisization of the Soviet people spilled out. Stalinism is Tbilisi-56. Anti-Stalinism is Tbilisi-89.

Another illustrative pair of similar events: Sumgait-63 and Sumgait-88. So, imagine the industrial centre on the Caspian coast with chemical plants, pipe-rolling and aluminum plants, with advanced machinery and construction materials, with the population of more than one hundred thousand... What happened here on November 7, 1963 during the celebration of the anniversary of the Great October Revolution?

By that time the bacchanalia of the Khrushchevites reached its climax. In 1961 at the XXII Congress of the CPSU, Khrushchev at last fulfilled his vengeance to the greatest Bolshevik after Lenin. Stalin's body was taken out of the Mausoleum. The last monuments to the leader were demolished, the last cities, streets, collective farms and state farms that bore his name were renamed. For the Soviet mind, such a move meant, at the very least, an unacceptable violation of ethical norms. Disoriented population did not cause an organized mass protest, but the indignation at the domestic level was colossal.

I personally recall an episode of scrapping of a monument to Stalin in one of the provincial cities. Bunches of flowers flew to the monument. A dejected crowd threw them from the rows of a dense police cordon. At that time, gray-haired veterans of the revolution were still alive, who were known in the city in person. "Today they are demolishing monuments to Stalin. But this is only the beginning. Tomorrow they will demolish the monuments to Lenin,"- I, as a schoolboy, did not believe these visionary words of one of the veterans, but I remembered them forever.

Dissatisfaction with power during all the post-Stalin years only ripened. Millions of workers despised and hated Khrushchev, during whose rule the prices were rising and wages - falling, churches were closing and household plots were cut, bureaucrats were disgracing and crime was growing. Even far from politics, poorly educated townsfolk, not penetrating into the nuances of ideology and economics, realized that the USSR had moved away and was rolling somewhere else. With a degree of naivety, they unambiguously painted the picture of life in black and white colours and declared: Stalin was good, and Khrushchev is bad. Well, that's right. Stalin was a symbol of a better life and a hope for catastrophically diminishing social justice - even for a Russian student, even for an Azerbaijani worker, even for a Georgian intellectual, even for a Tajik peasant...

No wonder, Stalinism was regarded by all as an antipode of Khrushchevism. The struggle between them was not for life, but for death, with the complete and unfortunate advantage of the Khrushchevites, who relied on unlimited possibilities of administrative leverage and on the entire repressive power of the state.

Soon enough, this would result in a very peculiar form of criticism of the regime. In shoemakers' booths (Stalin was a shoemaker in his youth), on the windshields of cars, on lapels of jackets, not to mention the people's apartments, the images of the leader, seemingly already eradicated from the memory of the people, would appear again. However, in Sumgait, something extraordinary happened at the official festive demonstration in honor of the anniversary of the Great October Socialist Revolution.

Before moving to the place of the event, I will bring a significant fact from an unexpected sphere – that of diplomacy.

On November 15, 1963, the Ambassador of the Republic of Cuba to the USSR Carlos Olivares Sanchez was admitted to the Central Committee of the CPSU at his request. This time, it was not about matter of bilateral cooperation, but about the unprecedented complaint of the ambassador. He told Soviet comrades that a few days ago the head of a group of Cubans who were interning at the Sumgait thermal power plant came to the embassy. This leader reported to Comrade Sanchez that the whole group observed anti-state protests on November 7. The interns were stunned by what they saw and heard: portraits of Stalin, anti-Khrushchev speeches. They witnessed how the crowd thundered institutions, shops, police stations, beat party and Komsomol leaders. The head of the Sumgait police was allegedly kidnapped and killed, and then there were clashes with regular troops.

One of the Cubans also suffered. He was attacked when he began to photograph a "strange demonstration" (ambassador's definition). Suspecting something amiss, the townspeople called him a Cuban informer, a traitor, and according to the ambassador, "threatened to teach him the laws of Caucasian hospitality." In general, the Cuban students asked to be transferred to another region of the USSR, "away from the Caucasus." The ambassador, shocked by the details of the incident, which the Cubans called a "Stalinist riot," worried for the safety of his compatriots. But, apparently, he was even more agitated by the fact that there was not a word in the Soviet mass media about such large-scale political incident.

It is hard to judge how honestly the ambassador was informed in the CPSU Central Committee. But the fact that the party leader of Azerbaijan at the time V. Akhundov was cunning while reporting to Moscow about Sumgait events, is beyond any doubt. He reassured the Union leadership that he personally traveled to Sumgait and talked with the rioters, that there were no devastations there but only minor hooliganism, that a bunch of wreckers had already been imprisoned for 15 days. He allegedly found out that the Cuban intern was beaten not for political, but for routine reasons: that he was courting a local guy's bride, and he got what he deserved. And in general, supposedly, the Cubans themselves acknowledged the erroneous behaviour of the hapless comrade and changed their mind about leaving Sumgait.

I have no information about whether the Cubans left the Azerbaijani city then. But there are many materials with a comprehensive analysis of many aspects of Stalin-era and post-Stalin-era reality. On their basis, one can safely say:

During the Stalin era, it was almost impossible to distort report-backs and lie to higher authorities. The punishment for such was severe and inevitable. But then with the accession of Khrushchev, lies, concealment of the truth, and fraud became an unpunished style of behaviour of party and state officials, including high-ranking officials.

To the above, we must add the following.

In Georgia and Azerbaijan, the notes of offended national feelings were objectively blended with the social outburst. Georgia could not forgive Khrushchev the political assassination of Stalin and the physical assassination of Stalin's associate Lavrenty Beria (who was slandered no less than Stalin himself). Both were Georgians. Azerbaijan shared similar experiences with respect to the shooting of Mir-Djafar Bagirov, an equally faithful ally of Stalin and a friend of Beria, one of the outstanding sons of the Azerbaijani people of the last century. An old Bolshevik and Chekist, and participant of the revolution and civil war, Bagirov served as first secretary of the Central Committee of the Communist Party of Azerbaijan for 20 years. He was arrested in 1956 on charges fabricated by the

Khrushchevites, and after the parody of the court was executed. Together with him, a huge number of employees of Azerbaijani party, state and law enforcement agencies, whose only fault was often that they were nominated by Bagirov were removed from their posts and excluded from the party. Meanwhile, Bagirov enjoyed immense popularity among workers and peasants. After his arrest, entire cities and villages of the republic wrote letters in his defence to the Supreme Soviet of the USSR. A popular favourite, Bagirov was the personification of the counterweight to the Khrushchev regime.

In a word, the most violent unrest of the workers took place on the territory of the Caucasus, which ended with a stern crackdown of pro-Soviet, i.e. pro-Stalin masses and individuals by the Khrushchevites. Coincidentally, during his stay in Pitsunda (Abkhazia) in 1964, Khrushchev was isolated and, in fact, involuntarily brought to Moscow, where he was retired at the Plenum of the Central Committee of the CPSU.

While the Kremlin branded Stalin, Sumgait residents showed love for him. In the course of a later investigation, the prosecutor of the Azerbaijan SSR S. Akperov informed the General Prosecutor of the USSR R. Rudenko (stated below):

In the city of Sumgait, it was not the first time that a portrait of Stalin was shown during a demonstration. Such cases already happened at the time of the May Day demonstrations of 1962 and 1963 and the October celebrations in 1962. Demonstrators usually carried small portraits of Stalin or simply postcards with him, which no one interfered with, but this time someone brought a giant cloth to the square.

I repeat that Khrushchevism with its fierce anti-Stalinism reigned in the country, and such indulgence towards defiant sedition - disagreement with official evaluations of Stalin - could be regarded by Moscow leaders as a crime. Local authorities, fearing accusations of indulging the Stalinists, which easily led to the end of their careers, expulsion from the party or something worse, decided to stop, as they expressed themselves, "the wrong folk tradition."

In other words, they could not stand the nerves. The city government decided to fight with people's love for Stalin in an unceremonious manner. Police officers, druzhinniki (public activists who helped the police), officials responsible for the passage of columns of demonstrators, were instructed to take away the portraits of Stalin, if they are to appear.

At 10 o'clock in the morning, a procession of columns of workers started along the central square of the city. The orchestra was playing. Slogans and toasts in honour of the CPSU and its leader - the "faithful Leninist" Nikita Khrushchev sounded from the speakers. The self-satisfied "faithful Leninist" looked at the demonstration from his huge portrait, which hung on the facade of the Palace of Culture located on the square. Nothing was breaking solemn order, when suddenly everything went awry. To the shock of the leaders standing on the podium and to the jubilation of ordinary spectators, a portrait of Stalin floated over the columns of demonstrators.

At 11:30 a.m., unrest arose in the square. According to the materials of the Azerbaijani prosecutor's office, the reason was not even the appearance of this portrait, but the fact that one of the demonstrators was wearing a pin with Stalin on it. The vigilant party functionary tried to pull off the pin. Worse than that. Druzhinniki wrist-locked the "Stalinist" and dragged him to the police car. But the demonstrators were not a timid ten. A lot of them stood up for their comrade. In a matter of seconds, they dispersed the druzhinniki, the boorish functionary was mashed, and the police car was stoned.

This rebuff made a great impression on the column of workers of the pipe-rolling plant. Encouraged by it, the column stopped, turned around, and walked to the podium. Intentions of the column did not bode well for the city officials standing on the platform, so they just ran. Later, justifying themselves, the city officials complained and assured various verification commissions that they had allegedly entered into a peaceful dialogue with the demonstrators, which softened their behaviour.

To the horror of party officials, instead of the usual slogans, calls were made for Khrushchev's dismissal and the resignation of the Politburo, as well as demands for the supply of food to the population from the loudspeaker. (As a result of market reforms initiated by the Khrushchevites, categorically contraindicated to the socialist economy, the supply situation was in a deplorable state not only in Azerbaijan but throughout the country.) Unscrupulous insults to Khrushchev were heard under approving whistles and ridicules of the arriving columns. But instead, jubilant toasts to the name of Stalin roared from the speakers.

On one of the festively decorated cars passing through the square, as it was said later in a closed information message of the Central Committee of the CPSU, "a young man suddenly sprang up, whose identity is not yet established, and began to wave Stalin's photograph. A group of druzhinniki tried to call the offender to order. In response to these actions, the crowd formed, numbering about 100 people, and rushed to the druzhinniki. A fight ensued."

In fact, the crowd consisted first of hundreds, and then of thousands of people, who fiercely resisted the guards of order. Soon, the demonstrators, gaining more and more support from townspeople, went over to a total offensive, and the police retreated. The aforementioned huge portrait of Khrushchev at the Palace of Culture was torn down and torn to shreds. Portraits of leaders of the CPSU, with loud approval of the entire area, were knocked down from the stands.

Soon, a deputy of the city police caught by the workers was brought to the platform. He was packed down, pushed into a bus, and driven to his office – most likely, for negotiations about the fate of several "rebels", whom the police managed to detain at the very beginning. At the same time, the protesters who climbed onto the roof of the bus shouted calls for an uprising against the Khrushchev regime.

Simultaneously, the sound of broken glass of police stations rang in the air. Police officers hesitated to fire bullets yet, they used their clubs, then they simply locked and barricaded themselves. But the city council (mayor's office) they could not defend. Furniture, document folders, and even some members of the City Council flew from the windows of buildings seized by the demonstrators.

As for the central police establishment, the residents of Sumgait gathered at its entrance began to break asphalt out of the pavement and to hurl them into the windows and in the guards. Resistance of the shooting guard was broken, and people broke into the service rooms and into the cells where the detainees were held. Two police cars standing in the courtyard were damaged, and motorcycles were burnt.

Later, the police assured that it was shooting at the air. However, not far from the building, a twelve-year-old teen was found with a gunshot wound. He is the only one of the officially registered victims of the attack on the central office of the Sumgait police. There were unregistered victims as well. The total number of 20-30 of wounded in those events was estimated by eyewitnesses. It is believed that the authorities concealed the murder of two attackers. In addition, it was officially reported that one serviceman of the internal troops was killed and one more was wounded.

Despite the fact that Sumgait is only 30 kilometres from the capital of Azerbaijan - Baku, local law enforcement forces had to wait a long time for reinforcements. Only towards evening, the armed units of internal troops arrived here, and the riots were suppressed. Until late night, raids and arrests continued, but it was impossible to arrest the entire city.

Khrushchev was furious. There was revolt of the people directed personally against him?! In this he saw the intrigues of organized Stalinists, who craved political revenge. Alas, there was no organized resistance to the opportunist course. If we talk about Khrushchev's displacement after a year, then, yes, it was carefully planned, but not by the Stalinists, but by the conductors of the same opportunist, revisionist line. Leaving the bridge from 1963 to the future, I will briefly explain.

Khrushchevshchina turned out to be too rabid, too poorly managed by behind-the-scenes puppeteers. If the cult of Stalin's personality was solemnly majestic, then Khrushchev's self-bloated cult looked excessively lurid and caricatured. Affairs in the country were getting worse and worse, and Khrushchev was rolling out abroad. With a huge retinue, squandering the people's money, he visited 36 countries, having visited all continents except Australia. He visited many countries multiple times. Even the most devoted sycophants got tired of the vagaries, fantasies and unpredictable somersaults of the adventurous Khrushchev.

The pro-Khrushchev part of the world's communist movement also degenerated and decomposed - the XX Congress of the CPSU did not simply disunite, split, but literally ripped and cut it. The foreign Khrushchevites, including those who proceeded seemingly out of good intentions, neglected the behests not only of Stalin, but also of Lenin and Marx, regarding the strictest obligation: to preserve the unity of the Communists as the apple of the eye.

Unfortunately, Khrushchev was not brought to trial for his crimes, but was just fired, He was replaced by Brezhnev in 1964. Having slowed down the catastrophic process of disintegration, the new leadership of the country did not prohibit, but only muffled anti-Stalinism, as an unpopular phenomenon. Dismantling of communist foundations through de-Stalinization in the economy and politics did not stop. The paradoxical Soviet-anti-Soviet training of cadres involuntarily reflected on the mentality of foreign communists and friends of the USSR. Outside of our country, the process of de-Stalinization was "cracked up" precisely under Brezhnev.

Arriving in Sumgait from Moscow under the orders of Khrushchev, investigators of the central apparatus of the KGB accused local law enforcers: a) of failure of their job; B) of an attempt to protect and justify the helpless and dishonest authorities of the republic. According to the

Azerbaijani authorities, nothing special happened: just little trouble. According to the version of the Moscow investigators, there was a riot with economic and political demands, and, perhaps, a premeditated insurrection. In their report, even such "trifles" as the mood and talk in the columns of the demonstrators were noted, where no one was smiling or having fun. But they discussed the rise in prices, the shortage of food products, corruption in power structures. And, of course, Stalin was remembered...

Since the demonstration was spontaneous, it was not possible to find the "orderers" of the riot. Six people were sentenced to imprisonment for a period of up to several years as "instigators of the unrest". Moreover, it was decided to judge them not by political, but by criminal articles. Thus, there was no need to punish the local party leadership, which would have lead to the inevitable and wide publicity of the pro-Stalinist speech of the working people of. Furthermore, a wave of discontent and even pronounced political strikes has already rolled across the Soviet Union. It seemed to the Khrushchevites that the best way out of the situation was to hush up the Sumgait history.

Perhaps it is worth mentioning the names of some ordinary participants of the event, preserved in the documents. These are young workers M. Alimirzoyev and Y. Makhmudov, who hammered down portraits of members of the Politburo, a worker N. Shevchenko, who convulsed a police officer, another worker A. Mahmudov who shouted into the microphone: "For the Motherland! For Stalin!" And then - calls for the overthrow of the government. Azeris, Armenians, Russians, Lezgins, Tatars, Ukrainians, Avars, Moldovans, representatives of other nationalities who lived and worked in Sumgait responded with thunderous "Hoorah!"

A. Kerimov's name is preserved in the archives and sad memories of the party functionary, boorishly tearing off the pin from the clothes of the demonstrator. Even the names of the wounded at the central police office boy - A. Aivazov, and the beaten Cuban student - D. Grant, are known. The latter was beaten, of course, not for the mythical courtship of someone's girlfriend.

Photographing of an angry mob by a foreigner could by no means be regarded as soothing. Well, what can one expect from the Cubans? Honest little ones, they, to put it mildly, did not understand a thing of Stalinism and completely trusted Khrushchev's propaganda. At the same time, revolutionary Cuba often behaved in a Stalinist manner on the international arena, and in many respects, in its internal life, it was going on in a truly communist, i.e. Stalinist way. Well, the fact that Fidel Castro was not aware of this and acted in the mainstream of Stalinism rather intuitively than scientifically does not detract from his outstanding merits. Under his leadership, a small island nation stood by the monstrous onslaught of imperialism, wiping off the noses of the three hundred million people of a powerful but surrendered enemy of the Soviet state. Many Cuban Communists are now embarrassed by their former criticism of Stalin and are silent about this unsightly page of their history. Moreover, they to some extent deserve the proud title of the Stalinists. And if some Cubans still do not perceive this circumstance adequately, then again this is due to their inadequate knowledge of the high philosophy of the Marx-Engels-Lenin-Stalin doctrine.

I repeat once again: the fact that the Azerbaijani workers, driven to despair, rushed with Stalin as their rifle, ready to smash the institutions, beat and drive away city officials, is not surprising. Khrushchev personified the failures in the development of the country and injustice, Stalin - successes and concern for the people. Therefore, in reality, the workers did not revolt against, but in defence of the Soviet power. They defended it from Khrushchev, from untruth, from the country's turning to the capitalist road. Without knowing it, they wanted to save it from the future debacle, committed under Gorbachev.

Therefore, other information, the details of which are buried in secret archives, is not surprising. The working people of Sumgait were going to repeat a similar pro-Stalinist speech on May 1, 1973, the year of the twentieth anniversary of the death of the leader. However, this time the KGB was on the alert and preventive measures prohibited the riots. Other factors also played a role in this. In particular, an increased craving for the consumer enrichment of significant sections of Soviet society, their amoralization and depoliticization, the declassing of workers and peasants...

And here it is - the tragic continuation of history. The same Sumgait, February 27-29, 1988.

The same? Oh no. The scene is the same, but the passions are now completely different. Gorbachevshchina reigns in the country, and now the city dwellers, among whom the tone is set not by workers but by semi-criminal elements, are in effect attacking the Soviet power. Outwardly this translates into a wild anti-Armenian pogrom. Armenians were the second largest nation in Azerbaijan. Before the October Revolution, hostilities and clashes between Azerbaijanis and Armenians were permanent. Wise and strictly scientific Leninist-Stalinist national policy liquidated this and other antagonisms. The incompetent Khrushchev-Brezhnev policy revived the conflict, something that Gorbachev took advantage of for his wrecking purposes.

As a result of the Sumgait pogrom in 1988, dozens of people were officially announced dead. In reality, hundreds were killed. Before that, the administrative authorities could not (read: they did not want to) protect the Azerbaijanis from the outburst of chauvinistic sentiments on the Armenian lands. When a resurgence of chauvinistic moods in the Azerbaijani lands occurred in revenge, they could not protect the Armenians there either.

It is more correct, however, to state – and there is plenty of evidence - that Gorbachev and his gang deliberately provoked the Azeri-Armenian slaughter, sabotaged the adoption of emergency measures to curb it. Troops, which were ordered to Sumgait with great delay, were forbidden to use weapons against the rioters. Suddenly it turned out that in a city that was once famous for its internationalism, the population did not have immunity against anti-Soviet, anti-socialist bacilli. Long-standing anti-Stalinism corrupted people.

The manifestations of ethnic intolerance were rare in the vast space of the multinational Stalinist USSR. The dictatorship of the proletariat knew how to deal with any social, national and other evils. But in the fifties this dictatorship, this core of the socialist state, was liquidated by the Kremlin revisionists at the legislative and executive levels.

The Stalin epoch was coming to an end - the new world was coming to an end, and its recoil began. This recoil was dialectical and long. Inside, it was accompanied not only by the senseless and destructive actions and inactions, but also by the periodic leaps of the USSR in development, by phenomenal acts of accelerated creation, by momentary upsurge in culture, science, and technology. Outside, its companions were separate successes in spreading communist influence on the globe. And yet, because of the general decay process caused by de-Stalinization, these leaps became weaker from year to year, occurred less frequently, while failures became more frequent.

A quarter of a century passed between the first Sumgait rebellion to the second. The daring anti-Stalin high life creaked, some were carefully cobbling about rotten, chauvinistic moods. So they cheered up, got prettier, blossomed. Humanism in the post-Stalin state disappeared, brutality returned. Soviet people in diverse parts of their homeland in different ways reaped the fruits of anti-Stalinism. We continue to reap them today on the wreckage of the power. I can say more than that. The anti-Stalin vector of development led the Soviet Union to collapse, which stimulated the unconcealed aggression of the West against the countries and nations that did not obey them, leading to millions of victims. Aggression expands and deepens. Thus those fruits are reaped, in effect, by the whole planet.

Translated from the Russian by Polina Brik. Edited by Kevin Kipp

Revolutionary Democracy is on sale at:

REPORT ON 22nd PARTY OF THE CPSU
(April 1962)

Jagjit Singh Lyallpuri
Promode Das Gupta.

The following is the minority report submitted by Jagjit Singh Lyallpuri and Promode Das Gupta to the CPI leadership on the 22nd Congress of the CPSU. These leaders of the CPI did not find the report presented by Z.A. Ahmed, S.G. Sardesai and Unni Raja to be an accurate rendering of the experiences of the Indian delegation in Moscow.

The report is self-explanatory. We may add one correction. The serial mendacity of Nikita Khrushchev is now established. The analysis by Grover Furr of the 'closed speech' at the 20th Congress of the CPSU in 1956 has not been controverted. One such shocking lie may be seen in the note presented by the CPSU to the delegates at the 22nd Congress in 1962. An example of Albanian repression was depicted in the case of Liri Gega who was allegedly executed whilst pregnant for spying for the Yugoslavs. This had already been denied by Enver Hoxha in Moscow in his speech at the Meeting of 81 Communist and Workers' Parties on November 16th 1960: 'To our amazement comrade Khrushchev came out in defense of these traitors and Yugoslav agents. He accused us of having shot the Yugoslav agent, the traitress Liri Gega, allegedly 'when she was pregnant, a thing which had not happened even in the time of the Czar and this had made a bad impression on world opinion'. These were slanders trumped up by the Yugoslavs in whom comrade Khrushchev had more faith than in us. We of course denied all these insinuations made by comrade Khrushchev'.[1] We may also point out that Promod Dasgupta later became a politbureau member of the CPI (M) and that Jagjit Singh Lyallpuri went on to hold the post of the General Secretary of the Marxist Communist Party of India (United). The original spellings in the text of the names of Communist leaders have been retained.

Vijay Singh.

COMMUNIST PARTY OF INDIA
Central Office: 7/4, Asaf Ali Road, New Delhi.

April, 1962.

National Council Meeting,
23-28, Apr. 1962.

For National Council Members only.

REPORT ON 22ND PARTY CONGRESS

Comrades,

There is a note already in the hands of the National Council members on 22nd Party Congress on behalf of three members of our delegation, Comrades Z. A. Ahmed, S.G. Sardesai and Unni Raja. This notes states that two members (namely we two) did not agree with this note, and hence the note by three comrades only.

We made a factual report of the work of delegation to the C.E.C. on which there were no differences between us. The C.E.C. directed us to make a report to the National Council as well on the basis of that report to the National Council and on similar lines. The report to the C.E.C. was made on the basis of three notes, one taken by Com. Sardesai, and the other two by Com. Lyallpuri. Comrades Ahmed and Promode added a few points but there was complete unanimity in our factual presentation. We asked Com. Sardesai to prepare a single consolidated report on the basis of these three reports, so that it can be presented before the National Council.

But as you find, instead of presenting a factual report, Comrade Sardesai prepares a report which seeks to plead a particular view point on various controversial matter raised in the 22nd Party Congress. In doing so, he seeks to place, before you some pieces of information which we never acquired during the course of work of our delegation (reference to certain speeches in 81 party Conference, impressions based on hearsay and so on), and also fails to convey certain information which our delegation collected during the course of its functioning. The note of these three comrades also fails to convey to you certain standpoints of our delegation which we took there after discussion amongst us. Naturally we could not agree to this type of report, and when a copy of the draft of this report was handed over to us, we expressed our inability to agree.

But at the same time, we suggested to Comrade Sardesai to call a meeting of all the members of the delegation present here so that we can arrive at a unified understanding about presentation of factual report. What we did in CEC, could in our opinion be done for the National Council as well. Later on, on the basis of these facts, each one of us can express his standpoint during the course of a discussion.

We regret to inform you that without holding any such meeting of the delegation as desired by us, these three members of the delegation have circulated their report to the National Council members. Under the circumstances, we are forced to submit a separate report here.

In any case, we will try to place before you a factual report without imparting any colour to it.

Sd/- Jagjit Singh Lyallpuri

Sd/- Promode Das Gupta

Our delegation to the 22nd Party Congress consisted of seven comrades selected by the C.E.C. in its September 1961 meeting. The members of delegation were Comrades Ajoy Ghosh, Z.A. Ahmed, S.G Sardesai, Promode Das Gupta, Jagjit Singh Lyallpuri, Unni Raja and Khandkar. Comrades Ajoy Ghosh and Sardesai left for Moscow oh 13th October and the other five members reached Moscow on 17th October, the day on which the Congress started. The Congress concluded on 30th. During the days between 17th to 30th; October, all members of our delegation except Comrade Ajoy Ghosh went to visit Leningrad for two days. After the Congress, Comrade Z. A. Ahmed and Comrade S.G.Sardesai came back via Tashkent and the four members of delegation (Promode Das Gupta, Unni Raja, Khandkar & Lyallpuri) went to visit Kiev for two days. We came back for the 7th November, Parade at Moscow, after which we departed.

Our daily programme during the Congress was too crowded. It was difficult to find time to exchange views with any other fraternal delegation. We were putting up along at a separate lodge. That also handicapped us in this manner. We had planned to meet many fraternal delegations, but it became difficult to meet all. Anyhow we could manage to meet members of the PB of CPSU, including Com. Khrushchov at a dinner at which they invited us along with two other delegations. We had also meetings with the Chinese, Greek, Indonesian delegations.

The Reports to the Congress, and speeches of the various leaders of CPSU as well as the messages of various fraternal delegations have already appeared in the Press. We need not go into those in our report. After his return Com.Ajoy also wrote an article giving some information as well as posing certain issues. Herein below will be given some information as a supplement to that.

In the reports of Comrade Khrushchov, besides the programme of building Communism, three other issues also got prominence. These were:

i. The question of personality cult

ii. The question of anti-Party Group and,

iii. The question of Soviet-Albanian relations.

The manner in which, all these three issues were displayed at the Congress were a surprise to us.

Our delegation discussed the message that Com. Ajoy wrote for the Congress. We unanimously came to the conclusion that we should not opine on the Soviet-Albanian controversy although various fraternal delegations had by that time, expressed themselves on that question. Com. Ajoy also reported to us that he had a talk with Com. Aidit, Chairman, C.P. of Indonesia who had also expressed his opinion that we do not intend to enter into this controversy. But at the same time, we decided to meet other fraternal delegations, especially Soviet as well as the Chinese comrades in order to get clarity on this controversy.

We had lengthy interview, with the Soviet comrades at the time of our meeting at a dinner, at which Com. Khrushchov explained to us various issues concerning the harmful effect of personality cult, the activities of anti-Party Group and also relations with Albanian Party of Labour. As it was a meeting at the dinner table, we could not take notes of this talk. Anyhow most of the information that they gave regarding Albania is there in the gist of the document that we submit below.

Com. Khrushchov also told us that in August 1961, Com. Ho-Chi-Minh came to Moscow, expressed concern over the turn the relations between these two Parties have taken, and expressed his desire to intervene if it could be helpful. Com. Ho-Chi-Minh told them that after meeting them in Moscow, he would like to go to Tirana to meet Albanian leaders. The Soviet comrades told Com. Ho-Chi-Minh, that if he wanted to resolve the differences, he should go to Peking instead of Tirana. After this Com. Ho-Chi-Minh returned back to Hanoi; he neither went to Peking nor Tirana.

As is known, while delivering the message of greetings Com. Chou-En-Lai disapproved of the unilateral condemnation by the Soviet Party of another brother Party. We could not meet Com. Chou En-Lai, but had an opportunity to meet Com. Pen Chang, a PB member, and requested him to throw some more light on this question. By that time Com. Khrushchov has also delivered his concluding speech in which he had stated that no one is in a better position than Chinese comrades to solve this controversy. The remark was once again a clear indication that Albanian comrades are taking a position which deteriorates the relations with Soviet Union and CPSU, at the instance of Chinese comrades. At the talk over the dinner also Comrade Khrushchov categorically stated so.

We asked Com. Pen Chang that we heard the speech of Com. Chou En-Lai. Would you like to say something more on the question of Albania. Com. Pen Chang expressed his views in the following manner.

"Regarding rights or wrongs of the two Parties, I do not want to say anything. It concerns these two Parties. Comrade Chou En-Lai expressed our opinion in his message. There, are many other delegations also who acted in a wise manner, that is to say, that they did not mention it. That includes Comrade Ghosh also.

"Even in a trial of a prisoner no judgement is passed in his absence. Even a State employs a lawyer to plead his case if he cannot do so. But this is a case of a brother Party. They (Albanian comrades) did not come to this Congress not because they did not intend to come, but because they were not invited to come."

"Those who are passing such unilateral judgements do not feel that they have firm ground for that. All fraternal parties are equal. How can we a Third Party express who is right and who is wrong between the two Parties, when one Party is absent. We only said it is not proper to express it publicly in this manner. I am worried about the consequences of such a behaviour since Soviet Party has today unilaterally condemned Albanian Party, who can guarantee they will not condemn this or that Party next time. Also, is it permissible for other Parties to condemn Soviet Party when they come to attend their Conference. If everybody is going to follow the same method as followed by CPSU in this Congress, just because it thinks a particular Party has committed mistake, then where is the guarantee of solidarity.

"Is this in conformity with Leninism and Moscow Declaration? What more could be done to discredit the movement? Our delegation is unhappy over it, not because it would create difficulties for People's Republic of China alone but because it would harm the common cause. As the Indian delegation knows, the Chinese Party was attacked at Bucharest and at Moscow Conferences, but this did no harm to a single hair on our body. Here we are worried because of other reasons."

"So much on consequences. If they continue like that, what, will happen to Soviet-Albanian relations. Just imagine if imperialism attacks Albania because differences are exposed, can this do any good to anybody. Will this not be condemned by history?"

"There is another possibility. It may be there are people who believe that by exerting pressure they can remove Com. Enver Hoxha and Sheikhu from the leadership. Suppose for a moment that they succeed. Will it not be vicious? It will create a precedent that one Party or a group of Parties can change-leadership of another Party and put anti-leadership people into power. If so where is the spirit of Moscow Declaration.

"We have been advising both the Parties to exercise restraint in their relations and solve the differences in atmosphere of mutual respect. We have not yet given up hope, whether we succeed or not, let us see."

"In his concluding speech, Com. Khrushchov remarked that if the Chinese Party is willing it can help..... If he means. what he says, we ask a question - Has he left any room for Chinese party to act. "

"Is it better to have 12 or 11 Socialist countries?"

In connection with Soviet-Albanian relations, CPSU prepared a lengthy note for information of the fraternal delegates. Summary of its important points is attached herewith.

When our delegation returned from Leningrad in the morning, we learnt that the previous evening a resolution had been passed in the Congress calling upon the Government to remove the body of Com. Stalin lying by the side of Com. Lenin. At that time, we were ignorant as to what they proposed to do with the body of Com. Stalin. We had a discussion and all except Dr. Ahmed came to the conclusion that Com. Ajoy should convey to the Soviet leaders, that Com. Stalin's body should not be buried or destroyed as it would be resented by the people in general, and if they have decided to remove it from there, as it cannot be placed equal to. Com.Lenin, then they should preserve it in some other Mausoleum. But as we came to the Congress Hall, we were informed that the body had already been buried besides the Kremlin Wall.

Our Delegation also decided to convey it through Com. Ghosh to the Soviet- leaders that the manner in which they have dealt with, the Soviet-Albanian relations is not proper.

C.C. of the C.P.S.U. prepared a note for information to the fraternal delegates regarding Soviet-Albanian Party disputes. The main contents read out to us are as below:

C.C. of the CPSU addressed a letter to the delegates of Moscow Conference on Dec.1, 1960. This letter gives evaluation of the Conference and regrets the stand taken and speech delivered by Enver Hoxha, Albanian Party leader.

It contained unsubstantiated attack on Soviet and other Parties. They try to force a discussion not in accord with the principles of Marxism and fraternal relations. It was natural that it was condemned by over-whelming majority.

CPSU did not deem it necessary to reply these allegations - Deliberate omission in N.S. Khrushchov's speech of Nov.23rd 1960.

If Albanian leaders really want friendship they must not resort to such methods.

The letter also deals with the history of relations between these two Parties. Relations were friendly till recently. A Conference was held in 1957 between the representatives of two parties and a communiqué was issued. It stated, "negotiations held in atmosphere of friendship ... Unity of views in all matters.... "

The same was registered in May, 1959, when Soviet Party and Govt. delegations visited Albania, headed by N.S. Khrushchov. It was stated in the communiqué issued:

The Soviet Union has rendered and, trained cadres for building socialism. CPSU always held that Albania be aided more in order to set an example to Muslim countries how Albania following socialism and aided by Socialist countries is able to raise its standard. Com. N.S. Khrushchov emphasized the significance of prosperous Albania.

Soviet Union advanced credits more than one billion rubles. In April 1957, wiped off past arrears of debts amounting to 422 million rubles.

In addition Soviet Union transferred: as a gift all industrial establishments built in Albania. Also helped in finding oil. Although quality of oil found was low, even then Soviet Union agreed to purchase it.

From 1951-60, 3027 Soviet specialists visited Albania. It also helped Albania in building defence. Provided 50 percent foodstuffs and equipment to Army free.

It played a great role in turning backward Albania in to agrarian-industrial country.

In his speech at 21st Congress, Enver Hoxha stated "Our profound gratitude for all Soviet Union has done for Albanian people."

Later on in one of his speeches, E. Hoxha stated that June 1960 Conference was convened unexpectedly. It is not true as proved by correspondence between - Socialist countries.

In a latter in June 1960 Soviet Union asked for the possibility of holding a conference at Bucharest to discuss political issues. All Parties including Albanian agreed.

On June 7, 1960 CPSU wrote a letter that all Parties of Socialist countries have agreed to it. It is known that 50 Parties participated, and a Communiqué is signed by all. Nevertheless, Com. Enver Hoxha says that this Conference was one sided and does not express collective opinion.

In view of the fact that differences had arisen CPSU made efforts to improve relations.

CPSU addressed a letter in Aug.1960 to Albanian leaders to come to Soviet Union to take rest and have talks. But they rejected invitation in view of the forthcoming Party Congress of Albanian Party.

Again on Aug.30, 1960, CPSU sent another letter saying "we deem it necessary that the Albanian Party of Labour and CPSU should reach unanimity at the forthcoming Moscow Conference. It would be correct to extinguish the fire till it grows into flames. That is why we should have talks before the Conference. If it is agreed we would like to meet your delegation."

This proposal was also rejected. As an excuse they said in a reply, "Marxism also teaches that if two Parties start negotiations among themselves which would aim at criticism of general line of any other Party that would be against principles of Marxism-Leninism."

Baselessness of this argument is proved by the fact that we did not suggest discussions of any line but to iron out the misunderstanding that had arisen between two Parties.

Later on Albanian Party of Labour started accusing Soviet diplomats of interference in internal affairs of Albania.

It was in those days that CPSU started receiving letter regarding changed attitude towards Soviet citizens in Albania.

They levelled unfounded allegations against C.C. of C.P.S.U.

The First; Secretary, of one of the District Party Committees of Albania in his talks-with Soviet citizens stated that the line adopted by CPSU on Yugoslavia is opportunistic.

There was arrogant attitude towards Soviet Military personnel.

There were some accusations in relation to Soviet Policy of War & Peace.

For example, Balucar, Albanian Defence Minister stated that Soviet policy was not sufficiently firm. He told a Soviet officer that Khrushchov said that we will blow U.S., and other bases if more American flights on

Soviet territory but when U.S. again violated the space, there was no, retaliation.

How can one evaluate such statement. If these words were not said by a Defence Minister of a friendly country, it would be considered as a provocation, meant, for pushing us into war.

He wanted to show that Soviet Govt. does not follow its words with deeds. Despite all this, CPSU continued its efforts.

On Nov.10, 1960, CPSU delegated Com. Mikoyan, Kozlov, Suslov and others to go to see Albanian comrades staying in Moscow. A meeting did take place but without any results.

Com. Mikoyan & Kozlov again met them and had lengthy talks. Then on Nov.12, Com. Khrushchov expressed a desire to meet them. A meeting took place. Com. Khrushchov, Mikoyan and others of CPSU. and Com. Enver Hoxha, Sheikhu, Kapo and others from Albania participated. At that meeting Albanian comrades conducted arrogantly. It. showed that they had no desire to iron out differences and in the middle of the discussion, they walked out.

CPSU again made efforts to meet them. On Nov.14 1960 another letter was sent to them.

Albanian comrades did not reply till Nov. 21 and met on Nov. 25. Enver Hoxha had left for Albania at that time but, Sheikhu and Kapo met Mikoyan and Kozlov.

At that meeting Albanian comrades did not show any desire to improve relations We told them that after Bucharest we have uttered no word against you whereas in Albania systematic campaign is conducted against us. We also told that there can be misunderstanding but it can be solved.

They accused us of applying pressure upon them. It was obvious that they do not intend to improve relations.

To sum up, all our attempts to improve our relations with them failed.

Instances of Repression in Albania.

1. **Liri Belishova:** A PB member removed from that position and also of Parliament membership. Her husband, Chomo - Minister of Agriculture also deprived of his post. It was towards the end of 1960.

Their sole guilt was that they supported the line of CPSU and Soviet Govt.

2. Koch Tashco. Chairman, Central Auditing Party Committee, a veteran Communist who was sentenced to death before liberation, was removed

from his position because he called upon Albanian leadership not to worsen relations with Soviet Union. He was expelled from the Party, expelled from Tirana with family and his son studying in Moscow recalled.

These facts resemble the deeds of Yugoslav leadership, earlier. (The document enumerates some detailed history of relations with Yugoslavia.)

Shipment of Soviet wheat.

Enver Hoxha stated that at difficult times Soviet Union refused to send wheat loan ...

It is wrong. He is silent to state that it is the Soviet Union which supplied them all the grains. In 1960, Soviet Union honoured its commitment ahead of time, i.e. by September 5th.

Liri Goga and Paliako Case.

In his speech Enver Hoxha alleged that Soviet Union supports agents of Tito. Indeed some time ago CPSU sent a letter to Albanian comrades trying to find out what had happens to a P.B.M, Liri Goga, who was condemned of high treason of spying for Yugoslavia. We asked the Albanian comrades not to execute a woman who was pregnant. Even Czar did not hang pregnant women. It would be impermissible in a Socialist country. We warned the Albanian comrades about the mistakes which would discredit the whole socialist world. Unfortunately they did not heed to it and executed her some times during 1960, some months before the Bucharest Conference. (The letter is silent whether CPSU believed she was guilty or not.)

Poliako another comrade fled to Yugoslavia in 1957 and from there sent a letter to CPSU why he had fled. CPSU immediately informed the Albanian comrades about this letter.

Enver HOXHA was in Moscow at that time. Copy was given to him. - The matter was dropped at that time; But later on, he wanted to raise it again. The comrade had applied for asylum in USSR but he was not granted.

"Much attention has been given to such facts which have not to be discussed in public. We do not want to supplement unprincipled discussion with some minor issues.

This is how the letter: to delegates sums up.-

A letter, to Albanian Party of Labour dated Aug 1960 relates history, of good relations with Albania and invites them for discussion before Moscow Conference.

Source: Kamgar Prakashan Library.

Endnote:

[1] Enver Hoxha, The Party of Labor of Albania in Battle with Modern Revisionism, Speeches and Articles, The Naim Frasheri Publishing House, Tirana 1972, p. 76-7.

THE QUESTION OF THE PEASANTRY AND INDUSTRIALISATION IN THE SOVIET UNION AND PEOPLE'S CHINA

Vijay Singh

In a recent discussion a comrade argued 'that Stalin engaged in the production of surplus value through the exploitation of the peasantry, and this funded and sustained urban industrialisation. Furthermore, this exploitation was exacerbated, as Bettelheim argues, due to the poor organisation amongst the peasantry of the Bolsheviks (this predates Stalin's ascendency as well), which results in an antagonising of contradictions amongst the people. Indeed, I do not think that Stalin was some tyrant who purposefully went around killing peasants for fun, but do think that the exigencies of developing urban industrialisation and poor relationship between the Bolsheviks and the peasantry resulted in a rather callous approach towards the difficulties that the peasantry faced. I think that this difference in approach with respect to the peasantry and industrialisation is a qualitative difference between the policies of Stalin and Mao'.

This is a not an uncommon view in progressive circles. But it has a tenuous relation with historical reality. The following response was made to this understanding.

But there is no evidence to suggest that Soviet industrialisation was financed by the 'production of surplus value through the exploitation of the peasantry'. Preobrazhensky, an ally of Trotsky, in the 1920s had called for the peasantry to be treated as an 'internal colony' of the Soviet working class. He proposed that surplus extracted from the peasantry should be utilised for 'super-industrialisation'. Stalin had rejected this view but he was charged later by Deutscher and then by many others of stealing the clothes of Preobrazhensky and implementing his policies in the First Five Year Plan. These views have also been repeated by those who were part of the marriage between Trotskyism and Maoism which was consummated in Paris in the late 1960s. Bettelheim as is known supported Trotskyism from the 1930s till the 20th Congress of the CPSU when he began to support the pro-Khrushchev Communist Party of France, and then he went on to give support to the cultural revolution of China. The ideological views of Bettelheim on Soviet history are a gallimaufry of each of the ideological trends that he had espoused from the 1930s. Many of these ideas are carried by fractions of the contemporary progressive intelligentsia. The only problem is that these notions have no basis in historical reality. The only serious study of this question based on Soviet materials and documents is by the Soviet economic historian A.A. Barsov in his book 'Balans stoimostnykh obmenov mezhdu gorodom i derevnei', Moscow, 1969. While this book and related documents are only available in Russian they have been reviewed by a number of specialists. See, for example, Michael Ellman 'Did the Agricultural Surplus Provide the Resources for the Increase in Investment in the USSR? (The Economic Journal, December 1975, 844-864.) and Arvind Vyas 'Primary accumulation in the USSR revisited' (Cambridge Journal of Economics 1979, 3,119-130).

This is what A.A. Barsov has to say:

'...the surplus product created by the labour of the Soviet peasantry played a big role in the establishment of a mighty socialist industry. The contribution of the Soviet peasantry to the solution of this immensely important historical task was great. Nevertheless, the majority of the accumulation, necessary for carrying out socialist industrialisation, was obtained from the non-agricultural branches of the economy and was created by the working class'.

Arvind Vyas indicates, on the basis of Barsov, in terms of Marxian values, that in the financing of Soviet industrialisation, two-thirds of the accumulation fund came from industry and one-third from the surplus product necessary for the development of industry. He also pointed out that the net agricultural surplus between the years 1928 and 1932 was negative. The evidence of Barsov negates the viewpoint of those who argued that Stalin followed the policies earlier recommended by Preobrazhensky to ensure 'primary socialist accumulation' at the expense of the peasantry. Vyas further points out that there was a drastic decline in the urban standard of living in the period of the First Five Year Plan, urban real wages falling by 49%, which permitted a very high rate of accumulation. It was primarily the sacrifices of the Soviet working class which ensured Soviet industrialisation.

Michael Ellman noted that during the First Five Year Plan it was not possible for agriculture to have provided the resources for industrialisation. He argued that ' ...during the First Five Year Plan the volume of investment more than quadrupled and rose from 14.8% of the national income in 1928 to 44.1% in 1932. Clearly, measuring in 1928 prices, agriculture could not possibly have provided the resources for industrialisation in 1928-32 because by the end of the First Five Year Plan annual investment was more than double annual agricultural output, and the increase in investment during the First Five Year Plan (i.e. the excess of investment in 1932 over investment in 1928) was substantially greater than the entire output of agriculture in any year. ...During the First Five Year Plan the Soviet national income rose by 60% and virtually all this income was used to increase investment.' Ellman, who is no sympathiser of Marxism, is clear that '...there is no basis whatsoever for the view that the increase in investment during the First Five Year Plan was financed by an increase in the agricultural surplus'.

It is correct to say that the Bolsheviks as a party of the industrial working class had a weak base amongst the Soviet peasantry just as it can be said that the CPC had a weak base in the Chinese working class. Lenin and the Bolsheviks considered that the industrial proletariat was the only class which could lead a socialist revolution and take it to communism. For this reason they privileged organisation of the industrial working class. They did not accept Narodnism. The Bolsheviks were concerned to ally with the whole peasantry in the struggle for revolutionary democracy and with the working peasantry in the fight for socialism. The October revolution and collectivisation (and the Great Patriotic war) showed that the working peasantry were important allies of the working class. There was no general antagonism, as you argue, between the working class and the peasantry as a whole in the Soviet Union during collectivisation. They were allies but it was not an objective of the Bolsheviks to create a party in which the working peasantry would be quantitatively important. Antagonistic relations existed only between the working class and the working peasantry at one side and the rich peasant class, the kulaks, whom Lenin had dubbed as the last capitalist class, on the other side. Lenin and the Bolsheviks did not consider that the kulaks were a part of the 'people' they were a part of the bourgeoisie. It is highly problematic to talk just in terms of the relationship of the Bolsheviks and the peasantry in general *as a whole*. The Bolsheviks followed Marx and Engels in excluding the rich peasantry from the collective farms and communes. Engels pointed out in *The Peasant Question in France and Germany* that collectives should be formed of the small peasantry. He also argued that: 'Marx and I never doubted that in the transition to the full communist economy we will have to use the cooperative system as an intermediate stage on a large scale. It must only be so organised that society, initially the state, retains the ownership of the means of production so that the private interests of the cooperative vis-a-vis society as a whole cannot establish themselves.' In the Soviet Union after collectivisation the means of production whether land or agricultural machinery was owned by the state sector which was under the control of the working class.

After 1927 the Communist Party of China (CPC) had a marginal membership from the working class for obvious reasons. It was not something wanted by the CPC; it was forced upon them by the massacres of the communists and workers instigated by the Kuomintang. The communists were driven out of the urban areas so that the work of the CPC in the towns was driven underground. The CPC consequently became in terms of its social composition a peasant party. Only after 1949 did the CPC attempt to rebuild a new industrial proletarian basis for itself though it did not in any way become a major part of its membership - despite its being the leading party holding state power. The CPC during the revolutionary wars, despite its almost non-existent industrial working class base, did have the benefit of real proletarian guidance and not just ideologically. It had the unmitigated support of the Soviet working class and the CPSU (b).

Soviet industrialisation under the Five Year Plans not only created the material basis for the defeat of Hitlerism in the west it also enabled Soviet (and Mongolian) troops to enter Manchuria and destroy the Japanese 4th Army. Had the CPSU (b) followed the policies of Bukharin of the late 1920s or of Mao after 1956 i.e. placing stress on the development of light industry and agriculture there would not have been a strong metallurgical and engineering base in the Soviet Union and it would have been difficult if not impossible to confront Nazi Germany and Tojo's Japan. The stunning Soviet victory in Manchuria over the Japanese had the consequence of enabling the Chinese People's Liberation Army to take shelter from the Kuomintang, saved it from physical destruction, and enabled it to receive from the Soviet Union Japanese armaments which could be used in the march south to defeat the Kuomintang. The Soviet army (and the Bulgarian) entry into eastern Yugoslavia and Manchuria ensured people's democratic victories in both Yugoslavia and China. Nationalist elements in both countries were to say (rather screech from the housetops) that their victory was based on the internal armed forces.

The ratio of forces between the Communist Party, the proletariat and the peasantry as well as the social composition of the party was determined by historical circumstances and it changed over time both in the Soviet Russia and China.

You argue that in comparison to Stalin, Mao had a qualitatively different approach on industrialisation and the attitude towards the peasantry. We pointed out that the arguments that Stalin had exploited the peasantry are unfounded. What you prefer in the Chinese exemplar it seems are the policies in China which were in consonance with the views of the Soviet leadership after Stalin. In both countries industrialisation (production of the means of production) was downgraded to the benefit of agriculture and light industry after 1957. Centralised directive planning was ended in both the countries and replaced by a decentralised 'co-ordinated planning'. In both states the socialised means of production in agriculture, the Machine Tractor Stations, were handed over to the collective farms/people's communes, thereby expanding the sphere of commodity-money relations in the economy. (It must be recognised though that in People's China collectivisation and the establishment of the people's communes had greatly reduced the area of operation of commodity-money relations in the economy). The collective farms in People's China after 1955 had a different social class basis from the Soviet and early Chinese collective farms. Whilst Marx and Engels had urged that the social class basis of the collective farms were the small peasantry the CPC leadership incorporated the kulaks and former landlords into the collective farms after 1955 as had earlier been done, to the horror of Cominform, by Tito in Yugoslavia in 1948. These relations of production were carried over to the people's communes which at the time of their being set up were a multi-class formation of the national bourgeoisie, the landlords, the kulaks and the working peasantry. The people's communes incorporated all kinds of rural industries including fertiliser factories as well as steel plants and steamship companies which meant that a 'gigantic' quantity of the means of production was outside the sector of state property which constituted the property of the whole people. The CPC in its policies not only distanced itself from the founders of Marxism in terms of the social class composition of the collective farms/people's communes but also from their views on the property relations in means of production in the collective farms/communes. Engels had stated in his letter to Bebel dated 20th January 1886: 'And Marx and I never doubted that in the transition to the full communist economy we will have to use the cooperative system as an intermediate stage on a large scale. It must only be so organised that society, initially the state, retains the ownership of the means of production so that the private interests of the cooperative vis-a-vis society as a whole cannot establish themselves.'

All this suggests that questions of the peasantry and industrialisation in the Soviet Union and People's China under Stalin, Khrushchev and Mao Zedong need to be looked at afresh with great care stripped of the rightist theories which have been spread since the 20th Congress of the CPSU.

TROTKYISM'S LATEST SORTIE

L. Kasharsky

In January and February 1932 the Institute of Economics of the Leningrad branch of the Communist Academy held meetings on the Trotskyist Theory on Imperialism (already translated and published in RD in April 2016) and the Universal Crisis of Capitalism. Here we publish the contribution of L. Kasharsky in this conference in which the author evaluated the recently published book by E.A. Preobrazhensky 'The Decline of Capitalism' which had been published in Moscow in 1931. (An English translation of this book was published in 1985: E. A. Preobrazhensky, 'The Decline of Capitalism', translated and edited with an introduction by Richard B. Day, M. E. Sharpe, Inc. Armonk, New York). Kasharsky argues that Preobrazhensky breaks with Marx and Lenin on a range of issues of political economy, on the crisis of capitalism, on the theory of reproduction of Marx, a rejection of Lenin's theory of imperialism, particularly of the theory of uneven development under imperialism and is heavily influenced by the theories of Karl Kautsky, Hilferding, Trotsky and Luxemburg. This paper, as that of V. Serebryakov published earlier in this journal, shows the valuable literature on political economy which was occluded after the 20th Congress of the CPSU.

Comrade Stalin's letter to the editorial board of "Proletarian Revolution" revealed, on the basis of historical component of the theoretical principles, that a counter-revolutionary Trotskyism, its counter-revolutionary nature demolished and unmasked, is powerless, in conditions of the worldwide historical victories of our country and the party in building socialism, when it speaks openly against the Leninist party, the Leninist Central Committee, and all the more persistently resorts, as a method of struggle, to a theoretical contraband, trying to mount an attack from the rear on the history of the party, on the theoretical principles of the party, trying to subject the axioms of Bolshevism to revision.

It goes without saying that the smuggling of counter-revolutionary Trotskyism is not limited to the historical front alone. In particular, on the economic front, recently, the former henchman of Trotskyism and Pope Trotsky's Cardinal for Economic Affairs - E. Preobrazhensky — has been made the peddler of Trotskyist contraband. At the end of 1931, he published the book *"The Decline of Capitalism"* that is heavily soaked with Trotskyist ideology.

E. Preobrazhensky's book is devoted to the theoretical coverage of the basic problems of modern capitalism in the phase of the general crisis of the capitalist system. In the preface E. Preobrazhensky pointed out that this book is only a part of a larger study on the issues of modern monopoly capitalism and its demise. "A characteristic feature - writes E. Preobrazhensky at the beginning of the first chapter -of the *post-war economy* is the huge size of the unused fixed capital and the monstrous absolute dimensions of unemployment" (page 5). These features of post-war capitalism, says Preobrazhensky, unwittingly posit before everyone the fundamental questions: why does it happen, what causes this phenomenon in capitalism? Getting to resolve these issues, Preobrazhensky says:

> *"Based on the theory of reproduction of Marx* and *Lenin's theory of imperialism*, as well as on an analysis of the conditions of expanded reproduction under monopolistic capitalism, I try to give an answer to the above questions, as well as to give a theoretical analysis of the causes of the current global financial crisis" (p. 5, my italics. LK later italic, belonging to the author, is not specified).

Let us first of all see, on whom does E. Preobrazhensky rests his analysis of the conditions of expanded reproduction under monopolistic capitalism and also his analysis of the causes of the current global crisis, so as to then proceed to a characterization of Preobrazhensky's findings on the truly fundamental questions of modern capitalism and contemporary global crisis.

1. THE THEORY OF REPRODUCTION OF MARX AND E. PREOBRAZHENSKY'S TROTSKYIST THEORY OF REPRODUCTION

In his book, E. Preobrazhensky repeatedly characterizes the inheritance of Marx's theory of reproduction of social capital and crises (pp. 54, 61, 82 etc). E. Preobrazhensky does not think much of this legacy. He persistently and in various ways develops and emphasizes the idea that Marx did not leave behind a complete theory of reproduction and crises and that, while specifying a method to understand these problems, Marx confined himself mainly to the most abstract statements and a number of individual observations, highly valuable and brilliant, but which still are of a fragmentary and partial nature. "*Marx's theory* of crises, - says Preobrazhensky, - *due to the incompleteness* of his work, as well as Marx's theory of reproduction need be *developed and framed* in the sense of proximation of the analysis to the real conditions of capitalism (p. 61). As we shall see below, E Preobrazhensky wants the *development* and the *formulation* of the theory of reproduction not only in terms of approximation to the real conditions of capitalism, and "development" in all its essential relations." This is not the place to defend Marx against Preobrazhensky. But here, at the outset it should be emphasized that before us is the old tried and tested method of revisionists — to justify their anti-Marxist constructions they usually declare one or the other side of Marx's theory "undeveloped" and "incomplete" and thus get an opportunity to pass on their own constructions as "*development*" and "*formulation*" of the ideas of the teacher.

What is the essence of Preobrazhensky's theory of reproduction and the theory of crises?

1. First of all, it should be noted that Preobrazhensky approaches the problem of reproduction and crises as a mechanic. Preobrazhensky in his book, as in his previous works, understands Marx's theory of reproduction as a theory, constructed on the principle of equilibrium[1]. Marx's schema of reproduction, according to Preobrazhensky are only "laws of proportionality" (p. 82), that just fix the process of distribution of capital in the process of reproduction[2], and so on. Of course, along with this Preobrazhensky also speaks of "*persistent imbalances*" but the decisive and determining factor in all his arguments is the fact that Marx's theory of reproduction Preobrazhensky interprets as a theory, resting on the postulate of equilibrium. Thus Preobrazhensky puts the whole Marxist methodology on its head. If for Marx "balance in a spontaneously emerging capitalist system of production is an accident" (Capital, vol. II, p. 302), if the balance appears only as a special case of the movement of social capital, if the movement is primary and balance and "proportionality" constitute only a moment of the latter, then for Preobrazhensky the movement itself becomes only one moment in maintainence of the balance, movement is subject to the balance, the balance has primacy over the imbalances.

For Marx, capitalist reproduction, even with ideal proportionality includes capitalist contradictions; therefore it involves movement - self-movement - of capitalist contradictions. The motion of contradictions constantly creates imbalances in the capitalist economy: the proportionality and disparities are inseparable from the contradictions of the capitalist system, from the motion of the latter. In this movement, "*proportionality*" and "*equilibrium*" occur as an accident, as one moment. Here, Preobrazhensky firmly holds on to his old mechanistic positions.

2. Treating the process of social reproduction of capitalism as a dynamic equilibrium of the capitalist system, not realizing that the process of reproduction of social capital is a self-movement of the basic capitalist contradictions, by taking in this regard a vulgar mechanistic position, Preobrazhensky naturally comes to consider the capitalist crisis as a temporary disorder of equilibrium of the capitalist system, the emergence of the capitalist system from this equilibrium as deviations from a major proportion. He writes: "*The crisis breaks out, which means a transition from a specific temporary equilibrium ...to a smoother process ...*" (p. 27), to new proportions. Elsewhere it is stated: "*In order to show how the general crises are possible under capitalism*, it is necessary from the schema revealing overall proportionality, to continue to study further and to proceed, firstly, from the fact that the fixed assets are not amortized over a period of one year, and secondly, from unevenness of recovery and of increasing unevenness in time "(p. 82).

Thus according to Preobrazehnsky it appears that capitalism is peacefully marching on according to the schema of expanded reproduction, and only the uneven reproduction of fixed capital pushes the system out of balance.

For anyone who is in the least even broadly familiar with Marx's theory of crises, it is clear that such representation has nothing in common with Marxism. According to Marx, as we know, crises are just a "*real connection and forced evening of all the contradictions of the bourgeois economy*." (*Theory*, Vol. II, Part 2, pp. 17 7–178)

3. Preobrazhensky exhibits monstrous theoretical carelessness on the question of the causes of capitalist crises. Periodic crises are known to represent the explosion of all the contradictions of capitalist society. It is also clear that the causes of these crises cannot be understood, if one ignores the movement of the main contradictions of capitalist society - the contradiction between the social character of production and the private character of appropriation. What is characteristic of Preobrazhensky in this regard is his manner of viewing capitalist crisis without, and separated from, the movement of the most basic, the most profound contradictions of capitalism. On the basic contradictions of capitalism, the real cause of the crises, the author does not say anything.

In one place he most clearly demonstrates the extent to which he is indifferent to the internal causes of capitalist crises: "*It is sufficient to have one deep economic crisis, whatever its reason, for subsequent crises to recur periodically."*

4. In order to uncouple the capitalist cycle and crises from the movement of the internal contradictions of capitalism, not understanding the contradictions of the process of reproduction of social capital, Preobrazhensky naturally is forced to seek other reasons for pushing the system out of balance, i.e. into a crisis. Such a reason, to some extent a reason for the external shock, he sees in the refurbishment and the creation of fixed capital.

There would be no harm if Preobrazhensky took into account the reproduction and an increase in fixed capital as one of the moments that make up the capitalist cycle. But a mechanical Preobrazhensky, by separating the crisis of the motion of capitalist contradictions is forced to raise an increase in the reproduction of fixed capital to the rank of the general and the main cause of the crisis. The cyclic form of motion of capitalism, according to the latest discovery of Preobrazhensky, is *"first of all connected with the uneven over time reproduction of fixed capital"* (p. 42). This uneven reproduction of fixed capital the author believes is the main immediate cause of the crisis: "The uneven recovery, and especially the increase of the capital in bourgeois society is the *main, immediate and proximate cause of the general economic crisis.*"

After this discovery Preobrazhensky thinks of course it is superfluous to refer to the real causes of the crisis, pointed out by Marx, Engels and Lenin. On these real, deeper causes the author is stubbornly silent. The slightest attempt by a mechanical Preobrazhensky to approach the nature of the real causes of the capitalist crises shows his complete inability to understand them. An isolated attempt by Preobrazhensky to break through in explaining the crises on the basis of a specific moment (of reproduction of capital) to the most common, deep, inclusive cause of the crisis - the main capitalist contradiction (between the social character of production and the private character of appropriation) ends a miserable fiasco. Preobrazhensky wrote: *"All of the above is not to mean that crises* or the state of crisis of the capitalist system have only the cause pointed out by us. The *anarchy of production under private management of firms* (obviously anarchy is possible with the public management of the company? LK), *but the social character of production* in its entirety and complexity of relationships of proportionality inevitably creates conditions not only for the above, but also for other causes of crises "(p. 84).

If anything that can be deducted from this awkward quote, then there are only two things. Firstly, Preobrazhensky agrees to allow, along with the reproduction of the fixed capital, also "*other causes of crises.*" Secondly, as Preobrazhensky touches upon as one of the "other reasons", the basic capitalist contradictions, he takes the last in a narrow and one-sided manner, imitating Hilferding. We would be looking in vain for (as the causes of the crisis) Preobrazhensky's other aspects of the mentioned main capitalist contradictions - for example, the contradiction between production and consumption, the contradictions between, the bourgeoisie and the proletariat, the contradiction expressed in the fall of the rate of profit, etc. The class characteristic of capitalist contradictions leading to a crisis is obscured, smeared, and it loses its defining importance.

At the same time, further, having allowed himself the above empty runaround about these "other reasons" Preobrazhensky here tends to annul them. "However, - he writes - these other imbalances usually exert their effects in the framework of the existing cyclicity of the entire process and either increases or decreases the process of expansion or contraction of production."

Thus the real causes of the crises are, at best, of secondary importance, including the already established cyclic movement subordinated to the main, immediate causes of the crisis - the uneven reproduction of fixed capital.

How disdainfully Preobrazhensky treats these "other causes" of the crisis is clear from what follows. He says, "To this is added the influence of environmental conditions on the reproductive process" (page 84.). Thus, the impact of "other" (in addition to the reproduction of capital) causes of crises is reduced to the influence of natural conditions.

5. According to Preobrazhensky reproduction of fixed capital is not only the main, a direct and immediate cause of crises, not only explains the necessity of crises, not only determines the structure of the capitalist cycle, but also explains the *frequency* of crises. Moreover, Preobrazhensky attributes his own discoveries to Marx. "He is (Marx. LK) credited with formulating the position that the *periodicity* of the capitalist crisis is due to the uneven distribution over time of reproduction of fixed capital" (p. 25).

Earlier we saw how Preobrazhensky supplemented Marx in those parts of the theory of crises, which, according to Preobrazhensky remained undeveloped in Marx. Now we are witnessing how our author attributes to Marx a position that Marx not only could not share, but against which he directly spoke with certainty. Marx points out conditions that make it necessary for the crisis to occur, and which determine the *frequency* of crises. The reproduction of fixed capital plays an important role but is not the main, not the basic, not the crucial factor, as it appears to Preobrazhensky. Below I will focus more on how Marx treats the problem of fixed capital in the cycle.

6. After all that has been mentioned it is clear that in his conception of a crisis, Preobrazhensky completely misses the point of how the transitory nature of the capitalist mode of production is established. Each cyclical crisis shaking the capitalist system, reminds us of the historical limitations of its existence and at the same time sharpens all capitalist tendencies and contradictions which bring capitalism to ruin. Preobrazhensky, at least for crises in pre-monopoly capitalism, stresses and gives prominence to the other side of crises, the ease with which they are overcome and their temporary nature, their narrow economic importance and, moreover, views them not so much negatively as positively. In other words, Preobrazhensky's assessment of the significance of the crisis for capitalism is essentially apologetic.

"For capitalism, once it already exists, it is not this alternation of highs and lows that is dangerous, what is dangerous is a standstill in the transition from a crisis to recovery, to depression, because a decline of production in itself is the greatest factor in long-term market contraction, if the system does not have sufficient incentives to break out of depression" ... *But - Preobrazhensky says soothingly - such a stimulus exists.*

"Lower prices and fast technical progress, mercilessly strangling all backward enterprises, is the mechanism that facilitates the preparation for a new upsurge on the basis of orders for new fixed capital" (p. 42).

7. It follows from the above that in Preobrazhensky's formulation, which can be described as an underestimation of the revolutionizing significance of each crisis, the significance of the crisis lies in changing the interclass relations, especially relations between the proletariat and the bourgeoisie, the significance of the crisis as a factor in the revolutionary upheavals of capitalist society. For Preobrazhensky crisis, at least in the environment of free competition, passes with barely perceptible consequences for the capitalist society. According to Preobrazhensky in a crisis the "real loss is ... reduced to ruination of some reserves of the means of production (e.g., spontaneous combustion of coal, etc...) and to insufficient employment of the potential labor force in the next cycle in the branches manufacturing means of production! (P. 22).

Elsewhere Preobrazhensky stresses that the negative impact of the crises on the working class is shortlived and gets over quickly - an assertion amazing for its frank apologetic conclusion. But Preobrazhensky makes and must make this conclusion, as he occupies a mechanistic and anti-Marxist position on the theory of reproduction and crises. Logic requires it. If the crisis is not due to the totality of capitalist contradictions - if it is not seen as something imposing its stamp on all aspects of capitalist reality, but is due to the conditions of reproduction of fixed capital, taken in isolation from the inherent capitalist antagonisms — then the revolutionary significance of the crisis is inevitably misunderstood and blurred.

Having developed his "the schema of economic cycle under free competition" (Ch. VI) and having proceeded to the presentation of the "economic cycle schema under monopoly conditions" (Ch. VII), our author in advance attacks the inevitable criticism that can be levelled against its theoretical constructs in the following angry tirade:

"In our economic literature, instead of laying bare the process of how a typical economic crisis under capitalism inherently follows from the general structure of capitalism, many often get off with a mere repetition of the general Marxist thesis that capitalist crises are explained by the contradiction between the social character of production and the private character of appropriation. Meanwhile, the whole problem is precisely to uncover the specific economic content of this formulation, and analyse it in relation to the cycle under classical capitalism, and in the period of imperialism ... In this paper, I give my version of the construction of this theme. I would consider it worthy of serious attention only to such criticism, which could counterpoise this construction by some other" (pp. 80-81).

Is it possible to counter Probrazhensky's constructions of the cycles in the epoch of free competition and in the era of imperialism? Is Marxist-Leninist economic thought so poor, that it can do nothing to oppose the impotent Trotskyist schema used by Preobrazhensky? Certainly it can. And it is no different against a boastful Trotskyism and it can and should be exposed by a genuine Marxist-Leninist understanding of the nature of the cycles and of crises in the different stages of development of capitalism.

Of course, if we restrict ourselves to multiple repetitions of the thesis of Marx - Engels - Lenin about the contradictions between the social character of production and the private form of appropriation for the understanding of the crises, then it gives us very little. It is just Preobrazhensky who in his book demonstrates that he is unable to concretize the initial argument. It is Preobrazhensky who fails to understand all the wealth, all the content and comprehensive strength of the Marxist-Leninist position and fails to discover its "specific economic content." That is why Preobrazhensky believes that Marx did not complete both his theory of reproduction and the theory of crisis and that Marx left behind, on the question of crises, just some general methodological positions and isolated views, some fragmentary notes.

Not having the possibility to reproduce here the Marxist-Leninist theory of cycles and of crises in all their brilliant versatility, I will confine myself to a brief depiction of the substance of this theory of crises and the *revolutionary character* of this theory; even a short reproduction of the Marxist-Leninist theory of crises will make it possible to see clearly that Preobrazhensky does not understand Marx and Lenin and that he is actually revising them and creating his own theory of cycles and crises – a caricature of Marxism.

From the standpoint of Marx, Engels and Lenin the common cause of crises — the contradiction between the social character of production and the private form of appropriation - is the 'really *basic, immanent* contradiction of capitalism, that *includes* all concrete contradictions of capitalism. This basic contradiction gets concretized in multiple individual contradictions of capitalism: between anarchy of the social and the despotism of the industrial division of labor; between the growth of productive forces, resulting in an increase of the organic composition of capital and a consequent lowering of the rate of profit; between the need for a limitless expansion of production and the limited size of available capital; between increasing production and increasing, at the other pole, of the working class poverty, in other words, between production and mass consumption; between the need for proportionality in the process of reproduction and the inevitable imbalances in conditions of the capitalist anarchy of production and so on.

All these contradictions are expressions, concrete moments of the main, the most profound, decisive contradiction - between the social character of production and the private form of appropriation.

And precisely because it is the basic contradiction contained in all the concrete contradictions, it involves these specific conflicts, which is why it is - and it alone - can act as causes of the crisis.

The movement, the self-movement of this fundamental contradiction leads inevitably to that that a certain stage capitalist production reaches its limit, the point where contradictions are exacerbated to an extreme degree.

And then the crisis breaks out, which represents a real connection and forceful equalization of all the contradictions of bourgeois economy. *"For capitalism a crisis is necessary to create a constantly disturbed proportion."* (Lenin. *Collected Works*, Vol. III, p. 511)

The crisis temporarily removes this limit and by providing existing capital *"delays the lowering of the rate of profit and accelerates the accumulation of capital value by the formation of new capital"*. But by forcibly equalizing the contradictions, the crisis at the same time makes it the only way in which the conditions for a new crisis are created.

Thus, the movement of the main capitalist contradiction between the social character of production and the private character of appropriation, not only reveals the deepest cause of the crisis, but also determines the periodicity of capitalist crises. The frequency of crises is created by the self-movement of the main contradictions of the capitalist mode of production. In the necessity of crises is given the necessity of their periodicity. The theory of crises of Marx, Engels, Lenin certainly is in irreconcilable conflict with all sorts of theories that try to explain the nature of the crises by any one feature of capitalism, whether under-consumption, reproduction of fixed capital or anything else ...

The theory of Marx - Engels - Lenin explains the capitalist crises by self-movement of this most general capitalist contradiction, and reveals at the same time the possibility of crises and their necessity under capitalism.

The same theory gives an exhaustive answer to the question about the actual role of the reproduction of fixed capital in the capitalist cycle and in the capitalist crisis. This theory does not underestimate the role of fixed capital in the capitalist cycle; it only fixes its proper place and importance in the overall effect of other conditions and factors. Let me remind you here of the two instances from two letters of Marx and Engels, where the former specifically examines the role of fixed capital in the capitalist cycle. In a letter dated 2 / III 1858 Marx asks Engels about the average duration in which the equipment is upgraded, and writes that this fact "is an important factor in explaining the multiple cycles through which industrial development occurs from the time that large scale industry was created". (Marx and Engels. *Collected Works*, Vol. XXII, p. 312)

In a letter dated 5 / III 1858, having received from Engels calculations made on the subject, Marx wrote: "The figure of 13 years corresponds to the theory, since such compliance is necessary, that it gives the *unit for measurement* of one epoch of industrial reproduction, coinciding more or less with periods of recurring large crises, the movement of which, of course, from the point of view of intervals between them, is determined by very different moments. But it is important for me that there is one point in the immediate material preconditions of large-scale industry, defining these cycles." (Italics Marx, ibid, pp. 315 -316.)

Marx does not underestimate the role of fixed capital in the cycle. He emphasizes the increase in the share of production of fixed capital in the total production. He notes that the industries producing the elements of fixed capital, played a leading role in the cycle. He shows that in this connection, the duration of the cycle more or less coincides with the average period of functioning of the fixed capital. But this does not mean that cyclical nature is due to the dynamics of fixed capital as Preobrazhensky tries to show. Upgradation of fixed capital is a consequence of the crisis. The movement of fixed capital reflected the general laws of the cycle and is composed of the totality of capitalist contradictions. The frequency of crises cannot be explained exclusively from the conditions of reproduction of fixed capital. It follows from the general causes of the crisis, and that is ultimately from the contradiction between the social character of production and the private form of appropriation, no, specific reason periodicity than the causes of the crisis does not exist.

The main features of the Marxist-Leninist explanation of crises consists in the fact that it:

1. Takes as a basis, the fact that the causes of the crisis are not an arbitrarily chosen single or a series of separate contradictions of capitalism, but the totality of capitalist contradictions, takes not the external reasons for the crisis, but reveals the inner, deepest reasons and takes into account not a what is derivative and secondary, but what is basic and important.

2. Consistently gives the *class* relations of productive relations of capitalism, emphasizes the class nature of the capitalist contradictions and thus expresses the laws of the dynamics of capitalism and crises in the language of the class struggle. Suffice it to recall Engels: "*The contradiction between socialized production and capitalist appropriation is expressed in the antagonism between the proletariat and the bourgeoisie.*" (Engels. *Anti-Dühring*, p. 256)

3. The theory of cycles and crises of Marx, Engels, Lenin is a revolutionary critique of capitalism, for it reveals the limitations of the capitalist mode of production, the movement and the growth of its contradictions, preparing the downfall of capitalism, for it sees every crisis, as Marx aptly puts it, to be a reminder to the bourgeoisie of the relativity and temporality of its domination.

4. This theory is strongly opposed to any attempt to treat the cycles and crises of capitalism as a monotonous repetition of the constant, always equal to themselves phenomena. Exposing the deepest foundations of the crises, reducing them to the movement of the internal contradictions of capitalism, this theory emphasizes in a crisis, firstly, that every crisis reveals the relativity and the historically limited nature of the capitalist mode of production; secondly the fact that crises are becoming more frequent; and thirdly the fact that each new capitalist crisis is a new step toward the collapse of capitalism, since it develops and sharpens all of the internal contradictions of capitalism.

5. This theory, while giving an explanation of capitalist cycles and crises, not only fully reveals their economic nature and the laws of motion, it always pays close attention to the aggravation of class antagonisms through crises, to processes escalating the crisis in the revolutionary upheavals, and so on. It is worth quoting here the most striking places from fundamental works of the founders.

"Finally, to the same extent that the above course of development is forcing the capitalists to exploit the already existing gigantic means of production on an ever larger scale and for purpose sets all the levers of credit in motion, to the same degree making the earthquakes more frequent, from which the trading world can only be saved by sacrificing to the underground gods a part of the wealth, products and even of productive forces, in short, frequently occurring crises ..." (Marx. *W*age Labour and Capital. *Coll. Works*., Vol. V, p. 444)

"Capital lives but not only due to labour: like a noble barbarian slaveholder, it carries with him into the grave the corpses of its slaves, whole hecatombs of workers who perish in the crises. * (Marx. Wage Labour and Capital. *Coll. Works*, Vol. V, p. 444)

"If capital is at a standstill, the industry not only stops, but is moved back and the worker is the first victim of this phenomenon. He dies before the capitalist." (Marx. On Freedom of Trade. *Coll. Works*, Vol.V, p. 454)

If it is impossible to argue for the inevitable co-occurence of a capitalist crisis with a revolution, if I cannot talk about the inevitability of the transformation of an economic crisis into a revolution, then one can and should consider crises, shaking the entire capitalist system, as periods when the preconditions for revolutionary upheavals are created.

"Since the beginning of this century, the industry is constantly fluctuating between ages of prosperity and times of crisis, and almost regularly every five to seven years such a crisis has occurred, which has always been connected to a terrible disaster for the workers, to the general revolutionary exuberance and to the greatest threat to the entirety of the existing situation ". (Engels. The Principles of Communism. *Coll. Works,* Vol.V, p. 571)

Elsewhere Engels wrote:
"Such a revolution (a real revolution. L. K) is possible only in such periods when both these factors, ie. the modern productive forces and the bourgeois forms of production, come into conflict with each other ... A new revolution is only possible after a new crisis. But its advance is as inevitable, as the last attack * (Vol.VIII, p. 239)

Marx and Engels specifically linked the Revolution of 1848 to the general crisis in England."
"The second great economic event that hastened the explosion of the revolution (LK talking about the revolution of 1848), was a general commercial and industrial crisis in England." (Marx. The Class Struggles in France. *Coll. Works*, Vol. VIII, p. 81)

"Anyway there is no doubt that the commercial crisis facilitated the revolution in 1848 far more, than the other way round, the revolution - trade crisis." (Vol. VIII, p 226)

Marx and Engels associated the future revolution with crises.
"In fact, the abolition of the law of 1847, will involve manufacturers in such a fever of accelerated production that crises will come one after another, so that very soon all the tools and resources of the modern system will be exhausted and a revolution will inevitably break out that will change the society much more radically than the revolution of 1793 and in 1848, and quickly lead to political and social domination of the proletariat." (Engels. Ten hour worktime. *Coll. Works*, Vol. VIII, p. 99)

In observations of international situation in 1850, Marx and Engels, asserting an impending crisis, again connected the crisis with large scale conflict on the continent, with the "revolution on the continent." (Collected Works, Vol. VIII). One of the reviews by Marx and Engels is concluded with the following summary:

"Political developments in the continent insistently need to be addressed with every passing day, and the coincidence of a commercial crisis and the revolution, which has repeatedly been asserted in this review becomes ever more inevitable." (*Coll. Works.*, Vol. VII, p. 218)

Lenin also always stressed the importance of crisis for the revolutionary struggle.

"Without a common ground of an agrarian crisis in the country and the depression in industry, there is no possibility of a deep political crisis. " (Coll. Works, Vol. III, p. 93)

"Capitalism successfully takes care that crises occur frequently, a situation which this army will make use of (the army of the proletariat. LK) for the destruction of capitalism."

After all of the above it s not difficult to give a general characterization of Preobrazhensky's theory of crises. Moreover, Preobrazhensky himself makes this task easier. Preobrazhensky twice (note on page 37 —38 and page 55) indicates the true source of his revisionist inspiration. "I consider it my duty to mention a very important service rendered by comrade Spectator in that he is among the few economists who stress the critical role of the main process of reproduction of fixed capital both for theory of reproduction and the theory of crises" (note on p. 38). Meanwhile, we all know that in the theory of crises Spectator slips into the positions of social-fascist Hilferding, who considers Marx's theory of reproduction to be a theory of proportionality and crises as a violation of that proportionality.

In addition to these basics, the roots of which go back to Hilferding, Preobrazhensky's theory of reproduction includes Luxemburgian motives. I shall mention only the most important. Contrary to the Marxist-Leninist method that correctly distinguishes the problem of reproduction and the problem of the significance of external markets for capitalist development, Preobrazhensky, following in the footsteps of Rosa Luxemburg, straight away sets the first — reproduction — in direct connection with the second: *"So, if the opening of various new territories for development of capitalism played a role in the issue of realisation, it is not the absolute value of these areas in capitalist trade, but because ultimately the expansion of markets in the colonies allowed a far greater amount of expansion of market for capitalism within capitalism itself "* (. 15). External market, Preobrazhensky writes in another place, plays the same supporting role for capitalism which a small projection between the steps of a staircase plays, that raises a man with a load; the ledge helps a man to rise up and stand on the next step; foreign markets help to raise the productive forces of capitalism onto following stage of expanded reproduction. It is easy to see, that the difference between Rosa Luxemburg and Preobrazhensky is a difference just one of magnitude, but in principle, both recognise the thesis of impossibility of reproduction and realisation within the capitalist circle, devoid of "projections".

Substituting Marx's theory of crises with an eclectic stew of Hilferding and Rosa Luxemburg, Preobrazhensky entirely follows his teacher Trotsky. In the report of comrade Serebryakov it has been shown that it is from Hilferding and Rosa Luxemburg that Trotsky draws his wisdom in explaining crises. When Preobrazhensky explains the crisis of reproduction of fixed capital, he again copies Trotsky. He echoes Trotsky and his arguments that Marx left no complete theory of crises, but only scattered hints. And even in the praise lavished on Spectator, Preobrazhensky follows Trotsky. Preobrazhensky's whole theory of crises - from a methodological starting point - "equilibrium theory" to its last findings - is *Trotskyist theory of crises.*

II. LENIN'S THEORY OF IMPERIALISM AND PREOBRAZHENSKY'S TROTSKYITE THEORY OF IMPERIALISM

In his theory of imperialism, while verbally recognizing the Leninist theory of imperialism, Preobrazhensky in fact breaks with Leninism and opposes it.

I. Lenin, in his theory of imperialism, gives a detailed description of all the contradictions of monopoly capitalism, because the great variety of internal contradictions, their exceptional sharpness and strength make up one of the most characteristic features of imperialism. Among these contradictions that Lenin with extreme urgency emphasizes and promotes as the most profound and fundamental is the contradiction between monopolies and the competition coexisting along with them. Lenin while fighting against opportunism, reveals the "most profound and fundamental contradictions of imperialism: the contradiction between the monopolies and free competition existing alongside them between gigantic "operations " (and gigantic profits) of finance capital and "honest" trade in the open market, between the cartels and trusts on the one hand and non-cartelized industry, on the other, and so on ". (Coll. Works, Vol. XIII, p. 328.)

The obligation to recognize this contradiction, as a characteristic feature of imperialism, in Lenin follows from his theory of capitalist monopolies - the essence of imperialism. According to Lenin, monopoly cannot completely oust competition and must exist above it and alongside it, because "it is a capitalist monopoly, i.e. it has grown out of capitalism and exists in the general environment of capitalism, commodity production and competition, in permanent and hopeless conflict with the overall situation. " (Coll. Works, Vol. XII, p. 314) Underlining this, Lenin mocked all sorts of schema (whether the schema of ultra renegade Kautsky or schema of "state capitalist trusts" of Bukharin) that originate from the possibility of destroying competition among monopolies, from the conception of a pure monopoly, a pure imperialism.

Preobrazhensky on this issue holds a different opinion. However, in his book, Preobrazhensky talks about many modes in imperialism, mentions that "the monopoly can never completely destroy free competition" (p. 32). But all such reservations and declarations by Preobrazhensky are irrelevant. They only cover up his anti-Leninist construction. In fact, when it comes to the theoretical analysis of certain aspects of imperialism, Preobrazhensky almost completely discards the contradiction between monopoly and competition. Thus, for example, posing for himself the question, "how can there be any industrial expansion under monopolism", Preobrazhensky accompanies it with the following methodological remark: "We will try to analyse this issue, first on the basis of the prerequisites of pure capitalism at the stage of monopolism." And not to leave any doubt about the fact that the theoretical analysis of Preobrazhensky comes from the schema of pure imperialism, in another part of his book he states bluntly: *"The question now is what elements of industrial expansion may exist in the era of monopoly? We will talk about pure monopoly* "(p. 43). Below I'll show that Preobrazhensky's conclusions regarding the sharp drop in the pace of development under imperialism, the resolution of cyclical form of movement of imperialism, the termination of economic development and so on are closely linked with the methodological approach of

Preobrazhensky to imperialism as a pure monopoly.

This approach can also be seen in the 'revisionist teachings of Preobrazhensky on the operation of the law of value under monopoly capitalism. Following his early tradition, Preobrazhensky in his latest book examines the law of value only as a regulator of the capitalist economy, i.e. examines it in a one-sided, mechanistic manner, rather than treat it as a law of contradictory motion of capitalism. With respect to the operation of the law of value in conditions of imperialism Preobrazhensky rests (p. 35) essentially on his old position, the essence of which boils down to the thesis that monopolies *limit* the effect of the law of value. Recall his argument of the "New Economy":

> *"Restrictions on freedom of competition also lead to limiting the operation of the law of value, to the fact that on a number of occasions it encounters obstacles to its manifestation and partially takes on only that form of production and distribution, which is possible under capitalism"* (p. 182).

Limitation of the law of value, i.e. the spontaneous law of motion of capitalism, means that spontaneity gives way to a monopolistic organization, that the movement of capitalism in its monopoly stage is not complicated by growing internal contradictions, and gradually becomes to from them. But these assertions represent pure revision of Leninism. Such an interpretation is at the same time deeply akin to the theory of "organized capitalism" and the conception of the automatic collapse of capitalism, which, as is known, are preached by Trotskyists.

It goes without saying that the Marxist-Leninist understanding of the law of motion of capitalism in its monopoly stage has nothing to do with the theory of limitation of the law of value. Everyone knows how vigorously he emphasized the idea that the movement of monopoly capitalism becomes ever more anarchic, conflictual, impetuous and catastrophic.

It is a hopeless enterprise to try to reconcile this statement of Lenin's theory of movement of imperialism with the theory of limitation of operation of the law of value in the epoch of imperialism. Between Lenin and Preobrazhensky there are no points of contact. The idea that each new stage of commodity-capitalist economy develops, complicates and distorts the operation of the law of value, rather than eliminate it, is brilliantly expressed by Engels, when he wrote in Anti-Duhring (page 257). With the appearance of capitalism on the historical stage, the laws of commodity production, as long as they were, immersed in slumber, began to act with more force and clarity ... Anarchy of social production emerged and took on larger and larger proportions. Meanwhile, the chief instrument by which capitalism has intensified the anarchy in social production, represented the direct opposite of anarchy: it consisted in strengthening the social organization of production in every individual enterprise. "

Monopoly capitalism propelled forward the "strengthening of the social organization of production," but, in spite of Preobrazhensky, it does not lead to restriction of the law of value, but to a deepening, expansion and increasing complexity of the law and of the contradictions contained in it.

2. Preobrazhensky breaks with Leninism also in his interpretation of the law of uneven development under imperialism. The law of uneven development occupies a prominent place in the Leninist theory of imperialism. As is well known, Lenin links with this law tension generated by all the contradictions of imperialism, the spontaneity, conflict and crisis in the movement of monopoly capitalism; he associated with it the trend towards stagnation under imperialism; on this basis he built his brilliant theory of the victory of socialism in several or even in one single country. Lenin's understanding of the law of uneven development of imperialism almost allowed the Leninist Party to achieve great successes in building socialism in the USSR and in the advancement of the world socialist revolution. On the other hand - anti-Leninist understanding of the law of uneven development was, along with everything else, based on theoretical and practical bankruptcy of the Trotskyist opposition.

What does Preobrazhensky contribute to the understanding of the law of uneven development under imperialism? Nothing, absolutely nothing, except for those trinkets and trifles that appear under the label "law of uneven development".

Indeed. Preobrazhensky mentions law of uneven development in a number of places (p. 134, 55-56, 60, 81, 82, 83, 84, 86, 95, 102 etc.). For the most part, however, the law is only mentioned by him, or he only declares the need to consider the impact of this law on the process of capitalist reproduction. Preobrazhensky makes just one or two attempts to speak on the substance of the law. But the facts that he provides here is a very weak shadow of the real law of uneven development under imperialism - this "decisive force" of monopoly capitalism.

Basically Preobrazhensky just reduces the law of uneven development, to the unevenness of the reproduction of fixed capital (p. 82, 83, etc.).

In his theoretical analysis of imperialism Preobrazhensky takes into account the law of unevenness and does so mostly and only in the sense of uneven reproduction and an increase of fixed capital. Meanwhile, there is no doubt that if it is impossible to confine the all-pervading[3] law of uneven development of capitalism (the uneven development of enterprises, industries, countries, uneven development, not only economic but also political, and so on) to the particular facts of uneven reproduction of capital, then, on the other hand, it is completely wrong to see only unevenness in the reproduction of the fixed capital. The unevenness of capitalist development - is only one side, is one of the definitions of the capitalist relations of production, seen in movement. And in the reproduction of fixed capital, along with the unevenness there is uniformity in the same way as for example, the law of value also includes the denial of the organization of capitalism and a particular kind of its spontaneous organization.

Preobrazhensky's understanding of the law of unevenness has nothing in common with Lenin's understanding of the law, as it can be seen from the opposite effects, which stem from the law of unevenness in Lenin and Preobrazhensky. The law of unevenness for Lenin causes spasmodic gain, crises and catastrophic development; For Preobrazhensky the consequence of the strengthening of the law of uneveness in the era of imperialism (the uneven reproduction of capital) is the attenuation of the capitalist curve, reducing the cyclic waves, breakdown of the cyclical form of movement and a return to the schema of simple reproduction. What is this, if not decisive negation of the significance of the law of unevenness in the era of imperialism?

New evidence of Preobrazhensky's misunderstanding the law of unevenness is his "objection" against the theory of ultra-imperialism (p. 34). It is known that the battering ram of the law of uneven development of Lenin completely defeated the Social-fascist theory of ultra-imperialism. It is clear that along with this argument against the mentioned theory, all other arguments appear as partial and less significant. Preobrazhensky held a different opinion. In the critique of ultra-imperialism he makes no mention of the law of unevenness at all. Preobrazhensky thinks it is sufficient to overturn the theory of ultra-capitalism merely by a reference to an assertion of "the impossibility of complete elimination of competition" (p. 34).

Thus, if we ignore some of Preobrazhensky's purely verbal, purely formal assertions on the recognition of uneven development under imperialism, and take the essence of Preobrazhensky's interpretation of the law of uneven development, one necessarily comes to the conclusion: Preobrazhensky does not understand the law of unevenness, and not only did he underestimate its operation (and strengthening) in the era of imperialism, but ultimately ignores the very law of unevenness for monopoly capitalism.

Thus, Preobrazhensky again finds himself in the company of Trotskyites and supporters of social-fascist theory of organized capitalism, who, as we know, deny the strengthening of the law of unevenness development under imperialism.

3. In his book, Preobrazhensky demonstrated a lack of understanding of the Leninist doctrine of the decay of imperialism. Lenin considered parasitism and decay of the latter as one of the essential aspects of imperialism.

Under imperialism the seal of *parasitism* is put on whole sections of the bourgeoisie, and even on whole countries i.e. the imprint of a complete separation of capital-property from its direct operation, imprint of coupon slicers. Appropriation of surplus value and its consumption - these are the characteristics of these layers and rentier countries. The *decay* of monopoly capitalism Lenin saw in the fact that the form of "private economic and private property relations" no longer corresponds to the content of "socialization of production," and therefore it decays. This decay occurs across the whole of private property relations. In particular, this decay is expressed in the tendency to stagnation in the development of the productive forces in individual enterprises, sectors, individual countries; more than that, "At a certain period of time, it (this trend. LK) has the upper hand." (*Coll. Works.*, 1st edition, Vol. XIII, p. 314)

It should be emphasized that Lenin never equated decay and complete stagnation, the decay and full suspension of growth of the productive forces. Based on the fact that monopoly can never eliminate competition, based on the fact that the increase in profits through technical improvements cannot but act in the direction of change, based finally on the fact that an enormous intensification of the contradictions characteristic of imperialism, are "a powerful driving force of the transitional historical period "(*Coll. Works*, Vol. XIII, page 333), Lenin comes to the following conclusion:

"It would be a mistake to think that this tendency to decay precludes rapid growth of capitalism: no, certain branches of industry, individual sections of the bourgeoisie and certain countries display in the era of imperialism, to a more or less degree, now one and then another of these tendencies. On the whole, capitalism invariably grows, faster than before, but this growth is not only becoming more and more uneven in general, but the unevenness is also evident, in particular, in the decay of the countries most abundant in capital (England)." (*Coll. Works*, Vol. XIII, p. 333)

Preobrazhensky, in contrast to Lenin, equates the rot and stoppage ("throttling") of development of the productive forces in the imperialist epoch.

"Monopolistic form of organization of production stifles development of the productive forces of society" (p 144) - says Preobrazhensky. And it is not an accidental slip of the pen, an unsuccessfully formulated phrase - such flowers decorate the whole of Preobrazhensky's book[4]. 'But to treat the capitalist monopolies, which, as we know, are neither absolute nor solid, as a form that excludes any progress, any movement, equal to stifling of the productive forces, it means to break also from evidence given in this respect by experience and at the same time, from the contribution of Lenin on this point. The capitalist monopolies, creating a tendency to decay, to a partial and temporary delay of the productive forces are still just a specific form of motion, rather than simple stagnation, of capitalism, unevenness, conflict, spontaneity, abruptness, but still a movement. E. Preobrazhensky holds a different opinion. Trotskyist wisdom: if there is a monopoly - then what follows is full suspension of movement, absolute stagnation, a complete stifling of development of productive forces – and this is completely reproduced by him.

The thesis equating the decay with the suspension of development of the productive forces in the epoch of imperialism, of course consistently follows from Preobrazhenky's representation of imperialism as a pure monopoly, of his representation of the limitation of operation of the law of value, of his ideas about the monopoly form, as the form excluding any movement of the productive forces, and so on. This thesis of course coincides with the statements of Trotsky, but this thesis has nothing to do with the actual tendencies of imperialism and serves as a theoretical basis for anti-communist practices.

4. Revisionists must admit to the views of Preobrazhensky, developed by him on the conditions of the working class. Preobrazhensky manages simultaneously to "revise" Marxism-Leninism on this issue both in terms of capitalism under free competition, and in relation to the era of monopoly capitalism. According to the theory of Marx and Lenin, in the course of capitalist development, accompanied by the displacement of humans by machines, the growth of division of labour, the growing use of female and child labour, decreasing qualification of the workers, increasing army of the unemployed, etc., pay cuts and lowering of the living standards of the working class occurs necessarily. This involves both relative and absolute impoverishment. For Marxist-Leninists, Marx's law is still considered axiomatic. Preobrazhensky - and we know he is not alone - holds a different opinion.

He bluntly rejects Marx's law of the deteriorating conditions of the working class, developed by Marx as a general tendency for capitalism as a whole, *i.e.* for capitalism in all its phases. Preobrazhensky wrote (for the era of imperialism): "*As a result, wage rise even of the top and the best paid workers in the advanced capitalist countries is suspended, replaced by a tendency to fall systematically*" (page 146). Already from this thesis it can be concluded that Preobrazhensky considers an increase in the level of wages and the improvement of the working class to be characteristic features for pre-monopoly capitalism. But in another place he openly expresses it himself:

> "*In the era of free competition ..., due to the rapid deployment of industry, big demand for labour was relatively higher than in the era of monopoly, and wages, albeit slowly, but increased in the developed capitalist countries also for this reason. This is not a conjunctural fact from concrete history of capitalism, irrelevant for theoretical analysis, but a very important fact of a fundamental nature, because a more rapid increase in production and a rapid retraction of the labour force in the production and growth of not only the number of workers and the total salary fund, but also of wages of separate workers - all are elements of a single whole, elements and characteristics of the entire system of capitalism in the era of free competition ... The growing number of workers and average wage growth in the advanced capitalist countries is an inseparable part of the peculiar and historically unique moment, that expanded*

reproduction was in the era free competition. " (pp. 41–42)

Our "theoretician", as we see, follows the apologetic bourgeois statistics, and can see only the dynamics of the wages of the top layer of the workers of individual advanced capitalist countries, and swims *against the current*, against the "conjectural" tendencies of capitalism under free competition, the tendency toward decreasing wages and deterioration of the position of the working class. Thus, in respect of pre-monopoly capitalism, Preobrazhensky frankly revises one of the central points of the Marxist-Leninist theory. He "courageously" joins in this regard the company of a number of top-notch revisionists and opportunists - Bernstein, Kautsky and all modern social-fascists.

But Preobrazhensky also tries to distort the question of trends in wages (and the position) of the working class) in the epoch of imperialism, although, as we have seen here, he talks about suspension of raise in wages, and even the tendency to systematic reduction. The fact is that whenever Preobrazhensky begins to explain the reasons for this feature of downward trend in wages in the period of imperialism, he slips into the position of the social theory of distribution that is now so fashionable among the social-fascists. Preobrazhensky wrote: "*In monopoly capitalism, the main change here is that the balance of forces between the capitalist class and the proletariat has changed to the disadvantage of the latter*" (p. 46), because at the same time that workers oppose capitalists with the old trade unions (weakened by the betrayal of the union officials), the capitalists oppose the workers using the increasing power of capital organised in trusts.

All of this, to say the least, is very ambiguously and suspiciously formulated. Wages depend on the balance of force? Good. Well, is the law of value of labour power valid or not valid in the epoch of imperialism? Preobrazhensky is silent, although he will have to speak out here, because we already know that he in all his works he holds the view of limitation of the law of value in the era of imperialism. Wages are determined by balance of forces? Good. Well, is labour power a commodity? Preobrazhensky is silent, although he should be saying something, for as slipping into the theory of "organized capitalism", he must by elementary logic arrive at the theory of constraints to transformation of labour power into a commodity. Underlining the dependence of wages on the balance of "force" while concealing fundamental problems of wages (The law of value of labour power, problems of exploitation, of capital accumulation, etc.) brings Preobrazhensky to the social theory of wages of Social Fascists: The fact that in this case the Social Fascists speak about the tendency of wages to increase, and Preobrazhensky – of a downward trend, is not critical: with the wrong approach to the problem contradictory findings often and quickly pass one into the other.

Certainly monopoly associations are an important factor in the deviations of wages below the cost of labour power, of course, and a number of other factors act in the same direction, but this is on the basis of the immanent laws of capitalism and all this is closely connected with the law of the value of labour power.

5. The centre of gravity of the Preobrazhensky's book lies undoubtedly in the analysis of natural *cycles and crises* of monopoly capitalism. In this area, the Preobrazhensky does not make mistakes "unexpectedly", but consciously puts forward a new theory of the development of imperialism, as he puts it (p. 43). "from the view of the general theory of capitalist reproduction by Marx applied to the era of imperialism".

The starting point here is Preobrazhensky's thesis of the accumulation of excess stock of fixed capital.

"It is precisely due to the existence of monopoly and competition next to each other that I explain partly such a rapid accumulation of excess fixed capital under imperialism - a fact having so much importance in the process of deformation of the cycle under imperialism, and in changing the nature capitalist crises. " (p. 35)

But how and why under imperialism does an excess of fixed capital accumulate? Monopoly, says Preobrazhensky, is characterised by the desire to meet the demand of cyclic expansions of existing enterprises by increased production and the desire to prevent the emergence of new enterprises during the upswings. Therefore, monopolies should always have maximum reserves of fixed capital. *The huge increase in reserves of fixed capital ... inherently derives from the very structure of monopoly capitalism "*(p. 36) and *"is of paramount importance for the understanding of the whole system of reproduction under imperialism"* (p. 54)

Due to this excess of fixed capital economic recovery is very rickety and *"rarely* able to grow automatically into an economic upswing" (p. 63). *Only in some countries* it may happen that the recovery will develop into an upswing.

But such an *upswing* will turn out to be very sluggish. If in the era of free competition, new construction began in period of early recovery (as determined by the free competition regime and the insignificant reserves of fixed capital), now upgradation and increase of fixed capital occurs - if it's going happen at all - at the time of the upswing itself, mainly in its second phase, just before another crisis. This postponement of reproduction of capital weakens the robustness of the upswing and along with it delays the "crisis".

The depressive phase of the cycle under monopoly conditions significantly changes its character. If the depression phase under free competition era of capitalism was characterized by the fact that within it the critical contraction of production mostly ended and that restarted the movement in an ascending trajectory, in the monopoly era, when there is no demand for fixed capital, depression functions to eliminate only that part of the excess in the production sphere, which was created by the crisis.

Changing the conditions of reproduction of fixed capital under imperialism leads to a change in the nature of the crisis. Since monopoly capitalism "*enters into a crisis after the increase of capital*" (p. 95), the presence of an excess of fixed capital "now weighs down on it and makes it difficult to move forward" (p. 95), i.e. makes it difficult to exit from the crisis. "The crisis has to eliminate the swelling of the productive apparatus, which happened during the upswing." But it's just hard to do so, since monopoly capitalism "*loses a very important incentive in terms of potency and time to end the crisis*" (p. 64). If in the pre-monopoly period re-equipment has always acted as an important natural impulse for the weakening of the crisis, then now, since the increase in demand for fixed capital does not come in times of crisis, but earlier, this incentive disappears - hence the tendency to a prolongation of the crisis and in fact to its transformation into a permanent crisis.

If Preobrazhensky had thought his "concept" through to the end, he would have inevitably come to the conclusion about the impossibility of direct recovery and cyclical movements in general. He does not want, however, to openly declare so soon this explicitly anti-Marxist thesis. He tries to find the possibility of recovery under imperialism. But here he is helpless to do so with the help of his theory.

"The question is (how can a long recovery turning into an upswing,

LK?) is of exceptional difficulty, and I must frankly confess to the reader that I have not understood it completely". (page 51 -52)

However, without explaining the question, Preobrazhensky tries to offer the readers options for its solutions. There are two options. Either an upswing on the basis of orders for new equipment: "*In this case, increasing reserves of fixed capital are deployed before the crisis. It is this process of increasing stock of fixed capital can either turn the economic recovery into an economic expansion or throttle and temporarily postpone the looming crisis*" (p. 53), or an upswing through expansion of the foreign market: "With just such a non-uniformity in the distribution of the rate of movement, separate parts of the world can experience the state of a long recovery, translating into an upswing, despite the countering factor in the form of accumulation of huge reserves of fixed capital". (p. 56)

But all this does not help Preobrazhensky. The first option comes into irreconcilable contradiction with his main thesis that it is the accumulation of fixed capital reserves specifically the shifting demand for fixed capital at the end of the upswing makes the next upswing impossible. The second option does not answer the question: how is a general upswing possible under imperialism? As a result, for Preobrazhensky, the upswing under monopoly capitalism must be impossible. Along with this crisis and cyclicity in general becomes impossible.

At the root of all relevant constructs of the Preobrazhensky is the bourgeois and social-fascist idea about the disappearance of cyclical form of movement under capitalism at the highest stage of its development, an idea, the strongest preacher of which has consistently been Trotsky. Preobrazhensky directly formulates this idea.

Under conditions of monopoly, "*the capitalist system will tend to incline more and more to the conditions of simple reproduction*" (p. 95). "The whole capitalist system ... must enter conditions when gradually the *cyclical form of movement itself is absorbed* (if capitalism survives until then), when the gradual economic development is suspended, and the trend to simple reproduction come to prevail more and more ..." (page 96 - 97)

The whole theory of Preobrazhensky, which is really the theory of Trotsky and social-fascists, is in complete contradiction with the teachings of Marx and Lenin. Com. Serebryakov in his report has revealed the apologetic and defeatist essence of the theory of non-cyclical development. This theory is strongly at odds with the real dynamics of capitalism. It confuses the proletariat. It imposes the conclusion that if the cycle is still there, then all is well with capitalism and the proletarian revolution is premature.

Thus the cycle of distortions in the conditions of monopoly capitalism acquires a totally perverted character with Preobrazhensky. Deformation of the cycle undoubtedly occurs in the era of monopoly, but it happens differently than it is presented by Preobrazhensky.

The development of the basic contradictions of capitalism in the epoch of imperialism lies in a dramatic, immeasurably more acute than ever before, contradiction that finds its expression in the exacerbation of the specific contradictions of monopoly capitalism, representing, as stated above, the form of expression of the basic contradiction. In view of all these changes, there is nothing surprising in the fact that monopolistic cycle and monopoly crises acquire a number of specific features; here it is possible to note the weakening intensity, universality and durability of upswings; acceleration and deepening of the crisis; deepening and protraction of depression. But there is nothing like a resolution or an ending of cycles and expanded reproduction. That is because there would be no cessation of expanded reproduction of capitalist contradictions.

6. In close connection with Preobrazhensky's teaching of cessation of the cyclical form of movement under monopoly capitalism are his views on the general trajectory of development of monopoly capitalism and about the pace of this development. Preobrazhensky in numerous places (pp. 11, 13, 16, 44, 45, 57, 58, 59, 85, 95 and 96, and so on.) dwells on how monopoly structure of capitalism obstructs the development of the productive forces. We can and must say that monopoly capitalism creates new barriers to the development of the social productive forces. But one cannot view these obstacles as absolute, it is impossible to come to a conclusion regarding stagnation (cessation) or the absolute inability of imperialism to move the latter forward. Meanwhile Preobrazhensky directly develops the Trotskyist theory of stagnation.

"Monopoly ... means a slower pace of economic development in general". (p. 44)

Economic development of capitalist society is slowed down, the lifting curve of the upswing turns more and more to a straight line of simple reproduction" (pp. 85-86); *"The gradual economic development is suspended* (p. 96).

"Monopoly, with the existence of categories of profit as a direct stimulus to production, is a constant source of blockage in the development of the productive forces of society, and here the desire for profits increasingly becomes a stimulus not for the development of production, but for a reduction". (p. 134)

This *"philosophy"* of the productive forces in the era of imperialism has nothing to do with Leninism. Lenin all the time emphasizes that with the increasing tendency to decay, to parasitism, imperialism also drives forward the productive forces, although this development is uneven, intermittent, irregular, that decay, which is expressed in the suspension of the development of the productive forces in some sectors in some countries, in some periods of time, does not preclude an overall growth. This development of productive forces in the process of contradictions rising to the extreme, in the exacerbated antagonism (class and imperialist), in the general "horror without end" is what makes imperialism the eve of the proletarian revolution.

But if Preobrazhensky's statements regarding the general line of development of the productive forces of imperialism are contrary to reality and the views of Leninism, then these statements are identical with Trotsky's conception. I will not give quotes, because they are contained in Com. Serebryakov report. Let me just note that Preobrazhensky is in solidarity with the Trotskyist theory of stagnation of the productive forces in contemporary capitalism, that he boldly raises the Trotskyist position to the rank of general laws of monopoly capitalism, applies them not only to the post-war imperialism, but also to the entire pre-war imperialism. Here Preobrazhensky attempts to become more Catholic than even the Pope himself

So, there is not a grain of Leninism in the conclusions arrived at by Preobrazhensky of the laws of motion of imperialism. Preobrazhensky here reveals the ideological connection, first, with the bourgeois theory of non-cyclical development of late capitalism (Sombart); secondly, the social-fascist theory of "organized capitalism"; thirdly, the general concept of counter revolutionary Trotskyism of the absolute cessation of all development of the productive forces under imperialism; fourth, with anti-Leninist, anti-revolutionary, Luxemburg's theory of automatic economic collapse of capitalism.

III. TIMID ALLUSION TO A GLOBAL CRISIS
AND THE BOLD DENIAL OF UNIVERSAL CRISIS
IN E. PREOBRAZHENSKY

Throughout the work of Preobrazhensky the most characteristic feature of the post-war imperialism is absent - namely that it has entered the phase of the general crisis of the capitalist system. What Preobrazhensky provides in the short chapter XIII, which is titled the "general crisis of capitalism," does not in the remotest degree resembles the interpretation of the general crisis, given in the works of com. Stalin, in the Comintern's programme and a number of other documents, the correct interpretation which is confirmed on a daily basis by the revolutionary practice of the world proletariat.

What does Preobrazhensky here speaks of? He talks about the failure of the mechanism in capitalism to emerge from a crisis, of the complete suspension of the development of productive forces, the intensification, due to this, of capitalist contradictions, the systematic increase in excess of the working population, a growing unproductive consumption while reducing the base of the exploited workers, the growing mountain of income titles while reducing the mass of surplus value and so on. It is easy to notice that in all these arguments Preobrazhensky remains within the framework of the anti-revolutionary theory of *automatic economic collapse* of capitalism, the theory which is known to be one element in the eclectic ideology of the counter-revolutionary Trotskyism. On the general crisis of capitalism in its Leninist understanding Preobrazhensky says nothing.

What is this, a random forgetfulness? Of course not. Not only in this book, but in all his prominent works on the post-war capitalism, the prospects of which he gives in the preface, Preobrazhensky does not say a word about the general crisis of capitalism.

Misunderstanding of, or rather the denial of, the universal crisis of capitalism by Preobrazhensky is already apparent from his very approach to the problems of modern capitalism. Whatever the issue, whether it is the problem of reproduction, crisis, working class, unemployment and so on, Preobrazhensky takes up for examination, he considers these always in terms of monopoly, as a whole, i.e. it being the same both for the pre-war imperialism and for the post-war one. This methodology is precisely what exposes Preobrazhensky. It just shows that Preobrazhensky does not understand or deliberately denies the general crisis of capitalism, as a specific phase of imperialism, of the era of proletarian revolutions.

Incidentally this manner to treat specific problems of contemporary capitalism from the standpoint of imperialism as a whole constantly misleads Preobrazhensky in his conclusions (if he did not even want to be misled), forcing him to carry the characteristics of the imperialism in the epoch of the general crisis over to the pre-war imperialism, and vice versa. But this is a different thing!

Misunderstanding and the denial of universal crisis of capitalism by Preobrazhensky is also reflected in the fact that Preobrazhensky views the crisis of 1929- 1932 as the first classic crisis of monopoly capitalism.

Of course fundamentally wrong is the attempt to consider the crisis of 1929 - 1932 only as monopoly crisis: it is a monopolistic crisis, but it is also something more. The crisis of 1929- 1932 is also a crisis that unfolded on the basis and in an atmosphere of a general crisis of the capitalist system.

Since Preobrazhensky declares the crisis of 1929 - 1932 as "the first typical economic crisis of imperialism", he thus casts aside all the specificity of the crisis and, consequently, all the specificity of capitalism in an era of a general crisis, i.e. denies the existence of this universal crisis.

But if by equating capitalism of the era of universal crisis with the pre-war monopoly capitalism Preobrazhensky denies global crisis, then at the same time by additional arguments he stresses and also develops a counter-revolutionary theory of automatic economic collapse of capitalism. Unable to understand the real forces that are now undermining capitalism, equating the elements of post-war capitalism with the corruption of the mechanism of capitalist reproduction, with an "increase in the force of friction" of the capitalist economic machine, Preobrazhensky on the one hand smudges the specific features of capitalism in the epoch of its collapse, and on the other hand, extends the features of the latter for the entire period of imperialism as a whole.

With what ease Probrazhensky carves up a stubborn reality for the sake of his schemata can be illustrated by the following examples.

In Preobrazhensky's theoretical schema it must follow that in the epoch of imperialism, "the capitalist system is forced into the next phase, one of slower pace of development" (p. 60), into a cessation of cyclicity and general upswings, into an end to the movement of the productive forces. In fact, however, the pre-war imperialism knew upswings, on the whole far more rapid ones than in classical capitalism, the productive forces developed and found the sharpest breaks in the cycle. This glaring contradiction between reality and his schemes Preobrazhensky overcomes by stating that the pre-war imperialism was transitional, not typical, not classical.

According to Preobrazhensky's theoretical schemata it must follow that in the era of imperialism the crises are protracted, and the exit from these is difficult and that "the global economic crisis is a disaster for the whole imperialist system" (p. 98). In fact monopoly capitalism was shaken by more frequent crises (1902, 1907, 1914, 1921) and deeper ones, although they do not automatically lead to the downfall of the capitalist system. It is a contradiction of his theoretical schemata with reality that Preobrazhensky destroys by simple way of denial of reality: he argues that monopoly capitalism essentially has not yet experienced monopolistic cycles and crises of monopoly. The crises in 1902 and 1907 were still one of "transition" from capitalism of free competition to monopolies, the crisis of 1914 turned into a war crisis and one in 1921 was a crisis of deflation. After this simple operation Preobrazhensky reveals even a more striking fact:

"Remarkably interesting fact! Imperialism as the latest "stage of capitalism has been in existence for more than 30 years. Meanwhile, during this time there was no deep economic crisis, which would allow to distinguish its most characteristic features". (p. 98)

Really remarkable discovery: there is monopoly capitalism without monopolistic cycles, which are known to occasionally lead to the explosion and resolution of all the contradictions of the system, there is monopoly without monopoly, by the grace of Preobrazhensky's theoretical fantasy. I will here "rehabilitate" the crises of the era of imperialism from the accusations that they were not deep crises: the available statistical material[5] is not in Preobrazhensky's favour, but in favour of Engels and Lenin, who strongly emphasized the inevitability of escalation of the crisis in the imperialist epoch.

Denial by E. Preobrazhensky of the general crisis of capitalism clearly emerges from his conception of fascism. Fascism "as a terrorist dictatorship of big capital", as a "method of suppressing the revolutionary movement" as "civil war against the workers" is a product and at the same time a sign of the general crisis of capitalism. Of the two methods of bourgeois rule ("violence" and "liberalism") in the era of monopoly capitalism " the first acquired precedence: political reaction corresponds to the dominance of monopolies in the economy, but only under specific historical conditions, this bourgeois-imperialist reaction takes the form of fascism. These are special conditions - the conditions of the general crisis of capitalism, with its characteristic features - the struggle between the two systems, a tense struggle of the working class against the capitalists, etc. Preobrazhensky does not agree with... such an interpretation of the nature of fascism. For him fascism is a - "form of bourgeois state in the period of monopoly capitalism, the last stage of the existence of capitalism "(p. 141), which replaced the" bourgeois-democratic state, definitively established in the XIX century", in the period of pre-monopoly capitalism. In other words, in interpreting fascism E. Preobrazhensky again takes up the Trotskyite position and considers the era of universal crisis of capitalism and the pre-war imperialism as a single whole, conflates the first with the second, and as it were denied the unique nature of general crisis of capitalism. At the same time, fascism too, according to Preobrazhensky, ceases to be a specific product of the era of the general crisis of the capitalist system and one of the most characteristic features of the latter. This is one aspect of the matter. On the other hand, Preobrazhensky strongly emphasizes the idea that fascism as a new form of the bourgeois state in its very foundation has "a narrow base of social production" (p. 145), the inability to "use all the means of production and all the labour power of society" (p .145) , due to the structure of monopoly capitalism, and so takes up the task to compensate the bourgeoisie for "weakening of the economic power" by doubling of its political forces, providing means "to increase the rate of exploitation of the proletariat and to lower its standard of life ... that it has reached, by destroying all its strength as an organized resistance "(p. 143).

It is easy to see that all these considerations are sequentially arranged in a particular row and with Preobrazhensky it appears that the fundamental question of modern capitalism (the general crisis of capitalism) in the relationship between the bourgeoisie and the proletariat is the increase in the rate of exploitation, the desire to bring the standard of living below the one existing, i.e. the struggle between the proletariat and the bourgeoisie over economic issues and, moreover, in such a form that the bourgeoisie is on the offensive, and the proletariat is on the defensive. This is certainly not true. It is clear that in the era of the general crisis there is, between the working class and the bourgeoisie, a struggle not only on economic issues, but above all on the question of whether or not capitalism should exist at all. It is clear that in the era of the general crisis of capitalism, the proletariat not only leads the economic struggle, even if a defensive one but one that increasingly sharpens economic conflicts so that they become political battles and conducts offensive operations against the bourgeoisie on an unprecedented scale. There is no need to prove that the characterization of the labour movement of the era of economic crisis, both in terms of its content and as defensive tactics is anti-Leninist, and a Trotskyist one.

As a last in order, but perhaps first in importance of the common arguments in support of the assertion that Preobrazhensky denies general crisis of capitalism, it is necessary to point out Preobrazhensky's interpretation of the struggle between the two systems, of the defining moment of general crisis of capitalism. Preobrazhensky's interpretation of the problems of struggle between the two systems is wrong. nonpartisan and obviously obscures the greatest impact of the rising system of socialism on the dying capitalist system, inevitably leads to smudging the line between pre-war and post-war imperialism, of imperialism in the epoch of general crisis, leading to a denial of the general crisis of capitalism, 'More of it, I show below

We have indicated above some general moments, that provide irrefutable evidence that Preobrazhensky denies the general crisis of capitalism. Along with this, we find in Preobrazhensky's book also his direct remarks to that effect. He writes:

"The general economic crisis under monopolism, if it does not lead to a world war or is not interrupted by technological revolution inevitably develops into a general, not only economic, but also a social crisis of the entire historical system of capitalism" (p. 97).

Preobrazhensky considers as the first typical crisis under monopolism, as we have seen, the crisis of 1929 - 1932. However, he argues that such a crisis inevitably develops into a general crisis of the capitalist system (and that to only in the absence of a war and technological revolution). Consequently, until now there was no general crisis. Is this not a denial of the general crisis of capitalism, the crisis, which began with the War of 1914-1918!

Elsewhere Preobrazhensky predicts like a professional scientist: *"Universal economic crisis threatens to turn into a (general) crisis of the capitalist system."*

According to Preobrazhensky in 1931, the global crisis threatens even more to turn into a global crisis of capitalism. Social Fascists, these rabid apologists of capitalism, its doctors and rescuers are known to have denied and continue to deny that capitalism has entered from 1914 - 1915 into a period of general crisis. A counter-revolutionary Trotskyism as a matter of fact does not recognize the existence of the general crisis of capitalism. Is it difficult to understand whose ideas are now being peddled by Preobrazhensky when he denies the existence of the universal crisis of capitalism?

So Preobrazhensky denies the universal crisis of capitalism. Those of his argument, where he asserts the hopelessness of modern capitalism, the absence of a mechanism to exit the crisis, fading economic development of society, and so on., has nothing in common with the theory of general crisis of capitalism. Here the theorist of the "decline of capitalism" (which is the *sunset* rather than the collapse, not the revolutionary overthrow) simply reproduces the theory of automatic, purely economic collapse of capitalism, a theory on the basis of which half hearted mensheviks and Luxemburgism and counter-revolutionary Trotskyism and skittish right opportunism and adventurist left opportunism converge.

Preobrazhensky does not recognize the general crisis of capitalism. But this makes it hopeless to attempt to understand the basic questions of modern capitalism that is in its stage of death. In particular, it deprives him of the possibility of anything like a satisfactory understanding of today's global crisis.

IV. MODERN WORLD CRISIS
IN PREOBRAZHENSKY'S ASSESSMENT

What serious repercussions the ignoring of the presence of the general crisis of capitalism has, is easy to show by the example of Preobrazhensky's analysis of the nature, causes and prospects of the current world crisis. The theoretical study of the problems of the modern world crisis - the crisis is highly peculiar - clearly falls short of "practice." Marxist literature on the universal crisis, created over the past two years, often gives a comprehensive answer to one or the other question, thrown up by the course of the crisis. But what is now presented by Preobrazhensky is striking even in comparison with the poor state of our literature about the global crisis.

Analysis of the contemporary global crisis by Preobrazhensky and its content is nothing less than a biased forcing of reality into a contrived schema of cycles in the era of monopoly capitalism. We know this schema: the overall rise is excluded; the strength of a partial upswing determines the volume of reserves of fixed capital; an end to production of these reserves signifies a crisis, the mechanism of exit from which (if there is no war or technological revolution) is non-existent. In this schema Preobrazhensky tries to fit in all the development of the world capitalist economy since 1923.

The matter is presented in the following form. The war years of 1914 - 1918 for the USA were years of enormous growth in exports. This was a "spike", leaning on which the USA then increased the capacity of its internal market. Because of this the crisis in 1921 it was quickly eliminated. In fact, the expansion of the domestic market has played a crucial role in the expansion of the industrial demand for new fixed capital[6]. On the basis of this expansion of fixed capital in the production sphere in the USA economic expansion lasted until the summer of 1927. By this time it had exhausted itself. There has been a crisis, but it ended with depression, for the monopoly system of the USA at that time moved to the rapid accumulation of reserves of fixed capital, which has overcome depression and prolonged the upswing in the USA for two more years.

In other words, the latest upswing in the USA, according to Preobrazhenksy's assurances developed in full accordance with his schema. But not only the upswing, says Preobrazhensky, is a confirmation of his schema, the crisis itself of 1929 -1932 also confirms the correctness of (Preobrazhensky's) constructs: the crisis began suddenly, dramatically, with heavy industry, and was very deep and long. As in the phase of upswing so in the phase of the crisis the strongest country of monopoly capitalism - the USA was in the lead. The prospects for the crisis, as far as they can be judged at all, according to Preobrazhensky, are in full accordance with his schema:

"Capitalism in the United States cannot count on a way out of the crisis from this end (with upgradation and an increase of fixed capital, that got over in 1929 by L. K). On the other hand, neither had any revolution in technology occurred that could have led to existing capital becoming technologically obsolete and hence to placing of large orders for new fixed capital. Even in expansion of foreign markets in new territories there is no hope. Thus it is expected that capitalism in the United States will have to pass through an extremely difficult and a long course of compression of the productive apparatus till it reaches the limits mentioned above. Branches of Department II must shrink enough to be able to adapt to new proportions of consumption so that existing reserves are depleted.

The branches, producing fixed assets may shrink to the level of depreciation of fixed capital".

"The question arises - says Preobrazhensky, - how much physical compression of products is necessary for the economy of the United States so that the limit of critical reduction of the production apparatus is reached and inventories from the period of the upswing are used up". (page 134)

On this issue Preobrazhensky gives the answer: *"The volume of production in the United States must shrink at the very least to the level that preceded the onset of recovery, i.e., up to about the level of 1922-23. Then, even the additional compression of a conjunctural character must get over, compression, whose task is to re-absorb the excessive inventory"* (p. 134 -135).

"This is a natural limit to the contraction of production, and hence the limit after which a recovery can begin, if the system is not eliminated, or in that part where it is not eliminated by a proletarian revolution "(p. 134).

Comparing further data on commodities in the USA over the past decade with the monthly data of 1931, Preobrazhensky comes to the conclusion that "this basic compression of production has *almost gotten over by the end of the second half of 1930* (my italics. LK), since December provides production levels below that for all of the last nine years "(p. 135). Moreover, Preobrazhensky believes that at the end of 1930 the additional compression, which was needed to eliminate the trade surplus in the USA also comes to an end. From this follows the general conclusion: "so the level of production *in the United States is unlikely to have significantly dropped in comparison with the current level*" (page 135.).

In Preobrazhensky's interpretation of the causes of the current world crisis what strikes us most is the narrow, a purely economic approach to the problem. In words Preobrazhensky recognizes the inadequacy of this method: "As it is impossible to examine the current economic crisis only as a purely economic process - it is just as impossible to give a purely economic outlook" (p. 133). In practice he limits himself to this (and only this). If in his projections Preobrazhensky tries to take into account the impact of these non-economic factors, then in explaining the causes of the global crisis, he remains stuck in the positions of pure war economy, moreover, he is interpreting it incorrectly. The role of the foreign market at the beginning of recovery, the significance of the domestic market later and then an increase in the reserves of the fixed capital at the end of recovery - that's the whole cocktail, of the biggest, distinctive global crisis according to Preobrazhensky.

Accounting for at least such a decisive fact that the economic development of the USA after the war is to some extent a function of the political, social, economic disturbances that characterized the post-war development of the capitalist countries of Europe and the colonial and semi-colonial countries of Asia, America and Africa we have certainly not seen in Preobrazhensky's works. Problems of higher mathematics Preobrazhensky tries to solve the by primitive methods of multiplication tables.

It was noted above that essentially Preobrazhensky denies the general crisis of capitalism. Preobrazhensky's analysis of the current world crisis has convinced us of that again. We know that the current global crisis unfolds in the new specific conditions, without which it is impossible to completely understand its nature. We know further that most of these features are reduced to the fact that, firstly, the current crisis hit the main capitalist countries the hardest, that secondly, *industrial crisis* got interwoven with the *agrarian crisis*, that, thirdly, the current crisis unfolds in conditions of *monopoly* capitalism, and that, fourthly, the current crisis unfolds on the *basis of the general crisis of capitalism*.

Of all these conditions Preobrazhensky takes into account only the third, and then, as we have seen, in the form of "pure monopoly". With regard to the crucial features of the current crisis, as a crisis on the basis of the general crisis of capitalism Preobrazhensky pays no attention. Such important aspects of general crisis of capitalism, as the existence of the Soviet Union, a chain of proletarian revolutions in European countries, colonial revolutions, general social and political instability created by the war, a chronic agrarian crisis, a unique price dynamic, structural unemployment, and so on., should also be considered in order to explain the present global crisis. To equate the current global crisis to the general basis of capitalist crises, even though monopolistic, means bypassing by its most important features.

Further. When taking into account these features of the general background in which the current global crisis has occurred, all those "limits" to the crisis in the USA which Preobrazhensky outlines in the form of "*basic*" (pre-level, prior to the present recovery) and "*incremental*" compression (to the extent necessary for the resolution of trade surpluses) must seem frivolous.

As always, practice is the best criterion of judging a theory. Preobrazhensky says that the level of production in the USA is unlikely to fall significantly in comparison with the level at the end of 1930. What are the facts? They speak against Preobrazhensky. It is sufficient to compare the data for December 1930 and December 1931 on key indicators of production in the USA, to see that the Preobrazhensky "limits" have been surpassed by far by the actual movement of the American crisis.

Manufacturing products		Steel	Automobiles	Electricity
December 1930	76.1	1971 thous. Tons	161 thous.	1979 mil. Kv
December 1931	65.5	1320 thous. Tons	120 thous.	1670 mill Kv

In between the scissors of production level in USA in the late 1930 which (level) for Preobrazhensky is the lowest in the present crisis, and the level for December 1931 it is easy to discern a complete average crisis. Meanwhile, there is no reason to believe that the level of December 1931 is the lowest level. The fall still continues.

Preobrazhensky's "forecast" proves that his theory of monopoly cycle and the crisis, with all his "revolutionary" talk (there is no exit from the crisis, capitalism is powerless to develop the productive forces and so on and on) in its very core is an opportunistic theory – it smudges the most acute contradictions of capitalism, blurs the scope of the explosion of these contradictions, leading to a thoroughly wrong, findings undermining the degree of the decline of capitalism, and predictions. In Preobrazhensky the crisis in the USA should have long had come to an end. In fact, it now has not yet reached the bottom.

V. THE FIGHT BETWEEN TWO SYSTEMS IN PREOBRAZHENSKY'S ASSESSMENT

With the victory of the October proletarian: the revolution in the USSR, the world economy has split into two antagonistic systems: socialist and capitalist. "Capitalism is no longer the sole and all-embracing system of world economy» (*Stalin*). Alongside of capitalism and in irreconcilable struggle with it there is developing and strengthening the system of socialism, the USSR is growing "- the citadel of world revolution. But the totally opposite, antagonistic systems of a growing socialism and a dying capitalism are not indifferent to each other. They are connected by a single process of the revolutionary transformation of world capitalism into a socialist world. They are related by a relentless struggle between them. The tremendous aggravation of inherent to capitalism basic contradiction between the social character of production and the private capitalist form of appropriation has led to a splitting of the world economy and has found its highest expression in the contradiction between the socialist and capitalist systems, in the struggle between these two systems. The struggle between the two systems is the defining moment of the entire modern history.

It is impossible to understand anything correctly either about the capitalism of the era of general crisis, nor about the expansion of the world socialist revolution without a proper accounting for the actual significance for both aspects of the first country of victorious socialism — USSR. "By its very existence it is revolutionizing the whole world" (*Stalin*), shakes the very foundations of capitalism, aggravates all its contradictions, narrows limits of exploitation, "it poses a threat to imperialism through socialist industrialization of the USSR" (resolution XI Plenum of the ECCI), by the rapid pace of socialist economic growth practically realises the slogan of catching up and overtaking the advanced capitalist countries technically and economically in the shortest historical period.

By destroying the system of imperialism, shaking its foundations, aggravating its contradictions, the Soviet Union thus at the same time serves as a base for further development of the world revolution. "*The international significance of the October Revolution is not only that it is a great beginning of one country as the first centre of socialism in the ocean of imperialist countries and of destruction of the system of imperialism, but also in the fact that it is the first stage of the world revolution and a mighty base for its further development "(Stalin)*.

The struggle between the two systems - socialism and capitalism - is the main contradiction of contemporary history, the basic core of contemporary international relations. Now, in a new phase of the general crisis of capitalism, and in the period of the greatest global crisis of 1929/ 32, the period of the huge success of building socialism — this contradiction is revealed with unprecedented sharpness of the struggle between the two systems as a defining moment has increased enormously. The enlarged

Plenum of the ECCI (February 1930), noting the huge success of construction in the USSR, pointed out: *"There can be no doubt that all this change in the balance of power between the two world economic systems in favour of international socialism makes the USSR, now more than ever, a powerful factor in the deepening crisis of capitalism, and in a revolutionary upsurge of the proletariat and the exploited masses all around the world."*

How does Preobrazhensky evaluate and take into account in his analysis the struggle between the two systems, this decisive factor in the totality of relationships and of the whole development of modern capitalism?

First of all, a reader is astonished by the extreme brevity of Preobrazhensky's analysis of the matter. Winding and unrestrained in discussions on all sorts of subtleties of his arbitrary theorizing, Preobrazhensky is incredibly silent as soon as he comes to the most essential, the most crucial issue of our time.

Suffice it to say that in his book, to the question of struggle between the two systems Preobrazhensky devotes nearly four pages in Chapter XIV and several cursory and fragmentary observations in two or three other places.

Preobrazhensky's brevity is not accidental in this important matter. And what he says on this subject, clearly shows that he did not understand the significance of the problem. As a proof of this last thesis I will cite a few examples.

First example. When Preobrazhensky tries to take into account "the fact of the existence of the USSR" for the further development of capitalism and the development of the world socialist revolution, for him the Soviet Union merely acts as a symbol of the fact that "the crust of the capitalist system is already broken in the USSR", or the fact that the proletariat of Russia "already is organized in a state." In 1931, in the decisive year of the first five-year period, at the threshold of the second five-year plan, to characterize the USSR's importance in the revolutionary transformation of the world only by such features as a "breaking of the capitalist system's crust," as "the organization of the working class in form of a state," - means falling behind by 14 years.

We have entered the period of socialism, and completed the construction of the foundation of the socialist economy. As a result of the victories of world-historical significance we have secured the victory of socialism in our country, and solved the problem of "who destroys whom" in the Soviet Union once and for all in favour of socialism. We stand today at the threshold of the second five-year plan, which will ensure the elimination of the capitalist elements and classes in the USSR. The majestic outlines of this five-year plan is hanging like a terrible nightmare over the perishing capitalist world. In these circumstances, to limit oneself, in the interpretation of the issue of the Soviet Union, to just an indicating the fact of breaking the crust of capitalist society and the organization of the proletariat into a state (because it was already in 1917) is to ignore the huge successes of socialism in the USSR and it means underestimating the importance of the Soviet Union as a powerful factor of universal crisis of the capitalist system, shaking and destroying capitalism.

Second example. In the aforementioned Chapter XIV Preobrazhensky emphasizes mainly the "propaganda value of our economic success "(p. 164). He is very reserved in assessing the direct impact of the economy of the Soviet Union on the capitalist world.

"In our press a lot is said about the whole absurdity of the accusations that we can overthrow capitalism by offering cheap prices through the mechanism of three percent participation in the higher world trade" (p. 161).

Rejecting the bourgeois' press defamation of Soviet dumping, one should not at the same time underestimate the economic impact of the USSR on capitalist countries. Thanks to the heroic growth rates of socialist production, and rapidly changing share of the USSR in world production, the share of the USSR in world production (in percent) constituted respectively for cast iron: 1928.- 1.7 and 1929 - 4.1, 6.2 in 1930, and in 1931 - 9.0, for steel respectively: 2.1; 3.9; 5.9; 7.5; oil, respectively: 6,4; 6.6; 9.5; 11.5.

Already at this stage, and even more with the next steps we can talk about increasing economic pressure of the Soviet Union on the decaying capitalist economy. The threat of Soviet Socialist industrialization for imperialism, about which XI Plenum of the ECCI talks, is not only a matter of propaganda, but a real, direct offensive of socialism against capitalism. Preobrazhensky blurs this aspect of the matter, and obscures and hides it.

A third example. The last page of his book, Preobrazhensky completes with this sentence: -

"Let the other countries announce a blockade of the new socialist country: now it will not disappear because of this, now she has a powerful ally and a socialist rear of the East" (meaning the USSR L.K.)

This thesis of the USSR as the rear of the next proletarian revolutions of course has nothing to do with party's assessment of the role and responsibilities of the USSR in the world socialist revolution. It is known that Lenin pointed out the active role and leadership of the victorious proletariat of one country in the spread of the international revolution. It is known that Stalin forcefully emphasized the importance of the Soviet Union as a basis for further development of the world revolution, as a lever to the further disintegration of imperialism.

The Soviet Union as a "socialist rear" of the "new socialist countries" - it's a kind of echo of the old Trotskyist conception that preaches the impossibility of the victory of socialism in one country, smudging of the international significance of our revolution, denies the role of the USSR as the bulwark and the most important factor in the global victory of socialism.

Preobrazhensky's distortion and underestimation outlined above of the role of the struggle between two systems, again, are not of chance. This underestimation stems from Preobrazhensky's poorly concealed doubts about the authenticity of the socialist nature of the Soviet economy. In most of Preobrazhenky's wording to that effect, we come across purely ambiguous characteristics such as "our economy", "our economic system shows example of what socialist organisation of Labour can provide" (page 139.), "The law of value ceases (!) to operate in our economy" and so on.

In the present-day discourse on the nature of the Soviet economy and the struggle between the two systems the load of ideas, perceptions, attitudes, which is developed by Preobrazhensky in the "New Economy" (1926) continues to be felt. The then conclusions about the pressure of the world economy (p. 37) on the economy of the USSR, the old idea of our economy being a commodity-socialist one, the old doctrine of the two regulators (p. 42), the old ideas about the development of our economy like a parallelogram of forces between socialism and capitalism, the old formulations on the restoration of pre-war contradictions between agriculture and industry, all of this and are now part of the silence about the huge success of socialist construction in the USSR, a pure and deliberate usage of a vague language in characterizing the socialist nature of the Soviet economy, in disregard of the new stage of our development, in denying the active destructive impact of the Soviet Union on the capitalist system, in belittling the role of the USSR as a base for further development of the world revolution.

In this underestimation of the socialist nature of the Soviet economy, tremendous achievements in socialist construction, the smudging of the world-historical significance of the fact of the USSR entering the stage of socialism, this blurring of the success of the world proletarian revolution - don't we feel that there is a motive of the same conception, which social-fascists and counter-revolutionary Trotskyites openly assert in the form of a direct maligning of the successful construction of socialism in the USSR?

Lets summarize the results of Preobrazhensky's new book. It contains:

Open trotskyite revision of the Marxist-Leninist theory of reproduction and the theory of crisis.

Support for R. Luxemburg's revisionist theory of realization.

Open revision of Lenin's theory of imperialism.

Echos of social fascist theory of "pure" imperialism.

Trotskyite negation of Lenin's theory of uneven development.

Social-fascist, Trotskyite theory of automatic collapse of capitalism.

Trotskyite theory of stagnation of productive forces in contemporary capitalism.

Bourgeois and social fascist theory of non cyclic development of contemporary capitalism

Social fascist and Trotskyite negation of the general crisis of capitalism.

Mechanistic explanation of the contemporary global crisis as the latest stage in the general crisis of capitalism.

An almost a complete ignoring of the struggle between the two system as the main trajectory of development of contemporary society and as the decisive moment in the general crisis of capitalism

It is not difficult to note that the latest book by Preobrazhensky is an eclectic work. Separate parts of his theory Preobrazhensky has collected from from a wide variety of (bourgeois, social fascist, Trotskyite and Menshevik) theoretical junkyards. But in all his eclecticism the Trotskyite "motive" is most prominent and constitutes the main stream. The Trotskyite formulations of this book must be ruthlessly exposed and defeated.

***

Source: Serebryakov. V, Kasharsky. L, ***Against the Trotskyite Conception of Imperialism***, Party Publication, Moscow-Leningrad, 1932, p.43-78.

Translated from the Russian by Tahir Asghar.

Endnotes:

[1] As it is known that his whole article "*Economic Equilibrium in Concrete Capitalism and in the System of the* USSR" is based on the postulate of equilibrium (Vestnik Komakademii, bks 17,18. "The New Economy" and "Economic Crisis under NEP" are also based on this idea.

[2] "Our example illustrates equilibrium in expanded reproduction" p.20.

[3] Evenness, harmony and proportionality never existed anywhere in the capitalist world nor could have ever existed. (Lenin. Coll. Works, vol. XVI, p.183)

[4] See following instances: "The capacity of the capitalist system in relation to the productive forces is so small ... that this situation leads, in the entire world economy, to a systematically increasing, organic, immobilisation of an ever increasing part of the capital and labour power" (p. 144).

".... The suspension of development of the productive forces of bourgeois society" and several other instances.

[5] It is sufficient to compare the fall (in percent) in 6 main countries: cast iron 1873 / 74 — 8%; 1907 / 08 - 23%; 1920 / 21 - 42 %; Foreign trade turnover: 1873 / 74 — 5%; 1883 / 84 — 4%; 1907 / 08 — 7%;. Price of Shares 1873 / 74 - 30%; 1833 / 34 — 29%; 1907 / 08 — 37%; 1921 / 22 — 41% and so on?

[6] Other factors here were: increase in exports of commodities and export of capital from the USA.

FIDEL CASTRO
1926-2016

ICMLPO

On January 1 1959 the Cuban revolution triumphed. Several years of guerrilla struggle waged in the mountains of the Island, courageous fights of the working class, youth and people developed in the cities culminated in victory. Ninety miles from Yankee imperialism, the Cuban revolutionaries broke with the thesis of "geographic fatalism" according to which, because of the proximity of the United States, it was not possible to make the revolution in Latin America.

The achievements of the Revolution, the agrarian reform, the nationalization of all the US enterprises, the eradication of illiteracy, the health care and education involved the working masses and the youth; these awakened the solidarity of the workers and peoples of the world, especially of Latin America. They pointed the way to the armed revolutionary struggle. But they also unleashed the hatred of international reaction, the war-like actions of the United States, the invasion of Playa Giron (Bay of Pigs) and hundreds of terrorist actions, the trade embargo, which failed, over almost sixty years, due to the heroic resistance of the Cuban people and revolutionaries.

The heroic deeds of the workers and peasants, of the Cuban youth, was able to develop and led to victory with the defeat of the tyranny and the establishment of people's power. It succeeded in promoting the achievements, social and economic transformations and resisting and overcoming all sorts of attacks by imperialism and reaction. All this was possible due to the formation and forging of a revolutionary party, the July 26th Movement, which was able to adopt correct and timely guidelines, which was able to lead the social and political forces to struggle and victory. Among the members of the revolutionary command were many political and military leaders, Camilo Cienfuegos, Che, Frank Pais, Raul Castro. Among all of them, Comandante FIDEL CASTRO stood out as the leader, who participated actively and directly from the first combats, playing the role of organizer, strategist, popular leader and head of state.

Social revolutions are the work of the masses, but they could not be possible without the guidance of the revolutionary leaders who arise in the heat of combat but who achieve dimensions that determine the course and development of the processes.

The workers and peasants, youth, revolutionaries, the "July 26" Movement, the revolutionary commanders and Comandante Fidel Castro led a popular revolution that took place in a small country that confronted the strongest power on the planet and was able to resist.

Fidel Castro died fulfilling his duties and responsibilities. His words and deeds throughout his long life as a combatant will endure, they constitute the testimony of the courage and tenacity of a people, they express the convictions and commitment of a revolutionary.

The Marxist Leninist Parties and Organizations integrated in the ICMLPO express their communist sentiments to the working class, the people and the Cuban revolutionaries.

Coordinating Committee of the International Conference of Marxist-Leninist Parties and Organizations, ICMLPO

November 2016

Obituary

YEVGENY YA. DZHUGASHVILI 1936-2016

Lavrentiy Gurdzhiev

Yevgeny Ya. Dzhugashvili was born on January 10, 1936, in Uryupinsk, Stalingrad region, RSFSR, and he died on December 22, 2016 in Moscow. He was a Soviet military engineer, scientist, an historian, and a Russian and Georgian public and political figure. Academically he was a candidate of the military sciences and the historical sciences. He was a professor and a colonel when he retired in 1991.

His parents separated before the war. His father was Yakov Dzhugashvili, the elder son of I.V. Stalin. He was an artillery officer. According to some reports, he died at the front in 1941, and, according to other sources, he was killed in 1943 in German captivity. He had refused to serve the Germans. His mother was Olga Golysheva who also took part in the Great Patriotic War and served at the front as a nurse. She died in 1961.

Yevgeny studied at school in his native city, then in Morskva. He was admitted to the Suvorov Military School in the city of Kalinin. (These schools were established in the USSR during the war for the maintenance and training of children and adolescents who had lost one or both parents).

He graduated from the Air Force Engineering Academy which was named after N.E. Zhukov in 1959, after which he worked in the military plants of the USSR holding the rank of engineer-lieutenant.

For more than ten years he worked in the system of military missions, and was engaged in the preparation and launching of space objects. For some times he was at the disposal of the head of the Soviet space rocket programme named after S.P. Korolyov, participating in the launches of satellites and cosmonauts from the Baikonur cosmodrome. He was an employee of the Central Administration of Space Facilities of the Ministry of Defence of the USSR.

He was trained in the adjunct of the V.I. Lenin Military and Political Academy, where he defended his thesis in the department of "Military Art" and, in 1973, he became a candidate of military sciences. In 1976, after completing a course at the Historical Section of the Military Academy of the General Staff of the Armed Forces, USSR, named after Voroshilov, he was sent to the Air Force Academy named after Gagarin in the city of

Monino near Moscow.

Yevgeny Dzhugashvili taught in a number of military schools. For 25 years he worked as a senior teacher of the history of wars and military art in the Academy of the General Staff of the Armed Forces of the USSR named after K.E. Voroshilov. He also worked in the Academy of the Armed Forces named after Malinovsky. In 1987 he moved to the Military Academy named after Frunze, from where he retired from the service in 1991 in the rank of a colonel. From that time onwards he carried out social and political activity.

In 1996, Yevgeny Dzhugashvili became Chairman of the Georgian Society of the Ideological Successors of Joseph Stalin. In 1996 he became the chairman of the People's Patriotic Union of Georgia, and in 2001, he acted as the general secretary of the "New Communist Party of Georgia". However, the party did not achieve special success. Its candidates failed to be elected to the parliament of the republic. In the same year he was elected as a member of the Central Coordinating Council of the All-Russian Social and Political Movement "Union".

Yevgeny Djugashvili was widely known as the grandson of I.V. Stalin, in whose defence, honour and dignity he spoke in the judicial bodies of the Russian Federation and Ukraine. In fact, of the numerous descendants of Stalin, he was and remained the only one who raised his voice in defence of the ideas and accomplishments of his grandfather. He managed to pass the baton of this to both his sons. The elder, Vissarion, graduated from the Tbilisi Agricultural Institute and the higher courses of directors and screenwriters at the Moscow Institute of Cinematography. His younger son is Yakov, a professional artist who graduated from educational institutions in Tbilisi (Georgia) and Glasgow (Great Britain).

The bourgeois courts, including the notorious European Court of Human Rights, regularly refused to satisfy his lawsuits against the slanderers who attacked not only the name of Stalin, but the entire Soviet past, the heroes of the revolution and the war. And he was not afraid to file more and more claims, or participate in meetings, conferences, rallies, casting well-reasoned accusations against his powerful enemies. He appealed to the highest Russian authorities, including the president, with the requirements of justice and respect for the rule of law.

It is noteworthy that in 1990, Yevgeny Dzhugashvili was asked to play the role of Stalin in a feature film that told of his father's feats: "Jacob, the son of Stalin." One of the motives for this proposal was the striking external resemblance between Yevgeny and the leader. The debut was successful. However, because of the anti-communist bacchanalia which was unleashed during perestroika, the film was not widely disseminated. In addition, he starred in a number of documentary films and TV shows.

In 2015, a book of memoirs by Yevgeny Dzhugashvili was published in Russian: "My Grandfather Stalin. He was a Saint!" (Yauza-Press, Moscow, 2015). In it, in particular, the author revealed some biographical details, and described the difficulties and misunderstandings that he had in his relationship with his relatives.

Yevgeny Dzhugashvili had dual citizenship - Russian and Georgian.

ELYA KERIMOVA
1952-2015

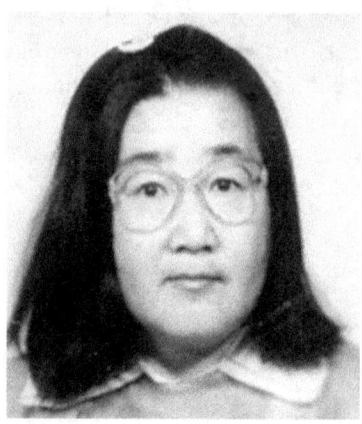

Elya Afanasievna Kerimova (maiden name Kim) was born on August 31, 1952, in the kolkhoz named Karl Marx, Postdargomsky region, Samarkand province, Uzbek SSR. According to her wish she went to the local Russian language School. Early in school she started to read books about the world workers' movement and seriously studied the political problems of society. In 1976 Elya graduated from Samarkand's Food College as a technician-technologist. For the last 30 years of her life she permanently lived and worked in Leningrad.

Almost immediately after her relocation to Leningrad, Elya Afanasievna started to actively participate in the political struggle of the working class. It was the time when the legalised so-called democratic bourgeoisie started its struggle for state power against Khrushchev-Brezhnev "Soviet" social-imperialism. In the minds of the petty bourgeoisie, as well as a number of workers, there was confusion and disorientation. The majority of ordinary citizens did not understand that it was not a struggle between "communists" and newly appeared "democrats", but between two groups of large capital.

In that difficult period in the life of our society Elya Afanasievna was convinced that Soviet socialism and the proletarian dictatorship were linked to the name of Lenin and Stalin. Her introduction to the works of Enver Hoxha made her conviction in the correctness of her chosen path even stronger. Until her death Elya never swayed from her political line. Because of this her comrades in the struggle called her "Iron Felix", as the workers called Felix Dzerzhinsky in his time.

Elya Afanasievna was one of the most active members of the 'Proletarskaya Gazeta' Editorial Board since its founding. She carried out the most difficult and responsible work of practical class revolutionary agitation amongst Leningrad's petty bourgeoisie and the workers of many cities of our country. She was well-known to the workers of Severodvinsk, Nizhniy Novgorod, Ryazan, Moscow, Donetsk and other cities. For her active and unyielding class revolutionary agitation she was arrested many times, went through several trials and was tortured and beaten by reactionary elements. However her will and convictions were not broken.

Comrades in struggle buried Elya Afanasievna Kerimova in Kovalevsky Cemetery with all honours befitting to the memory of an advanced fighter for the revolutionary cause of the working class of our time. Her name will be placed in the ranks of the revolutionary fighters of our epoch.

AGAINST FORMALISM
AND 'LEFTIST' UGLINESS IN ART

In the upbringing of a new socialist, art plays a huge role. This is why questions about art and its creative development are so important to the Leninist Young Communist League. Members cannot stand apart from Soviet art, one must know his tasks, and must contribute to its flowering. This relates fully to all Soviet youths. It is unsurprising therefore, that the speeches of 'Pravda' about the compositions of the composer Shostakovich – the opera 'Lady Macbeth of the Mtsensk District' and the ballet 'The Bright Stream' – deeply concern the Soviet youth and put in front of them a series of serious issues.

Indeed, what is it about these works, and why are they subjected to such harsh criticism from the central organ of the Party? 'Lady Macbeth of Mtsensk District' – an opera, is written about a story of the same name by Leskov. However, the composer Shostakovich completely changed the basic plot of Leskov's story, and in his words, set himself the task of rehabilitating the heroine of the story – the merchant's wife Katherine Izmailova. The merchant's wife Katherine Izmailova is represented by Leskov as an evil, carnivorous creature, a child-killer, towering over the foul environment and the dark kingdom. Shostakovich, by all means, tries to make the Soviet public sympathise with the crude, half-animal image of Katherine Izmailova.

Followed by convulsive, hysterical, clanking and roaring music, people wander across the stage, whose whole lives go by in food, drunkenness and debauchery. It is characterised by the expressiveness of Shostakovich's music, which must portray the love of the clerk Sergei and the merchant's wife Katherine Izmailova, or the scene of the torture of Sergei in a formalist way. Music in this opera is turned inside out, turned into a crippling tearing noise for ears, and is a collection of chaotic sounds.

But no better is the music of the ballet 'Bright Stream'. The authors of this ballet aim to portray kolkhoz life, and kolkhoz holidays. But they did not bother to study ballet or the life of kolkhoz farmers. They added the old ballet cliché to the new plot, and on the scene arose a vulgar and puppet-like show. The ballet's falsehood and nonsense prevails on both the stage and the orchestra. But perhaps, in 'Bright Stream' it is clearly obvious why the composer builds his own music in a formalist way, because of the foibles and tricks that he gives out and takes from contemporary music. He does not know or appreciate national creations, and doesn't like or respect the musical language of the people. But meanwhile, the history of worldwide musical culture, and all art, teaches us that only these artistic works (which are inseparably linked with national creations, national poetry, songs and etc.), are important. This thought was expressed brilliantly by the great Russian critic Belinsky, writing that:

> 'National character is not just a virtue, but an essential condition for a truly creative work: if by national character, we are to understand the truth of the depiction of morals, customs and character of one or another nation, of this or that country'

But this is nowhere to be found in Shostakovich's work. 'Lady Macbeth', 'Bright Stream' and things like them are unable to deliver any joy to us at all. They do not carry with themselves realistic images, they are devoid of lively language and full of sickly, savage, ugly images. Look at the brilliant works of classical masters, and you will see that, together with great joy of aesthetic pleasure, they bring current knowledge, evoking thoughts about how to live. After all, in the words of Belinsky, 'art consciousness can help no less than science'. But only this art, which in a highly artistic form truthfully depicts reality, only such art is loved by the masses.

> 'It should leave its deepest roots in the thick of the wide, working masses' -Lenin

Exposing the lack of principles, poverty of ideas, the 'Leftist' ugliness seen in 'Lady Macbeth', and the falseness and puppetry seen in 'Bright Stream' is essential not just in music, but in paintings, sculpture, theatre, playwriting and literature. Indeed, formalist gamesmanship, together with crude naturalism, finds itself a place in artistic exhibitions, on the stage of the theatre, and in literary publications. Everyone still wants to convince us that a wooden mannequin with huge shoulders and a tiny head is better and more beautiful than a sculptural portrayal of a living person, but the wonderful beauty of the mighty human body is stored in classic clear proportions. How often lack of talent and pitiful ignorance hide behind formal innovation!

However, critics are sometimes unable to expose the lack of talent of artists who cram their work with countless gimmicks and flourishes. There was once an exhibition of the artist Barto in Moscow, filled with dark daubs in the frames. Absolutely nobody could understand what the artist shows in his paintings, and only the critics went, gasped and admired them, just like in the witty tale of A. Tolstoy, 'The Pig-Artist'. Even now, the school of Filinov in Leningrad has not disappeared, having gained scandalous glory with its portrayals of six-legged tarantula-like people, with heads but without skulls.

We have people coming forward, fearfully astounded that, in the opera of Shostakovich, both the naturalism and formalism are exposed at the same time. It is said that formalism and naturalism are phenomena that are mutually exclusive of one another. But in fact, naturalism and formalism are brothers, and often accompany one another. This is easily seen reading, for example, several chapters of the work of a Western-European arch-formalist. Excerpts from this, apparently, as the best example of literature, are published by the Moscow journal 'Foreign Literature'. This work is written in such English, that he does not understand the English themselves; and the style reminds one of delirious ravings of a crazy linguist, stirring up all well-known languages in a monstrous mixture. However, the obliging translator still tried as hard as possible to clearly recount the disgustingly natural scene of the hero of the story's visit to the toilet and all physiological details of this visit. Not by chance, we mentioned Jones:

> *'The petty bourgeois Western roots of formalism are clear to us in all its forms and transformations. Undercover, crawling slowly and slyly, dragging our country to a poisonous rot, to a formalist mould.'*

Not without reason, the 'untiring troubadour' of 'Leftist Ugliness', Sollertinsky, glorified the formless, wild music of the decadent German composer Alban Berg, and the psychopathic nonsense of the composer Krenek. And even now, we have people quietly admiring the most reactionary of the works of the emigrant composer Stravinsky, his 'Symphony of Psalms', full of orthodox Catholic spirits, whose headline bears the dedication: *'In the name of Almighty God'*.

> *'In art, the dead hold the living in their grasp, especially, when we do not fight hard enough against the tendencies of the hostile-class, which are arising in art, or which are filtering through to us from the bourgeoisie formalists of the capitalist West, and are sometimes carefully-masked by all kinds of 'Hallelujah' verbiage.'*

There are people, who do not understand at all, nor want to understand. Uninvited lawyers, trying to defend the errors of Shostakovich, make an effort to prove that 'they beat the talented composer' and others in the same spirit. The remarkable Soviet pianist and pedagogue, professor Heinrich Neuhaus, at the meeting of Moscow's composers, said correctly that:

> *'The young composer Shostakovich must have the greatest gratitude*

for the party because it corrected him on time, and showed him the correct way.'

Shostakovich should in his creation entirely free himself from the disastrous influence of the ideologists of the 'Leftist Ugliness' type of Sollertinsky and take the road of truthful Soviet art, to advance in a new direction, leading to the sunny kingdom of Soviet art.

There are however people wishing in their own way to return the huge movement of Soviet art, wishing to direct it to the incorrect course. There are very few of them, but they should receive a strong rebuke. At the same meeting, the former head of the Russian Association of Proletarian Musicians, L. Lebedinsky, stood out, trying to retroactively rehabilitate the direction condemned by the party. Lebedinsky has tried to falsify the problem of the creation of Soviet musical classics, claiming that the late composer Davydenko was a Soviet model. He had courage to publicly call for Soviet composers to follow the orientation of Davydenko, and 'his direction'.

There is no doubt that Davydenko himself, if he was alive, would sharply protest against the attempts to return Soviet music to this path, from which Davydenko distanced himself in his own posthumous and highly-talented works. No, the vulgarisers and simplifiers will not succeed in twisting Soviet music from its path.

Never before have perspectives of Soviet art been so bright and clear, as they are today. The words of the leader of the people, of comrade Stalin; of the leader of the Soviet government, comrade Molotov; with the composer Dzerzhinsky and conductor Samosud, and the central organ of the Party's criticism of the opera and ballet of Shostakovich; set up great and difficult tasks for Soviet Art. Socialist realism in art can be born only to the fertile, rich juices and forces of the soil of the national creation. The combination of the great skill of past classics with the simple, immensely rich, mighty and clear language of the national, artistic creation, — only such a combination can give birth to art of a high, socialist realism. To learn from Shakespeare and Beethoven, from Pushkin and Glinka, Ostrovsky and Mussorgsky, to draw upon the inexhaustible source of the creation of all people of our homeland – here is the task of the workers of art, from the young student to the grey master.

Source: 'Komsomolskaya Pravda' 14th February 1936.

Translated from the Russian by Nikhil Sharma

HO CHI MINH ON THE SONG 'MOUNT STALIN'

Peking July 10, 1950

Comrade Timofeev,

I am sending you herewith a short letter from President Ho Chi Minh (Din) and a new song "The Stalin Hill".

I wish you a very happy summer holiday'.

Sincerely yours,

[Signed]
Ngo Dien

Mount STALIN

Mount STALIN is located in the upper region of North Vietnam.

Here is its story:

A party cadre conference was to meet, the fifth one. To avoid espionage and bombardment by the French colonialists, the organizers had chosen, as a meeting place, one of the high mountains, almost impenetrable and, in any case, never penetrated before.

At this place, well-protected by nature, volunteer worker comrades had built a small town, small villas with radio, electricity and running water (words in Vietnamese).

On the appointed date, August 8, 1948, a hundred active militants arrived, men and women, young and old, with a rucksack on their back and a notebook in their pocket. All had crossed mountains and streams, jungles and rivers to get there. Some of them had walked for 5 or 6 months and had crossed several enemy lines to attend the conference. Those were the activists coming from the South and from overseas.

All were amazed to find this little, new and almost luxurious city in this wild and picturesque environment, surrounded by lush vegetation and a grandiose landscape.

All agreed that this was the best organized conference in years.

-x-x-x-

The entire agenda is summarized under the heading:
"We are fighting for independence and democracy"

The main issues discussed were:

- The international movement for democracy and for independence.
- Indochina and New Democracy.
- Our struggle for national independence and our immediate tasks.
- The National United front.
- The unification of the Viet Minh and the Lien-Viet (The Viet-Minh being the former national front, and the Lien-Viet, the new enlarged national front, having the Viet Minh as centre, and made of about 12 million members)
- Internal affairs of the party: organization, internal democracy, education of members, discipline, policy on cadres, reform of the work system, criticism and self-criticism, etc.

Towards the end of the conference, a delegate proposed to name the place "MOUNT STALIN" in recognition of the beloved leader of the world proletariat. The proposal was greeted by a storm of applause and endless "Hurrah!" Inspired, comrades Xuân-Oanh and Ngoc-My composed on the spot the words and the music of the song "MOUNT STALIN". Here is its translation:

> Here are proletarians,
> Who came here and are singing joyfully in this formerly silent jungle.
> Here is the strength of man and the worker's hand
> They came here with the overflowing and joyful force of life.
> They came in large numbers.
> In this forest, where man never set foot before, and whose top touches the sky and the clouds.
> Today, this forest is brightened by small villas, which have just grown.
> It seems the wild land is becoming a volcano.
> We are standing on MOUNT STALIN.
> Our eyes see, in this distant sky, the image of the One who guides.
> Groups of men gather here, laughing,
> Esteeming each other.
> Shaking hands, greeting each other.
> This MOUNT STALIN is the omen of victory, they sing the victorious song.

With their arrival here, life has become fresh and cheerful,
Joy is shining.
Waiting for the day they will come back to this place.
This is the Day of the Man of Peace
Where the heart
Shines everywhere like the sun on this Mount.

Learning that the Father has arrived,
The mountains forget to be silent,
The sun in this wild place rises radiant.
The birds sing merrily,
Life is enlightened.
The new sun is not as beautiful as its broad forehead,
Shaking his hand, we feel fully confident seeing his shining eyes.
And the inexhaustible strength to fight for the victory of Vietnam.
Arise, ye slaves of the earth!
Turn your eyes to this distant sky
The Mount is bathed by sunlight, the shade is cool, the birds are
    chirping.
See this joy as if we live in the future,
See this exaltation as if we celebrate tomorrow's victory.
We walk laughing along the long road.
We are overcoming the difficulties, we are building the future.

President Ho

Source: RGASPI, Fond 17, Opis 137, Delo 425, LL. 95-98.

Translated from the French by Antonio Artuso.